Programming in an
Object-Oriented
Environment

Programming in an Object-Oriented Environment

R A I M U N D   K .   E G E

School of Computer Science
Florida International University
Miami, Florida

ACADEMIC PRESS, INC.
Harcourt Brace Jovanovich, Publishers

San Diego   New York   Boston   London   Sydney   Tokyo   Toronto

Copyright © 1992 by ACADEMIC PRESS, INC.

Academic Press, Inc.
San Diego, California 92101

United Kingdom Edition published by
Academic Press Limited
24–28 Oval Road, London NW1 7DX

Library of Congress Cataloging-in-Publication Data

Ege, Raimund K.
    Programming in an object-oriented environment / Raimund K. Ege.
       p.   cm.
    Includes bibliographical references and index.
    ISBN 0-12-232930-9
    1. Object-orieented programming (Computer science)   I. Title.
QA76.64.E42   1991
005.1--dc20   91-34206
                                                         CIP

PRINTED IN THE UNITED STATES OF AMERICA
91 92 93 94   9 8 7 6 5 4 3 2 1

To my wife Jacqueline,
she makes it all worthwhile

Contents

Conclusion   257

Appendixes

Preface

This book is about the exciting new technology of object-oriented programming. It provides software professionals with an in-depth look at the concepts behind this emerging technology. This book explains why object-oriented programming has the potential to vastly improve the productivity of programmers and shows how to apply the new technology in a practical environment. Many programming examples are provided, and special attention is given to how different programming languages support the core of object-oriented concepts. C++ is used as the main sample language throughout the book.

This book is intended for those software professionals who are interested in learning the fundamental concepts of object-oriented programming, as well as in learning how to apply the concepts in a practical computer environment. The book assumes that the reader has a fundamental background in computer science (not necessarily academic) and is familiar with one or more of the modern structured programming languages, such as C, Pascal, or Ada. In addition, the book addresses the advanced student, who wishes to be prepared for the programming tasks of the next decade.

The need for this book arises from the growing attention that software professionals are lending to object-oriented programming. There is a general agreement that the new technology will increase the productivity of programmers; however, the programmers have to be trained to be able to apply the new concepts and to use the new programming languages. Whereas others still attempt to justify the new concepts in an academic context, this book shows how to apply the concepts in a practical environment.

This book has two major parts: (1) an introduction to object-oriented concepts, their rationale, and their implementation in programming languages; and (2) a detailed discussion of the object-oriented approach to programming in an object-oriented environment.

In Part I, the book introduces basic object-oriented concepts, such as object, message, method, class, hierarchy, and inheritance. Advanced features, such as multiple inheritance, polymorphism, and dynamic (late) binding, are discussed in detail. A special model of computation, including message sending and method lookup, is illustrated with many examples. The book uses the C++ programming language in its examples (as far as it implements the concepts), but should not be considered a complete coverage of C++. C++ is compared to other major object-oriented languages, such as Smalltalk, Objective-C, Eiffel, and Object Pascal.

Part II covers programming in an object-oriented environment. The global view is adopted that all entities of concern are objects. Programming therefore becomes the task of mapping objects in the problem domain into elements (objects) of the computer system. Elements of object-oriented systems and applications, such as object-oriented database and user-interface systems, as well as the appropriate software engineering techniques are covered.

Overall, the book is introductory in nature. The more interested scholar will find more detailed coverage in the references listed in the bibliography at the end of the book.

Throughout the book we use a number of registered trademarks: Smalltalk-80 and ObjectWorks(ParcPlace Systems, Inc.), Ada (US Department of Defense), C++ (AT&T), Objective-C (Stepstone Corporation), Smalltalk/V (Digitalk, Inc.), Eiffel (Interactive Software Engineering, Inc.), Actor (The Whitewater Group, Inc.), Turbo Pascal (Borland International, Inc.), QuickPascal (Microsoft), GemStone (Servio Logic Corporation), the X Window System (MIT).

List of Figures

List of Tables

Introduction

Object-oriented programming is a natural extension to existing programming technology. The introduction traces its history back to the early programming languages, and discusses how each new generation incorporated new features up to today's generation of languages. The desire to bridge the semantic gap — the gap between the concepts that humans know and understand and the concepts that computer systems know and understand — is described as the driving force of development. The introduction concludes with a simple example of a program task, which illustrates the overall nature and the basic concepts of the object-oriented programming paradigm.

This book is about programming in an object-oriented environment. Such an environment is based on the concepts of object-oriented programming. This new era in programming technology has been steadily developed since the late 1960s and promises to be one of the major ingredients in the response to the ongoing software crisis.

Ever since computers became available in the 1950s, it has been software that exploited its power to solve application problems. Machine code, capable of driving the raw hardware, was the first language available to programmers. Sequences of code statements were the earliest form of software. It was soon recognized that the communication medium between programmer and computer is a critical factor in the programming productivity and quality of the overall software product.

While computers, the hardware, underwent revolution after revolution, using faster and ever more powerful components, the software technology has significantly lagged behind in matching these advances. Hardware technology has been revolutionized several times: from tubes to discrete transistors, resistors and capacitors to board-level integration to integrated circuits. Even integrated circuits have undergone several significant evolutionary steps: from large scale integration (LSI) technology to very large scale integration (VLSI), and eventually wafer scale integration. Hardware engineering was able to keep up with this pace by developing new techniques to manage the exploding complexity of a modern computer system.

Software engineering has not been able to keep up with the speed of advancements and increases in computing power. Most programmers in this day and age still use techniques that are little more advanced than the programming techniques applied by the first programmers. This is why we face the software crisis: software becomes increasingly expensive, is of insufficient quality, is hard to estimate and schedule, and is almost impossible to manage. Some software projects have been judged impossible — beyond the scope of today's software engineering technology. While no "silver bullet" [Bro87] that promises to solve the software crisis is on the horizon, it is the new technology of "object-oriented programming" that is viewed as a possible step toward significantly advancing software technology.

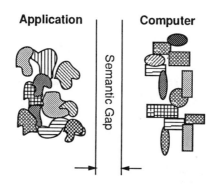

Figure 0.1   The Semantic Gap

Ever since computers were used to solve application problems, it was the task of software to bridge the gap between concepts in an application and computer concepts. Figure 0.1 illustrates this semantic gap. On one side of the gap are the concepts of an application: for example, customer files to organize, accounts to maintain, or rockets to launch. On the other side are the concepts understood by a computer system: electric impulses, micro code, machine code instructions, and programming language constructs. The typical programming task is to translate the application concepts into computer concepts. If the translation succeeds and the computer solves the application problem, a successful software product has been developed.

Early software projects were of limited complexity. Their software solution was possible. With the rapid increase in available computing power, ever more complex software projects are envisioned and undertaken. Bridging the semantic gap, however, becomes increasingly more difficult.

Advances in software technology are driven by the desire to make the transition from application concepts to computer concepts easier. Advances in software technology have narrowed the gap from both sides. On one side they provided software design principles and techniques that allow the programmer to express an application problem closer to computer system terms. Software design principles, such as abstraction, information hiding, modularization and stepwise refinement, allow the programmer to conceptualize application concepts and to ease their transformation into computer system concepts.

On the other side, software technology has advanced the expressive power of the tools used to manipulate a computer system: the programming languages. Programming languages have evolved since their conception in the late 1950s. Basic control structures, procedures and functions, data structures, block structure and nesting, and user definable types were some of the milestones that increased the expressiveness of programming languages.

In the late 1960s it was recognized that a combination of both forces — software design technology and advances in programming languages — may be possible. The resulting language construct was a *class*. A class implements the concepts of abstraction, modularization, and data hiding. It does so by grouping a user-defined type with all procedures and functions that can be applied to it. Classes allow *inheritance*. The concept of inheritance relates to the design concept of stepwise refinement and also allows the reuse of existing code and data structures in a class.

The engineering of a class concept represents a step to software technology similar to the development of an integrated circuit (IC) to hardware. As new hardware systems can be built by using (or modifying) off-the-shelf ICs, it is now possible to build software systems by reusing (or extending) off-the-shelf classes.[1] "Class" is the central concept in object-oriented programming. Object-oriented programming promises to significantly narrow the semantic gap.

Simula was the first object-oriented programming language. It was developed in the mid to late 1960s in Norway [DMN68]. Smalltalk, the language that popularized object-oriented concepts, was developed in the early 1970s. The artificial intelligence research community embraced this new programming technology early on: many flavors and dialects of the LISP programming language provide object-oriented extension. In the 1970s, these languages were available only within research laboratories. With the beginning of the 1980s came the real dawn of the object-oriented programming era. Smalltalk-80 [GR83] was introduced commercially in 1983. Other object-oriented programming languages, such as C++, Objective-C, Eiffel, the CommonLisp Object System, and Actor became commercially available.

---

[1]Brad Cox coined the term Software IC [Cox86].

The task at hand now is to educate the many programmers who still use yesterday's software technology to solve today's software problems. Object-oriented programming requires a new attitude toward problem solving. Problem solving with a computer system becomes more natural. Application concepts can directly be translated into classes. Although it is commonly believed that it will be easier to train new programmers to use object-oriented techniques than to retrain programmers who have substantial experience in applying conventional programming language constructs, this book will attempt to accomplish just this.

Illustration

Object-oriented programming represents a new approach to programming. In the following we will provide an informal look at its basic concepts: object, class, inheritance, encapsulation, and polymorphism. This example is meant to give the reader a skeleton on which to hang the more detailed and conceptual flesh he receives in the rest of the book.

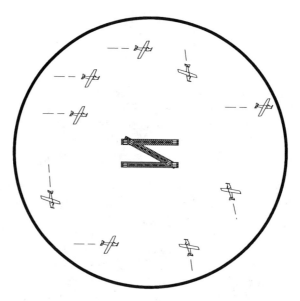

Figure 0.2   Illustration: Air Traffic Control

Consider that you are faced with the task to develop new software that drives a simple version of the radar screens used by air traffic controllers.

The screens depict the airspace around and over an airport and visualize the location and movement of airplanes. Figure 0.2 shows such a screen: it shows the airport layout in its center, and displays all planes that are flying within the controlled airspace.

A conventional approach to such a software development might first focus on the functionalities that are to be provided by the system: to gather radar information and to update the display. The major functionalities would be used to derive an overall functional decomposition of the system. Not so with object orientation: if we take an object-oriented look at the problem, we focus on the entities that occur in the application. Instead of looking at global functionalities, we look at much smaller pieces: entities, or *objects*, that occur in the application. Each object packages some small functionality and some small piece of data. Figure 0.3 shows the goals and results of the two different

Design Approach	
Conventional	Object–oriented

	Conventional	Object–oriented
Goal	identify major functions	identify major objects
Result	gather radar info update display	planes display screen radar receiver

Figure 0.3   Two Approaches to Software Design

approaches.

In our example, the airplanes become objects; they pack information, such as their identification, location, altitude, direction, and speed.   Figure 0.4 shows a plane object with specific values for its identification, location, speed, and altitude attributes. In addition, planes have functionalities or behavior: in the real world planes "fly"; in our application example, they change their location, speed, direction, or altitude. Movement of a plane is recognized by a radar system that senses these data and updates the display of each individual plane. Another behavior of plane objects is that they are displayed on the air traffic control screen. In summary, planes make fine objects.

At the center of our application is the plane object. Instead of describing each individual plane, it makes more sense to describe all planes as a group

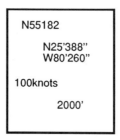

Figure 0.4   A Plane Object

or class. Classes are the major components of an object-oriented program. Most programming deals with defining classes.   Figure 0.5 shows a diagram

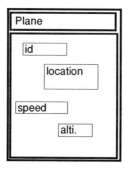

Figure 0.5   The Plane Class

that captures all features that are common to all plane objects. The diagram specifies that class. Classes are used to create objects. Any object is created from a class, and an object is said to be an *instance* of a class. We can view our system as a collection of plane objects. The overall main program operates as a simple loop that updates the plane locations from the radar returns and then calls on the planes to display themselves on the screen.   Figure 0.6 outline the simple pseudocode control loop.

In this context we can observe another important property of object orientation: *encapsulation*. We can think of an object as if it had a rigid boundary around it that protected the inside by making it invisible. The class of an object defines which aspects of an object are visible and accessible. For example, the

For all plane objects:

update location of each plane
display each plane on screen

Figure 0.6   The Control Loop

plane class can define that only two operations are accessible for plane objects: to update the location information, and to display the plane onto the display screen. This separation of *inside* and *outside* of an object is one of the major benefits of object-oriented programming.

But wait, object-oriented programming offers more. The example dealt with only one type of aircraft: an airplane. Rarely is the world so simple: there are gliders, balloons, helicopters, single and multi-engine planes, jets and more. In our example, it might be necessary to distinguish between light and heavy aircraft, between commercial and general aviation aircraft, or between aircraft operation under visual or instrument flight rule. Individual planes belong to different categories. When defining a class, object-oriented programming allows that one class inherits from another. What is inherited is the structure of data and the functionalities. To specify general aviation airplanes, for example, it suffices to identify how they are different from regular planes. For example, general aviation airplanes use their aircraft tail number for identification, whereas commercial aircraft use their scheduled flight number.

A new version of our air traffic control software might specify three classes: a general "plane" class as described above, and two subclasses that inherit all features from the "plane" class and add a new feature each that specifies how each is identified. In addition, the two new classes can refine their display behavior, which might include a display of the airplane identification.

Here we can observe another important property of object orientation: polymorphism. Polymorphism is Greek and means "many shapes." It refers to the fact that, while all objects that are displayed on the air traffic control are planes, they can be more: they can have more than one shape or type, or they can belong to more than one class. Some planes are general aviation planes, and some are commercial aircraft. As far as our overall control loop (see Figure 0.6) is concerned, it still is a loop that retrieves the radar information and redisplays the plane objects. Planes are redisplayed by invoking their "display" functionality. As far as this loop is concerned, it suffices that the "plane" class defines the display functionality. That the general aviation and commercial aircraft classes did refine this "display" functionality, does not change the control loop.

Some of the benefits and flexibility of object-oriented programming stem from this separation of function invocation and implementation. The invocation of a functionality is termed "the sending of a message to an object." The execution of its implementation is termed "the receiver of the message executes the corresponding method." The separation of message and method greatly adds to the flexibility possible in an object-oriented program. In our example messages are sent to the plane objects. Each plane object receives a message and executes its desired behavior. In effect, our program "computes" by sending messages to all participating objects. In general, we can observe an object-oriented program as a collection of objects that communicate by sending messages.

The Structure of This Book

We hope that this introductory example has whetted your appetite for what is the topic of this book: programming in an object-oriented environment. In the following chapters we will present step by step and detailed explanation and illustration of the concepts. The chapters are organized into two parts: (1) an introduction to object-oriented concepts, their rationale, and their implementation in programming languages; and (2) a detailed discussion of the object-oriented approach to programming in an object-oriented environment.

In Part I, we introduce basic object-oriented concepts, such as object, message, method, class, hierarchy, and inheritance. Advanced features, such as multiple inheritance, polymorphism, and dynamic (late) binding, are discussed in detail. The special model of computation, such as message sending and method lookup, is illustrated with many examples. The book uses the C++ programming language in its examples (as far as it implements the concepts), but should not be considered a complete coverage of C++. Chapter 5 presents a complete programming example. In Chapter 6, we give an overview of different flavors of object-oriented programming languages and how they compare to C++.

Part II covers programming in an object-oriented environment. Chapter 7 discusses the advantages that can be gained from applying modern engineering principles to programming. Elements of object-oriented systems and applications, such as reusable data structures and algorithms, object-oriented user interface, and database systems are introduced in Chapter 8 and covered in detail in the subsequent chapters. Chapter 12 closes our perusal of object-oriented topics with a discussion of new software engineering techniques in an object-oriented sense.

Part I

Object-Oriented Concepts

Chapter 1

Basic Concepts

Starting out with the familiar "hello world" program example, this chapter transforms the example into an object method, thereby introducing the notions of object and method. It also serves as an initial introduction to the object diagrams and to the C++ syntax. The importance of object identity is illustrated. More examples follow, introducing the notions of object structure, captured by instance variables. The need to describe groups of objects, instead of single objects, introduces the notion of class. How to create objects from classes is explained and illustrated. A first taste of other programming languages is given with a discussion of how they use slightly different terms for the same basic concepts.

1.1 A World Full of Objects

Indeed, everywhere in daily life you will find objects. Consider the chair on which you are sitting, the pen you are writing with, or the book that you are reading. They are all objects.

Object Anatomy

An object is something that is identifiable. It has a shape, a texture, a certain behavior. Your chair, for example, is an identifiable object and it serves a purpose. The same is true for this book. The pen that you use is also an object. Its behavior may be that you can use it to write sentences on paper.

If you reflect upon this "object" idea, you will agree that the world is full of objects that serve some purpose and that have their own behavior. Even people are objects. They are uniquely identifiable, have properties and behavior. People communicate with each other. Without communication we would

11

achieve nothing in this world. If objects want to achieve something together they too need to communicate. Through communication it is possible to guide the behavior of individual objects toward a common goal.

This is the basic idea behind object-oriented programming: to model an application as a collection of objects that communicate to achieve a common goal. In the following sections we will develop an argument to show how it is possible to model the diverse objects that make up an everyday application problem on a computer.

1.2 Modeling with Objects

Object-oriented programming has its roots in simulation. The first object-oriented programming language, Simula [DN66, Kir89], was developed to provide simulation facilities within a general purpose programming language. A simulation typically models an application as a collection of entities. For example, a simulation application can be an assembly line on a factory floor with workstations and queues, a bank with tellers and customers, an operating system that provides services, etc. — each entity in the application is represented as one entity in the simulation model. Changes to the state of the application are typically expressed as events. For example, it is an event that a customer arrives at the bank and requests service. The state of the application is changed when this event occurs; it has to react to it.

Object orientation views such a system as a collection of objects, where each object models an entity or event in an application problem, and where all objects work together to achieve the goal and task of the overall system. The central software concept is "object." An object captures the identity, structure, and behavior of the application entities that it represents.

Another important observation is that in the real world there are many objects that are similar. They share properties and exhibit common behavior. However, each object has its own identity and its own unique values to fill common properties. For example, consider a savings account and view it as an object. While there are many savings account objects that share common properties — such as having a balance, being able to deposit and withdraw — each particular account is different from another. Each account object has its own value for the "balance" property and is unique.

Apart from an individual object's unique identifier and values, it makes more sense to describe objects in groups. An object-oriented program describes objects that occur in an application. It does so with *classes*; its instances are *objects*. Now, "object" is a software concept that models an application entity. A "class" is a software concept that describes a set of objects.

1.3   Software Objects

Objects in software can be compared to variables in traditional programming languages. As we will discover in this chapter, there is a significant difference between an object and a regular variable, in that a regular variable only captures the data structure aspect of an object, and not its behavior, Throughout this chapter we will be using the C++ programming language [Str86] to illustrate our objects and classes. We chose C++ since it is the object-oriented programming language that enjoys the widest acceptance. In the following sections we will first explain the central concept in object-oriented programming: the *object*.

1.3.1   Hello World

To start out, let us consider the familiar "hello world" program [KR88] in its usual C style. Since C++ is a superset of C, the "hello world" program is also acceptable as a C++ program. It consists of a main program containing a single print statement:[1]

```
main(){
    printf("hello world \n");
}
```

It might not be apparent, but we can view the simple code fragment as an object. It models some application entity; its purpose is to announce a message to the world. It is important to recognize that there are two views of this object: (1) the outside view and (2) the inside view. Part of the outside view is the identity of the object: it is the "main" program. Part of the outside view is also the visible behavior of the object: for the main program its visible behavior is the fact that it can be executed. Part of the inside view is a description of how this object is structured. The "main" object does not have much structure: there is an internal string containing "hello world" plus a line feed character, and a description of how to achieve the behavior of the object, that is, to print the string upon execution.

A better and more sophisticated version of this object has the capability to store a text string, print it on demand, and change it to a different string. Consider such an object in "C" notation:

---

[1]We assume that the reader has some basic knowledge of C. In this code segment we define the function `main()` with no parameters. It contains one call to the library function `printf()` to print the string `"hello world"`. In order to keep our code examples brief, we list only the essential aspects necessary to understand our argument. For example, we omitted the include statement `#include <stdio.h>` that defines the `printf()` library function. Table 1.1 summarizes the differences between C and C++. Appendices B and D elaborate on how to create, compile, and run a complete C++ program.

```
char *message = "hello world";
void announce(){
    printf("%s \n", message);
}
void change(char *newmessage){
    message = newmessage;
}
```

The resulting object has a more complex structure, the capability to store a text string in the variable message, and a more diverse behavior, described by the functions announce and change. The name of the variable message serves as the identification of the object. To bring the object to life, we need another main object that performs the functions:

```
main(){
    announce();
    change("still alive");
    announce();
}
```

The output upon execution will be

```
hello world
still alive
```

1.3.2   Hello World Structure

We can extend this idea to describe groups of objects, their structure and behavior. For example:

```
struct HelloWorld {
    char *message;
};
```

The C declaration struct describes a data structure that is common to all its instances. It defines one field to refer to a character string. Variables that conform to this data structure can be declared with

```
struct HelloWorld hw;
```

Elements of the data structure can be accessed using the "." operation.

```
hw.message
```

refers to the message field inside the hw variable. The following functions allow the manipulation of HelloWorld variables:

```
void announce(struct HelloWorld& hw){
    printf("%s \n", hw.message);
}
void change(struct HelloWorld& hw, char *newmessage){
    hw.message = newmessage;
}
```

The functions announce and change accept HelloWorld structure references[2] as parameters. The references are denoted using the "&" character. A main program is needed to create instances and to call the functions:

```
main(){
    struct HelloWorld hw1, hw2;
    change(hw1, "hello world");
    change(hw2, "hello world");
    announce(hw1);
    announce(hw2);
    change(hw1, "this is hw1");
    change(hw2, "different object");
    announce(hw1);
    announce(hw2);
}
```

The execution of this program yields this output:

```
hello world
hello world
this is hw1
different object
```

The example illustrates two objects hw1 and hw2. It shows the description of their structure and behavior. The structure is given by a data structure description, a struct in C parlance; the behavior is given by function declarations.

1.3.3 Hello World Class

The combination of data structure and function declaration, together with the capability to create identifiable instances from it, is called a "class" in an

---

[2]The ANSI C programming language lacks the call-by-reference parameter passing mechanism found in all modern programming languages. All arguments to functions are strictly passed as call-by-value. C usually simulates call-by-reference by passing pointers as values and by manipulating the variables that the pointers point to. C++ provides a *reference* type constructor that allows the declaration of call-by-reference semantics.

object-oriented programming language. A class bundles data structures and their associated functions closely together. For example, consider the previous "hello world" example, now as C++ class:

```
class HelloWorld {      // comments start like this
public:
    char *message;
    void announce(){
        printf("%s \n", message);
    }
    void change(char *newmessage){
        message = newmessage;
    }
};
```

The keyword `class` begins the declaration of a class. It is followed by the name of the new class. The body of the class declaration gives the fields and the functions, collectively called features, of a class. The body also contains the keyword `public`, which makes all features of the class accessible. A class differs from a struct declaration in that it allows the inclusion of functions. Note that there is no need to include a parameter identifying a hello world object for the functions `announce` and `change`. The correct `message` variable is locally known to all elements of a class declaration. A class implicitly declares a type that can be used in variable declarations. To create objects from this class we need a main program:

```
main(){
    HelloWorld hw1, hw2;      // two variables: hw1 and hw2
                              // of class HelloWorld
    hw1.change("hello world");
    hw2.change("hello world");
    hw1.announce();
    hw2.announce();
    hw1.change("this is hw1");
    hw2.change("different object");
    hw1.announce();
    hw2.announce();
}
```

The syntax to invoke a function for a specific object is akin to the access to a field within a class structure. The statement `hw1.announce()` invokes the announce function for object hw1; that is, the content of its local `message` variable is printed. The execution of this program yields this output:

```
hello world
hello world
this is hw1
different object
```

Two distinct objects are created: `hw1` and `hw2`. Both are instances of class `HelloWorld`, but hold different values in their message string.

1.4 Basic Terminology

The "hello world" example served as an introduction to the basic terms: object and class. An object models some entity of concern in an application, it encapsulates its structure and its behavior through its data structure and functions. A class describes a group of similar objects. It names and types the components of the data structure of each object in the class and declares the functions that can be applied to them.

Object and class compare to *variable* and *type* in conventional programming languages. A variable is an instance of a type, as an object is an instance of a class; but a class is more expressive than a type. It expresses the structure and all of the procedures and functions that can be applied to one of its instances.

One could argue that in conventional programming this is also the case. Consider the type *integer* found in almost any programming language. It defines the structure of an integer variable, e.g., as a sequence of 16 bits, and the procedures and functions that can be performed on integers. According to our definition of "class," the type integer would be a class. However, in these programming languages it is not possible to group new types and their corresponding new functions and procedures into a single unit. In an object-oriented programming language a class provides this service.

Object and class are not the only terms in object-oriented terminology. Variables or fields that are declared inside a class are called *member fields* in C++; other languages refer to them as *instance variables*. The functions that are declared inside a class are called *member functions* in C++; other languages use the term *method*. Member fields and functions (instance variables and methods) are collectively referred to as *member features*, or simply *members*. Sometimes the words are reversed, and member functions are referred to as *function members*, and member fields are called *data members*.

It is useful to illustrate objects and classes with diagrams. The diagrams further highlight an object as something with a boundary, where there is an "inside" and an "outside" aspect to it. Figure 1.1 shows the general outline of an object diagram. An object is depicted as a box. The box is labeled with the name of the object. The box denotes the boundary between the inside and

Table 1.1   Summary of C++ Syntax Features

To help the reader follow the C++ examples used in this book, here is a partial list of how C++ extends C. While efforts are under way to standardize C++ , C has been standardized into ANSI C, the de facto standard is set by Bjarne Stroustrup's original book "The C++ Programming Language [Str86]," the current version of the AT&T C++ compiler, and "The Annotated C++ Reference Manual [ES90]" by Mary Ellis and Bjarne Stroustrup.

C++'s syntax rules are very close to ANSI C. We assume that the reader is somewhat familiar with C syntax, so it suffices to summarize the C++ extensions to C. The object-oriented features of C++ are not listed here; they are explained throughout the text.

Comments	In addition to the character combinations `/*` and `*/` used to delimit a comment, C++ allows the character combination `//` to start a comment. The comment extends to the end of the line.
Function prototypes	Also present in ANSI C, it was C++ that introduced this feature to C. It allows the specification of formal parameter types inside the parenthesis following the function name. Example:

```
double vector_add(double v[], int size) {...}
```

All formal parameters need to be declared. The declaration `vector_add()` would declare a function *without* parameters.

Default values	The function prototype allows the specification of default values for parameters. If a function is called with less arguments than specified, the default value is used. Example:

```
int test(char one[], int size=0){...}
```

can be called as `test("text")`. The omitted second argument defaults to zero.

Inline functions	A function can be defined as `inline`, which will cause the compiler to insert the function code wherever it is called, instead of inserting a function call. This feature increases execution speed but also the size of the executable file. It is only useful for small functions.
Constants	Variable declarations can be preceded by the `const` keyword, which declares them to be constants. They need to be initialized when declared, and cannot be changed afterwards.
References	C++ introduces call-by-reference semantics. The operator `&` can be used in declarations to denote a reference. Example:

```
int ref_test(int &i){...}
```

`ref_test` can be called with an integer variable as argument. The integer variable can be changed inside the function. The change is visible outside.

Table 1.1   Summary of C++ Syntax Features (continued)

Scope
C++ distinguishes three varieties of scope: local, global and class. The class scope refers to members of a class. To refer to a member of a class from outside the class it has to be prefixed by the class name and the scope resolution operator ": :". Example:

```
Person::print()
```

refers to the print member function of class `Person`.

Operators
C++ allows the specification of user-defined operators.   The keyword `operator` is used to label the operator function. Example:

```
vector operator + (vector v_1, vector v_2) {...}
```

which allows

```
vector v1, v2, result;
result = v1 + v2;
```

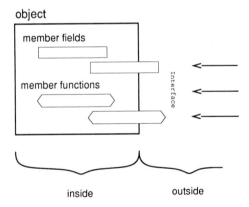

object

member fields

member functions

Interface

inside   outside

Figure 1.1   Object Diagram

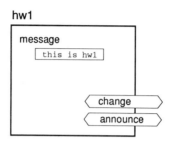

Figure 1.2   The "hello world" Object

outside of an object. Inside an object are the local variables — the member fields and functions. A field is depicted by a rectangular box, a function by a lengthy hexagon. Fields and functions are labeled with their names. If a rectangular box contains something, then it denotes the value of the field for the depicted object. Everything, i.e., the member fields and functions, that is completely inside the object box is hidden from the outside, which means these features are *encapsulated*. (Encapsulation is discussed in detail in Section 4.1.) Fields or functions that extend outside the object box are accessible; they make up the object interface. Access to the member features (fields and functions) is possible through the interface to the object. In a C++ class, the interface is made up from all the features that are listed after the public keyword; they can be functions and fields.

Figure 1.2 shows the object diagram for the "hello world" object example. Its is named hw1 and allows access to its internal state through the change and announce public member functions. The private member field message contains the value "this is hw1".

To summarize, it is an object that captures the structure, behavior, and identity of an application concept. It is the class, however, that describes the structure and behavior of more than one object. The next section will explain the concept of *class* in more detail.

1.5   Classes

As we have seen so far, an object-oriented system is a collection of objects that collectively achieve the goal of the overall system. An object-oriented program is a description of these objects, their structure and behavior. The structure of an object is described by member fields. The behavior is described by member functions. Member fields and functions are not described for individual objects; instead, the description is in terms of classes for each group of similar objects. A class is a description of what structure and behavior its instances exhibit. The task of programming, then, is to identify entities and concepts in an application and to model them using classes.

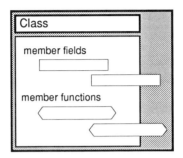

Figure 1.3   Class Diagram

Figure 1.3 shows the general layout of a diagram depicting a class. A class diagram somewhat resembles an object diagram. The top box inside the class diagram displays the class name. The lower box gives the structural details of objects of the class. It shows what member fields and functions objects of this class have and which features are private or public. The features are labeled with their names inside the box or hexagon.[3]

As an example of how to use classes to model a system, consider the following simple application: a course scheduling system. The goal of the system is to allow the scheduling of courses, to show their teachers and students, and to keep adequate record. The entities and concepts that are involved are schedule, course, teacher, and student. An object-oriented program mirrors these entities as classes. The classes describe the structure and functionality of schedules, courses, teachers, and students.

First, consider the concept *teacher*. Let's assume that every teacher has a name. The name is part of the information structure of a teacher. A teacher also has a specific behavior. To simplify the example, let's assume that a teacher can set and report his name. Figure 1.4 shows an object and a class diagram for a teacher. His name is "John Prof." Parts of his interface are the

---

[3]To save space in a class diagram, we put the feature name of a member field inside its box. However, there will be a need to express a common value of a field for all instances of a class, i.e., a class variable or static member field. We will later introduce a special notation for this special case (see Section 1.6.3).

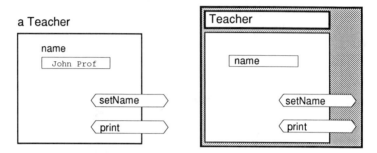

Figure 1.4   Teacher Object and Class

two functions "setName" and "print." Note, this object diagram is labeled "a Teacher," which temporarily serves as the unique identifier for this object.

Here is the C++ class description for teachers:

```
class Teacher {
   char *name;                    // name of teacher
public:
   void setName(char *newName){    // member function
      name = newName;
   };
   void print(){
      printf("the teachers name is: %s \n", name);
   };
};
```

It specifies one member field name as a pointer to a character string, and member functions setName to set a teacher's name and print to print the teacher's name. The name field is listed before the public keyword, which disallows access to the field from outside the object; the member field name is not part of the interface of a teacher, it is a private field. Given an instance t of class Teacher the access t.name is invalid. The idea is to protect aspects of the actual implementation of the teacher class from users of a class. Inside the class, that is, within member functions, the name field is accessible as usual. Section 4.1 (Encapsulation) explains this concept in more detail.

The student class is very simple. It defines one member field to contain the student's name:

```
class Student{
   char *name;         // name of student
```

```
};
```

The student class hides the single member field. There are no member fields or functions in the public interface.

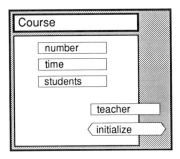

Figure 1.5   Course Class Diagram

Other classes can make use of existing classes. Consider the class description for courses (see also the class diagram in Figure 1.5). A course has a number, a regular time when it is taught, a number of students taking it, and a teacher. In the following class description, note that it defines two member fields — namely, students and teacher — that use the newly declared classes Student and Teacher:

```
class Course {
    char *number;         // course number as string
    char *time;           // time slot as string
    Student *students[25]; // array of students in class
public:
    Teacher *teacher;     // teacher for class
    void initialize(char *n, char *t){
        number = n;
        time = t;
    };
};
```

The Course class specifies three private fields (number, time, and students[4]), a public field (teacher), and a function (initialize) to assign initial values to the private fields.

---

[4]The students field is actually an array of pointers to student objects. We did not use a special notation in the diagrams in order to keep them simple.

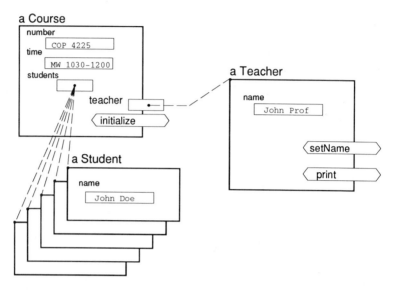

Figure 1.6   A Course with Students And a Teacher

Figure 1.6 shows an example course object together with student and teacher objects. The values for member fields are shown inside their boxes; e.g., the number field contains the value "COP 4225", or the teacher field contains a pointer to a teacher object (depicted as a dotted line to the teacher object it refers to). As the figure shows, object aCourse has one teacher aTeacher and five students. The first student's name is "John Doe." To complete our example we need one more class, the class Schedule:

```
class Schedule {
  Course *offerings[10];     // array of courses
  int offered;               // number of courses offered
public:
  void assign(Course *c, Teacher *t){
    if (offered < 10) {
      offerings[offered++] = c;
      c->teacher = t;         // NOTE: teacher field of course c
                              //  is accessed with operator "->"
    } else
      printf("Schedule full ! \n");
  };
```

```
};
```

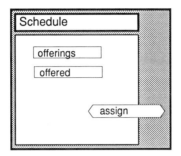

Figure 1.7   Schedule Class Diagram

Figure 1.7 shows the corresponding class diagram. The class Schedule keeps track of the courses that are being offered with the member field offered.[5] Its member function assign checks whether the maximum number of courses has been reached, assigns a teacher to a course, or prints an error message. Note that the assignment of t to field teacher of course c uses the dereferencing operator "->" since c is a pointer to a course object.

So far in this example, only classes have been specified. The classes establish the structure of possible instances. To form an executable system, a main program has to be constructed that defines instances of these classes and performs their functions. Consider this fragment of a possible main program:

```
main() {
    Schedule s;              // a schedule object
    Teacher t1, t2;          // teacher objects
    Course c1, c2;           // course objects

    t1.setName("Joe Teach");
    t2.setName("John Prof");
    c1.initialize("COP 4225","MW 1030-1200");
    c2.initialize("COP 6611","TR 1030-1200");

    printf("Welcome to the Course Scheduling system\n");
```

---

[5]This field is not yet initialized. Section 1.6.1 will show a way to conveniently initialize instances of a class.

```
    s.assign(&c1, &t1);        // assign function expects
    s.assign(&c2, &t2);        // pointer arguments

    printf("Teacher of first course: ");
    c1.teacher->print();
    printf("Teacher of second course: ");
    c2.teacher->print();

    // ... rest of application
}
```

The program defines instances of a schedule, teachers, and courses. It sets the names of the two teachers, and the number and time slots of the two courses. Then it assigns the two teachers to the two courses by invoking the `assign` member function for schedule s. Finally, it prints two messages identifying which teacher teaches what course:

```
Welcome to the Course Scheduling system
Teacher of first course: the teachers name is: Joe Teach
Teacher of second course: the teachers name is: John Prof
```

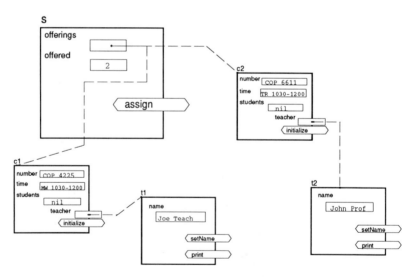

Figure 1.8   Schedule, Course, and Teacher Objects

Figure 1.8 shows the objects that are set up by the example main program. One schedule object refers to two course objects, each of which refers to a teacher object.

1.6   Creating Objects from Classes

The above example raised the question of how to create instances of classes. In general, object-oriented programming languages offer two ways to achieve the creation of objects. As seen in the sample main program in the previous section, it is simple to define variables by using the class name as their type.

```
Teacher t;
```

This usage is similar to defining a variable in a conventional programming language. Here, the variable t refers to an object that is an instance of class Teacher. When an object is created, it occupies storage space to keep the values for its member fields. The compiler reserves the necessary memory for the instance.

It is sometimes prudent not to reserve memory space for an object at compile-time, but rather to allocate it dynamically at run-time. At compile-time, all that needs to be declared is a variable that may hold a pointer to an instance of the class. Programming languages provide run-time support to allocate the instance dynamically. In C, for example, this can be achieved with calling the malloc library function. C++ provides the special operator new to create instances of classes at run-time. The new operator is applied to a class name. It allocates enough memory to hold the newly created instance and returns a pointer to the new instance of the class.

Consider the following code fragment:

```
Teacher *t;                        \\ same as:
t = new Teacher;                   \\      Teacher t;
```

The first statement defines t as a variable that can contain a pointer to a teacher object. In the second statement, t is assigned the address of a teacher object that is returned by the new operator.

An object's lifetime, that is, the time from its creation to its disposal, depends on how it is created. Objects that are created with a variable definition are sometimes called *static*,[6] or statically allocated. Their definition occurred within a certain scope: a block, a function, a class, or a file. Such an object lives as long as the scope (block, function, class, file) is active. When the

---

[6]Be aware that the C++ jargon continues the time honored practice of C to use terms such as "static" in different contexts with different meanings.

scope is exited, then the object is discarded, that is, the storage space that it occupied is released.

Objects that are created explicitly with the new operator are called *dynamic*, or dynamically allocated. Memory allocated for dynamic objects remains occupied until it is explicitly deallocated by the program (or the whole program exits). Explicit deallocation is achieved by applying the delete operator to a variable that holds a pointer to an object. For the example above, the teacher object can be discarded and its memory freed with

```
delete t;
```

The memory that was occupied by the teacher object is now freed and available.

The variable t does not contain a teacher object. It contains a pointer to a teacher object. To access any of a teacher's member features, the feature has to be dereferenced with the "->" operator. For example:

```
t->print();
```

executes the print() member function for the teacher object that t points to.

1.6.1 Object Initialization

After an object has been created it is desirable and good programming practice to initialize its member fields. In the course scheduling example above, the classes for course and teacher were declared member functions to initialize some of their fields. Most object-oriented programming languages provide a mechanism to simplify and automate this initialization. C++ uses special member functions, called *constructors*, that are automatically invoked when an instance of a class is created. At the time an instance is created, it is even possible to supply parameters to the automatically invoked constructor.

Consider the following new declaration of the course class:

```
class Course {
  char *number;
  char *time;
  Student students[25];
public:
  Teacher *teacher;
  Course(){                  // NEW:
    number = "unassigned";   // constructor with no parameters
    time = "TBA";
  };
  Course(char *n, char *t){  // constructor with parameters
    number = n;
```

```
    time = t;
  };
  void print(){
    printf("Course number: %s, at: %s \n", number, time);
  };
};
```

Constructors in C++ are member functions of a class that have the same name as the class. In the example, all member functions with the name Course are constructors.[7] The first constructor, Course(), does not declare any parameters; instead, it assigns dummy values to the two member fields. The second constructor, Course(char *n, char *t), declares two parameters, one for the number member field and one for time. Constructors are automatically invoked when an instance of the class is created. Consider the following program:

```
main() {
  Course c1;                        // constructor is called
                                    // with no parameters
  Course c2("COP 4225","MW 1030-1200");
                                    // constructor is called
                                    // with two explicit parameters
  c1.print();
  c2.print();

  Course *c3;                       // C++ allows to mix
  Course *c4;                       //   declarations and statements

  c3 = new Course;                  // constructor is called
                                    // with no parameters
  c4 = new Course("COP 6611","TR 1030-1200");
                                    // constructor is called
                                    // with two explicit parameters
  c3->print();
  c4->print();
}
```

Here, two objects (c1 and c2) are defined statically. Course object c1 is defined without providing any initialization parameters; therefore, the constructor Course() is called and the member fields number and time are initialized

---

[7]The fact that there are two functions with the same name poses no problem in C++. C++ supports *overloading*, which selects the appropriate function based on the types of the parameters supplied when the function is called. See also the discussion of overloading in Section 2.5.

to `"unassigned"` and `"TBA"`. Course object c2 is defined with two arguments. These arguments are used as parameters for the `Course` constructor, by setting the member fields to `"COP4225"` and `"MW 1030-1200"`. Then, two objects (c3 and c4) are created dynamically. Again, the program shows a parameterless call and a call with two arguments to the constructors of the course class. The program produces this output:

```
Course number: unassigned, at: TBA
Course number: COP 4225, at: MW 1030-1200
Course number: unassigned, at: TBA
Course number: COP 6611, at: TR 1030-1200
```

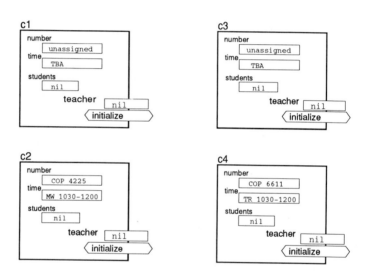

Figure 1.9   Four Different Course Objects

Figure 1.9 shows the four courses with object diagrams.

In analogy to a constructor, it is possible to declare a member function that is invoked whenever an object is discarded. Such a member function is called a *destructor*. In C++, the name of a destructor is the class name prepended with a "~" character. For example, consider yet another version of the course class, as it defines the ~Course destructor:

```
class Course {
  char *number;
  char *time;
```

```
    Student *students;              // NEW: variable number of
                                    //       students allowed
public:
    Teacher *teacher;
    Course(){                       // constructor
        number = "unassigned";      //     with no parameters
        time = "TBA";
        students = new Student[25];  // create 25 students
    };
    Course(char *n, char *t, int s){ // constructor
        number = n;                  //       with parameters
        time = t;
        students = new Student[s];   // create a specified
    };                               //     number of students
    ~Course(){
        delete students;            // free all students
    };
    void print(){
        printf("Course number: %s, at: %s \n", number, time);
    };
};
```

In the previous version of the course class, the students field was an array of 25 student objects. Now, the member field students receives the address of a block of memory for the array of students. It is done dynamically within the constructor whenever an instance is created. Note that there are two constructors: one — parameterless — allocates 25 students using the new operator; the other — taking the course number, time, and number of students as parameters — allocates only the specified number of students. When a course object is deleted, then the destructor performs any necessary cleanup. The destructor ~Course frees the memory that was allocated for the student array. Assume that a course object was created like this:

```
Course c("COP 4225","MW 1030-1200",20);
```

which allocates memory for 20 students, and later deleted with

```
delete c;
```

The delete operation would automatically call the destructor member function of the course class, which would in turn delete the previously allocated student array.

1.6.2 Object Management

Most object-oriented programming languages provide ways to manage objects. There are two factions: one group of languages provides a manual facility, such as explicit operators to create and dispose of objects; another group of languages provides an automatic facility, such as a garbage collector that automatically disposes of unneeded objects.

C++ and Turbo Pascal are examples of the first group. As we have seen in the previous section, constructors and destructors are used to explicitly define what occurs at object creation and disposal time. This places the burden of object space management on the designer of a class, and frees the user of instances of a class from concerns over allocation and deallocation of sufficient memory. This is in line with the information-hiding aspect of a class.

Eiffel and Smalltalk are examples of the second group. These languages provide an automatic facility to allocate memory for objects based on their size as determined by their features. They also provide a mechanism that disposes of objects once they are no longer needed; i.e., they are classified as garbage. The question is when is an object no longer needed. The common definition is that if no other object refers to the object in question, i.e., no object holds a reference or pointer to it, then the object can be disposed of. This mechanism of determining when objects are ready to be disposed of and actually disposing of them, is called *garbage collection*.

Smalltalk and Objective-C are examples of yet another group that allows even more flexibility when dealing with the creation of objects. Both languages allow the specification of functions for a class itself. The functions do not operate on instances of a class, but rather on the class itself. The new operator in C++ can be viewed as such a function. It uses the class description and returns an instance of the class. In Objective-C and Smalltalk it is possible to define such a function new for the class Course that returns an instance of class course. Such functions are called *factory* or *class* functions (methods).[8] Of course, these functions can perform any necessary initialization and can be defined to accept parameters. C++ has a notion of static members that is related to class or factory methods (see next section).

1.6.3 Class Level Members

Member fields (some object-oriented programming languages call them *instance variables*) have unique values for each instance of a class. To express fields that have a common value for all instances of a class, it is useful to have *class variables*. A class variable can be accessed or set by any instance of a

---

[8]Chapter 6 gives more details about these other object-oriented programming languages and their special features.

class. It is visible to any member function, but does not carry a unique value
in each instance. A class variable is different from a global variable in that it
is only visible within the scope of a class; i.e., only the member functions of
the class may use it.

C++ uses the keyword *static* to denote fields that are class variables. Consider the following extension to the teacher class:

```
class Teacher {
   char *name;
   int courses;                // number of assigned courses
                               // Class variable:
   static int MaxCourses;      // maximum courses taught by
                               // any teacher
public:
   Teacher() {
      courses = 0;
   }
   void addCourse() {
      if (courses < MaxCourses)
         courses++;
   }
};
```

The class defines two new member fields: `courses` and `MaxCourses`. The
member field `courses` can have a unique value for each instance of the teacher
class, whereas the static member field `MaxCourses` is global to all instances
of the teacher class. Any static member field is implicitly initialized to zero. It
can be explicitly initialized with the statement:

```
int Teacher::MaxCourses = 2;
```

which sets the static member `maxCourses` in class `Teacher` to 2 and initializes
the field for all instances of the class. If it is changed, for example, to 3, then
all teachers would have a course limit of three.   Figure 1.10 shows the class
diagram for the modified teacher class. The static member field is highlighted
with a double box.

Static member functions are class functions that can be defined to access
static member fields of a class. They may not contain any reference to a non-
static member feature of a class. For example, the following is a static member
function that can be used to access the `MaxCourses` field of class `Teacher`:

```
static int Teacher::currentMaxCourses() {
   return MaxCourses;
};
```

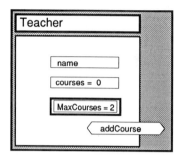

Figure 1.10   Teacher Class with Static Member Field

The function returns the current setting of the static member field. Since there is nothing instance specific in this function it is invoked relative to the class, not relative to a teacher object. For example:

```
Teacher::currentMaxCourses();
```

returns the maximum number of courses taught by a teacher of this class.

1.7   Composing an Object-Oriented Program

An object-oriented program is a collection of classes. In addition, there needs to be a main function that creates some objects and starts the computation by invoking their member functions. This organization lends itself nicely to separate different parts of an application into different files. The idea is to put the class description for each class into a separate file. The main function is also put into a separate file. The compiler will then assemble the complete program from the separate files into a single unit. Of course, classes that are in separate files can be used in more than one application. Appendix D presents a simple version of the course scheduling example used in this chapter as a collection of files. It also explains how to compile them into a single executable system using the C++ compiler.

1.8   Summary of Chapter

This chapter introduced the two key concepts of object-oriented programming: *object* and *class*. An object is a single, identifiable logical unit that combines data and functionality. A class is a description of a set of similar objects.

All objects in a class have the same data structure and functionality. An *instance* is an object that belongs to a class. Elements of an object are called member fields, data members, or instance variables. The functions that can be performed on an object are called member functions, function member, or instance methods.

Chapter 2

The Object-Oriented Model of Computation

The basic notion presented in this chapter is message passing. It is compared to the traditional procedure (function) call. Message passing and method lookup represent the binding of a procedure name to a procedure body. Examples illustrate this central notion with object diagrams and C++ code. Other critical terms, such as static and dynamic binding and overloading, are introduced, illustrated, and compared.

2.1 Objects Are Actors

In object-oriented programming we assume a radically different view of how computing is achieved. Instead of considering a thread of control that steps through a program and manipulates data, we view a program as a collection of independent objects. Each object maintains its own share of the data and has its own program pieces to manipulate it. The objects are active; they behave like actors, each following its own script and guided by the ever present hand of the director. The actors are basically independent, but their behavior is stimulated by interactions among themselves. They influence each other in that an action by one actor may cause another to start or change a behavior.

The scripts that guide the actors — the member functions — are similar to functions and procedures in traditional programming languages: they contain control structures to express how to achieve an actor's task. Parameters can be supplied to a procedure or function, thus making it useful in different contexts. Local variables can be specified within the procedure to capture local data that are germane to the task that the procedure is written for. These local variables are accessible only from within the procedure, i.e., the scope, where they are defined. The parameters and local variables comprise the state of a procedure. This state, however, does not persist after the procedure exits, i.e., returns. The only way that a procedure can gain a persistent state is through global variables.

The invocation of a procedure (function) is termed a *procedure call* (*function call*). In Chapter 1, we have seen functions as they occur in an object-oriented programming language.[1] Functions are declared for a class. These functions are somewhat different from their counterparts in conventional programming languages. In addition to any local variables that they might define, all functions for a class share the member fields of the class; i.e., all member functions have access to the member fields. Thus, an object gains state that can be shared by all its member functions.

Member functions are invoked relative to an instance of a class. In order to reflect the relativeness of an object-oriented function call, it is rephrased as "*the sending of a message to an instance of a class that results in the execution of a member function.*" In the following we will illustrate how messages are sent and received among objects.

2.2 Message Passing

"Message passing" is the term referring to the invocation of a member function of an object. It is similar to a function call in conventional programming languages. This notion of message passing is central to all object-oriented programming languages. For example, consider the following class description for `Teacher`:

```
class Teacher {
   char *name;
   int courses;                  // number of assigned courses
                                 // Class variable:
   static int MaxCourses;        // maximum courses taught by
                                 // any teacher
public:
   Teacher() {
     courses = 0;
   }
   setName(char *newName){       // member function to set name
     name = newName;             // of teacher
   }
```

---

[1]Procedures may appear to be missing from object-oriented programming, but they are not: a procedure is just a function where the caller does not care about the return value.

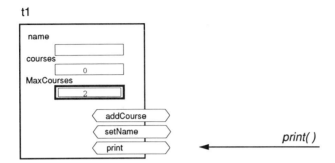

Figure 2.1   Teacher is Receiving Message

```
print(){                          // print name
   printf("the teacher's name is: %s \n", name);
}
bool addCourse(){                 // check whether limit of
   if (courses < MaxCourses) {    // courses is reached
      courses++;
      return TRUE;
   } else
      return FALSE;
}
};
```

```
static int Teacher::MaxCourses = 2;
```
This class defines the public member function `print`, among others. Figure 2.1 shows an object diagram with object t1, which is about to receive the message `print()`. In C++ this would be expressed as

```
t1.print();
```

This C++ statement is read as "sending the message `print` to object t1." The object t1 reacts to the message by executing the member function with the same name as the message. In this case t1 will execute `print`, i.e., print the teacher's name.

Now consider this invocation (see Figure 2.2):

```
t1.setName("John Prof");
```

This statement is expressed as *sending* the *message* `setName` to the object t1 with argument "John Prof." The object t1 is the *receiver* of the message

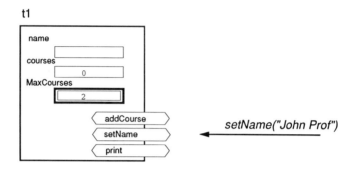

Figure 2.2   Teacher Receiving Message: setName

and — as response to the message — executes its member function `setName` with the passed parameter. To further stress the difference between the two notions, object-oriented languages use the term *method* to refer to the member function that is executed as the result of a received message.   In colloquial

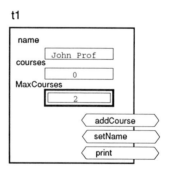

Figure 2.3   Teacher after Receiving Message: setName

terms, an object knows what method to use in order to respond to a message it receives. Inside an object, computation is achieved by sending messages to other objects. Figure 2.3 shows teacher `t1` after it has executed the `setName` method. Note that the name member field now contains the teacher's name.

2.3 Message Sending

A message originates from a *sender*. In our example, we assumed that the statements:

```
t1.print();
t1.setName("John Prof");
```

occur somewhere in a main program. The main program would then be the *sender* of the message. In the example, t1 is the receiver of the message. t1 needs to be an object, so we assume that a suitable declaration occurs within the scope of where the message sending happens.

```
Teacher t1;
```

would be such a declaration, which could occur inside the main program or could be a member field declaration within another class.

To illustrate how messages are sent among objects, let us consider yet another version of our old schedule, course, and teacher classes. First, a new version of the schedule class is given:

```
class Schedule {
  Course *offerings[10];     // array of courses
  int offered;               // number of courses offered
public:
  Schedule() {
    offered = 0;
  }
  assign(Course *c, Teacher *t){
    if (offered < 10) {
      if (t->addCourse()) {
        offerings[offered++] = c;
        c->teacher = t;        // NOTE: teacher field of course c
                               //  is accessed with operator "->"
      } else
        printf("Teacher unavailable ! \n");
    } else
      printf("Schedule full ! \n");
  }
};
```

The schedule class declares the function assign, which assigns a teacher to a course. It does that by sending the message addCourse() to teacher t provided by the argument. This checks whether or not the teacher is available to teach the course. Teacher t returns *true* or *false* depending on whether he wants another course or not. If *true* was the answer, the schedule object then sends a message to course c, also provided as argument, to assign the teacher to the course. Here is the class description for the course:

```
class Course {
  char *number;
  char *time;
  Student students[25];
public:
  Teacher *teacher;

  // ... more stuff

  print(){
    printf("Course number: %s, at: %s \n", number, time);
  }
};
```

Now assume that there are the following instances of these classes:

```
Schedule s;
Course c;
Teacher t;
```

Figure 2.4 shows their object diagrams. The intent of the example is to illustrate how the three objects are tied together by sending messages among them. First, consider that the main program sends the message assign to schedule object s.

```
s.assign(c, t);
```

Teacher object t and course object c are provided as arguments to the message, meaning to assign teacher t to course c for schedule s. Figure 2.4 shows this first message with the arrow labeled "assign(t,c)". Schedule s receives the message and executes its member function assign. Inside this function, s checks whether the teacher is available by sending the message addCourse to object t. Figure 2.4 shows this second message with the arrow labeled "addCourse( )". If the teacher has not reached a maximum, the teacher's courses field is increased and returns true. The schedule checks the maximum number of courses and then assigns teacher t to course c by assigning t to the teacher field of c. The course has a public member field teacher. Access to this field can also be viewed as sending a message to the object, which results in the field being set. Figure 2.4 shows this third message with the arrow labeled teacher. Note also, that in the figure the objects contain values for

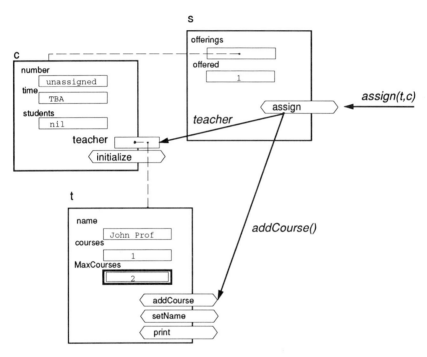

Figure 2.4   Object Diagrams: s, c and t

their member fields that reflect the state after the messages have been sent. The `offerings` member field of schedule `s` points to the course `c`, and the `teacher` member field of object `c` points to teacher `t`.

2.4 Method Lookup and Binding

The separation of procedure call (message sending) and procedure invocation (method execution) is central to object-oriented programming. For an object to respond to a message it has to look up the appropriate method. In conventional programming languages this binding of a procedure name to a procedure body is routinely done by the compiler. In object-oriented programming languages this is not necessarily the case. Here, we distinguish between *static* and *dynamic* binding. Static binding is done at compile-time, whereas dynamic binding is done at run-time.

To illustrate this concept, consider a teacher object `t` that receives the message `print`. In the case of static binding the compiler determines that there is a member function `print` defined in the class `Teacher`. The compiler will therefore generate the necessary code to execute the function. In the case of dynamic binding, what will be generated is code to determine at run-time whether the teacher object `t` has a member function `print` and code to invoke it. If the teacher object and its class do not change between compile and run-time then the two ways of binding should yield the same result: the `print` member function is executed. One difference exists, however; if there is no member function `print` defined in the interface to object `t` then static binding will report a compile error, whereas dynamic binding will result in a run-time error.

C++ is a strongly typed programming language. If object `t` is declared with

```
Teacher t;
```

then `t` will always refer to a `Teacher`. So there is little chance that `t` will change its class between compile and run-time. Not all object-oriented programming languages are strongly typed. Smalltalk, for example, allows the definition of variables that are untyped. In this case, a variable `t` could hold a teacher object at one time and a course object at another. So there is no guarantee that the object is the same, or even that its class is the same, as they were at compile-time. Imagine that `t` refers to a course object at some time during execution. If it receives the `print` message, it will respond by executing the `print` member function defined by class `Course` rather than the `print` member function of class `Teacher`.

Dynamic binding therefore allows significantly more freedom when an algorithm is specified. For example, consider a list of objects. In order to express an algorithm to have all objects in the list print their current state, one has to consider the class of each individual object. With static binding this will be a tedious and inflexible programming task. With dynamic binding, however, the algorithm would just specify (in a loop) to send a `print` message to each element in the list, leaving it up to the individual objects how to respond, i.e., what member functions to execute, at run-time.

It may seem that dynamic binding is of value only for untyped programming languages. Not true. In the context of class hierarchies (see next chapter), where a class inherits member functions from its superclasses, dynamic binding will gain the important stature that it has among the concepts of object-oriented programming.

It may also seem that dynamic binding incurs a performance penalty since it involves an extra lookup at run-time, however, current object-oriented compiler technology has shown that the performance penalty is neglectable [DS84] considering the rapid increase in hardware performance.

2.5 Overloading

A related concept is *overloading*. It usually refers to overloading of operators[2] or functions. Overloading allows the selection of a function or operator based on the type of arguments that are used. As an example, consider the following declaration of three integer and three floating-point variables:

```
int result, i1 = 10, i2 = 20;
float fresult, f1 = 10.123, f2 = 20.34;
```

Now consider using these variables in simple addition statements:

```
result = i1 + i2;
fresult = f1 + f2;
```

The operator + is overloaded. It is used to add two integers and two floating-point numbers. For integer arguments it invokes an integer addition; for floating point arguments it invokes a floating-point operation. The compiler selects the correct operation based on the type of arguments; that is, in object-oriented terms it binds the method to the message, based on the class of arguments. Overloading can actually be viewed as a generalization of binding. Binding selects a method for a message based on the class of the receiver of a message, whereas overloading also considers the argument types. Again, the question

---

[2]Operator and function overloading are semantically the same, since the operator can be viewed as a function name. It just happens that most conventional programming languages, such as Pascal, only support overloading of their predefined operators.

remains: does the selection occur at run or compile time? Most programming languages perform a static resolution of overloaded function calls at compile time. Smalltalk does not provide this feature. Ingals [Ing86] reports on how to add dynamic overloading to Smalltalk-80.

Overloading, of course, applies to member functions within a class. Member functions with the same name are selected based on the types of arguments that appear in the function call. The constructor example discussed in Section 1.6.1 for class `Course` was an example with an overloaded `Course` member function. As an additional illustration, consider this new class description for `Teacher`:

```
class Teacher {
  char *name;
  int courses;
  static int MaxCourses;
public:

  // ...
  // see other teacher classes

  bool addCourse(){
    printf("no argument \n");
  }
  bool addCourse(Course *c){
    printf("one argument \n");
  }
};
```

Here two `addCourse` member functions are defined, one without parameters and one with a course parameter. The compiler will select the correct member function based on the number and type of arguments provided. The following two statements invoke the two member functions:

```
Teacher t;
Course c;
t.addCourse();
t.addCourse(c);
```

The member function `addCourse` is *overloaded*. When executed, the statements print:

```
no argument
one argument
```

2.6 Object Identity

One of the foremost properties of an object is that it is *uniquely* identifiable. The unique identifier depends on the context where an object occurs: an object may be a variable in a function or a value for a member field in another object. It is used to communicate with an object. The identifier marks the receiver of a message that is sent among objects.

The obvious vehicle for keeping object identifiers in programming languages is a variable or data field. The variable is a repository that contains the unique identifier of an object. In most object-oriented programming languages it appears that a variable contains the object itself, hiding the fact that only the object identifier is stored in the variable.

C++ allows the programmer to specify how an object is referenced by a variable or data field. There are three ways to specify the type of variable used to identify an object:

1. The variable contains a complete object.

2. The variable contains a pointer to an object.

3. The variable contains a reference to an object.

A variable that contains an object is specified in C++ as:

```
Teacher t;
```

This declaration creates a teacher object. Variable t is declared to contain the complete teacher object. For sending messages, it can be denoted as

```
t.print();      // sending message print to object t
```

Such a variable declaration can occur inside a class description. Consider this modified version of the Course class:

```
class Course {
  char *number;
  char *time;
  Student students[25];
public:
  Teacher teacher;   // not a pointer !

  // ... more stuff

  print(){
    printf("Course number: %s, at: %s \n", number, time);
```

```
  };
};
```

Instances of class Course contain an instance of a teacher object.   Figure

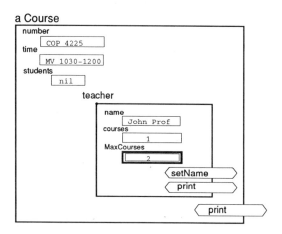

Figure 2.5   Course Object Containing Teacher Object

2.5 shows such a course object. Whenever a course object is created, a teacher object is also created and placed inside it. Therefore, it is not recommended to declare class members that contain instances of other objects. Imagine if the teacher class would specify a member field that contains a course object: infinite recursion would result.

A variable that contains a pointer to an object is specified as

```
Teacher *teacher_pointer;
```

The variable teacher_pointer is declared to be a "pointer to Teacher;" it will contain a pointer to a teacher object. To send a message to such an identified teacher object, the object has to be created first. This code fragment creates a teacher and sends a message to it:

```
teacher_pointer = new Teacher;
teacher_pointer->print();
```

If such a variable declaration occurs inside a class description, it defines a member field. The old Course class description that we used in Chapter 1 contains such a declaration. The `teacher` member field can hold a pointer to a teacher object.

C++ allows a third way to specify how an object identifier is kept. A variable can contain a reference to an object. It is specified as

```
teacher &teacher_reference;
```

The variable `teacher_reference` may contain a reference to a teacher object. We can view this declaration as a compromise between cases 1 and 2 illustrated above. The variable, in effect, contains a pointer to an object, but is used as if it contains the object. When a reference variable is declared it has to be initialized. We can think of a reference variable as just a second name for the same object. The correct declaration for our example is

```
Teacher real_teacher;
Teacher &teacher_reference = real_teacher;
```

To send a message to this teacher object, we state:

```
teacher_reference.print();
```

Most object-oriented programming languages treat variables that are used to refer to objects in this fashion: the variable contains the object identifier (implemented as pointer to its memory location), but can be used in message sending expressions without a "dereferencing" operation.

2.7 Object Assignment

Most object-oriented programming languages treat the assignment operation differently than a regular message received by an object. In C++, for example, the "=" has different effects depending on what kind of variable (see the three cases above) it is applied to.

In the case where the variable is a pointer variable, it copies the right-hand side — interpreted as a pointer — into the left-hand side of the operation. For example, consider this code fragment:

```
Teacher *t1, *t2;
t1 = new Teacher("John Prof");
t2 = t1;
t1->print();
t2->setName("Joe Teach");
t1->print();
t2->print();
```

Variables t1 and t2 refer to the same teacher object. If the teacher's name is changed through t2, it will affect t1's name. The output from this piece of code is

```
the teacher's name is John Prof
the teacher's name is Joe Teach
the teacher's name is Joe Teach
```

In the case where the variable contains an object, the assignment operation performs a member-wise copy[3] of all member fields of the source object (on the right-hand side) into the member fields of the variable on the left-hand side. The right-hand side and left-hand side of the assignment operation then contain two distinct objects. For example:

```
Teacher t1, t2;
t1.setName("John Prof");
t2 = t1;
t1.print();
t2.setName("Joe Teach");
t1.print();
t2.print();
```

which results in:

```
the teacher's name is John Prof
the teacher's name is John Prof
the teacher's name is Joe Teach
```

The assignment "t2 = t1" copies all member fields of t1 into t2.

As a more complex example consider a course object that contains a pointer to a teacher object constructed like this:

```
Teacher *teacher_pointer;
Course c1;
teacher_pointer = new Teacher;
teacher_pointer->setName("Jose Fernandez");
c1.teacher = teacher_pointer;
```

Now assume that we declare a second variable, c2, to contain a course object and assign c1 to it:

```
Course c2;
c2 = c1;
```

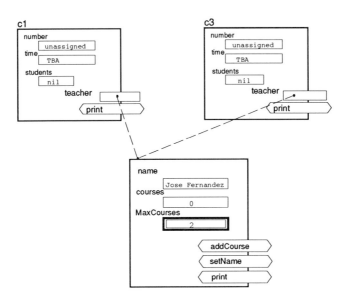

Figure 2.6   Two Courses and One Teacher Object Diagrams

The assignment copies all member fields of `c1` into the corresponding member fields of `c2`. Since the `teacher` field is a pointer variable, only the pointer is copied. Figure 2.6 illustrates the two course and one teacher objects. Therefore, `c2.teacher` refers to the same teacher object as `c1.teacher`. The following code fragment:

```
c2.teacher->setName("John Prof");
c1.teacher->print();
```

will result in:

```
the teacher's name is John Prof
```

The last case we need to consider is when the assignment involves reference variables. While the variables actually contain references (pointers), they still behave as if they refer to the object itself. For instance:

```
Teacher rt1, rt2;
Teacher &t1 = rt1, &t2 = rt2;
t1.setName("John Prof");
t2 = t1;
t1.print().
t2.setName("Joe Teach");
t1.print();
t2.print();
```

which results in:

```
the teacher's name is John Prof
the teacher's name is John Prof
the teacher's name is Joe Teach
```

The assignment "`t2 = t1`" performs a member-wise copy of all member fields of teacher `t1` to `t2`.

In summary, most object-oriented programming languages behave as illustrated in the last case: a variable declared to be of class `x` contains object identifiers of `x` instances. These object identifiers can be thought of as pointers. The variable, however, can be used as though it stood for the object.

2.8   Object Self-Reference

Inside a member function all member fields are accessible. Other member functions from the same class are also callable. This call of member functions

---

[3]Older C++ versions (before AT&T C++ 2.0) performed a bit-wise copy.

that perform on the same instance, can also be phrased as message send-ing. To send a message to the current instance, object-oriented programming languages provide a predefined member field that refers to the current object. Most object-oriented programming languages refer to the current object as *self*. In a C++ class there exists a predefined member field called this, which contains a pointer to the current object. In Eiffel this feature is called current.

Consider this extended definition of the teacher class (note that the member function addCourse has an additional parameter):

```
class Teacher {
    char *name;
    int courses;             // number of assigned course
    static int MaxCourses;   // maximum courses taught by
                             // any teacher
public:
    Teacher() {
        courses = 0;
    }
    bool check(){
        return this->courses < MaxCourses;
    }
    bool addCourse(Course *c){
        if (this->check()) {   // sends message check to itself
            this->courses++;    // retrieves and updates local field
            c->teacher = this;  // updates teacher field in course
            return true;
        } else
            return false;
    }
};
```

An explicit send of message check() to object this occurs inside the addCourse member function. The receiver (this) is the instance of the class Teacher at the time of executing addCourse. The "this" is a reference to the sending object *itself*. In this case, the receiver and the sender of the message is the same object. In effect, the message check() is sent by the teacher object to itself. The expression this->courses++ explicitly refers to the courses member field of the current instance. Of course, both usages of this are not necessary in the example, since the compiler defaults local references to this.

There are circumstances, however, where a method needs to pass a reference of the current object to another object. Consider the statement:

```
c->teacher = this;
```

which assigns a pointer to the current teacher object to the public `teacher` field of course `c`. In effect, the `teacher` field of course `c` points back to the teacher object that sent the message.

The member field that refers to the object's own identity is a regular, though private, member field. Changing its value also changes the identity of the object. This contradicts the principle that an object has a unique identity. It should be strongly discouraged. Most compilers for object-oriented programming languages disallow reassignment to `this`, `self`, or `current`.

2.9 Summary of Chapter

In this chapter we presented the basic concepts of *message passing* and object identity. Together, they form the cornerstones in understanding how an object-oriented system computes.

A function call is divided into two separate tasks: (1) a message is sent to an object, and (2) the object executes a method as a response to the message. A message is sent by a *sender* and received by a *receiver*. The selection of method for a message is called binding and can be performed at compile time (static binding) or at run time (dynamic binding). A function can be overloaded — i.e., there may be more than one function with the same name — and the selection is based on the types of the arguments.

An object is uniquely identifiable. Its identity can be represented in different ways in variables and member fields. An object's identity is affected by assignment operations. An object also knows about its own identity.

Chapter 3

Class Hierarchy

Comparing classes to conventional ways of categorization gives rise
to the notion of class hierarchy. Subclasses are explained and illustrated as extensions and specializations of existing classes; it is
natural that subclasses "inherit" features from their superclasses.
Examples using class diagrams and C++ class descriptions show
the benefits of inheriting structure and behavior from superclasses.
The model of computation is extended to explain method lookup in
the context of class hierarchies. Multiple inheritance is not treated
as a special case or extension of inheritance; instead, single inheritance is treated as a limitation of the overall concept imposed by
some programming languages.

3.1 Categorization

Object-oriented programming languages use classes to categorize entities that
occur in applications. This is very natural and commonplace in conventional
representation of knowledge, such as zoology. For example, zoologists refer
to categories of animals such as bears and cats. Moreover, zoologists create
hierarchies of related categories to adequately represent relationships between
categories. For example, leopards belong to a subcategory of the category of
cats; cats and bears are subcategories of the overall category of mammals.
The relationship among categories is usually "*is a*": a bear *is an* animal, a
leopard *is a* cat. The related categories form hierarchies that make it easier to
understand the represented knowledge.

Once a hierarchy is established it is easy to extend it. To describe a new
concept it is not necessary to describe all its attributes. It suffices to describe
its differences from a concept in an existing hierarchy. Imagine that a new kind
of animal is discovered in the Brazilian jungle. Researchers who observed the

animal determine it to belong the category of monkeys. Once the discovery
is reported in the newspaper, we will all have some idea what the animal is
like. We base our understanding on the monkey category: a monkey is hairy,
has two arms, two legs, and a certain behavior. We assume that the newly
discovered animal inherits all these features.

Object-oriented programming is built on the idea of relating classes with
such an *is-a* relationship. For example, consider the student and the teacher
class discussed in the previous chapters. Both students and teachers *are*[1]
persons. So why not define a class to capture the data structure and functionality of persons first, and then derive the student and teacher classes from it ?
Here are the necessary class descriptions in C++ notation, beginning with the
class for persons:

```
// Class definition for Person
class Person {
  char* name;
public:
  Person();                  // constructor
  Person(char *n);           //      bodies declared elsewhere
  void print();              // member function
};
```

In C++ it is possible to separate the header declarations of member functions
from their bodies. It is not necessary to fully list the member functions in a
class description. Member functions can be defined outside a class description. When the member function is then later declared, it needs to identify its
class (note the `Person::` prefixes):

```
// Body for class Person
 Person::Person(){          // constructor
   name = "";
 }
 Person::Person(char *n){   // constructor
   name = n;
 };
 void Person::print(){      // member functions
   printf("my name is: %s \n", name);
 };
```

The scope resolution operator "`::`" is used to label the member functions
with their corresponding class. The person class declares all features that
are common to all persons in the desired application. In this example, we

---

[1] *are* == plural of *is-a*

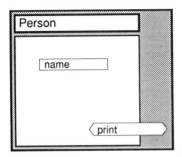

Figure 3.1 The Person Class

represent the name of a person as a string, and provide a member function to print the name of a person in a sentence. Figure 3.1 shows the class diagram for the person class. The class `Person` can now serve as the *base* class, from which the student and teacher classes can be derived.

3.2 Extension

The simplest case of subclassing an existing class is when the base class is extended into a new derived class. The subclass intends to extend the features that are defined by the base class. Again, consider zoology: a cat is an animal. Certainly a cat possesses all the features of a common animal. A cat adds certain features to the animal category that make the concept of "cat" stand out. Zoology therefore created a category for cats, extending the base category of all animals.

Consider our sample application concepts. Let us define a class for teachers. The teacher need not be a stand-alone concept. It can inherit all the features of a person: a teacher *is a* person. A teacher adds its own features; therefore, the creation of a derived class is warranted:

```
// Class definition for Teacher
                          // Teacher is derived
class Teacher: public Person {  //          from Person
   int courses;
   static int MaxCourses;
public:
   Teacher(char *name):Person(name){
     courses = 0;
```

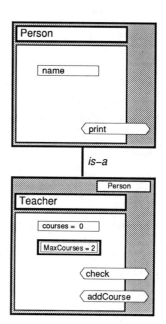

Figure 3.2   The Teacher and Person Classes

```
  }
  bool check();
  void addCourse();
};
// Body for class Teacher
bool Teacher::check(){
    return (bool) (courses < MaxCourses);
}
void Teacher::addCourse() {
    if (check())
      courses++;
}
```

The teacher class is declared as subclass of the person class. The first line in the class description:

```
class Teacher: public Person
```

lists `Person` as its base class. The base class `Person` is preceded by the keyword `public`, which makes known the fact that `Teacher` is derived from `Person`. Figure 3.2 shows both class diagrams in an *is-a* relationship. The teacher class extends the declaration with its own features, such as a local and a static member field and two member functions. Any instance of class `Teacher` has these features. In addition, any instance also *inherits* all features that are defined for the person class. Therefore a teacher also has a name and is able to respond to a `print` message, which is defined by the `Person` class.[2]

Constructors are not inherited by derived classes. In the example, the `Teacher` class defines its `Teacher` constructor. C++ allows passing parameters to constructors of base classes from the constructor of the derived class. For example,

```
Teacher(char *name): Person(name) ...
```

uses the base class constructor (`Person`) to initialize the inherited `name` member field.

Figure 3.3 shows a teacher object as it receives a `print()` message. Note that the teacher object diagram shows all features of a teacher — those that are defined by the teacher class and those that are inherited from the person class. The inherited features are drawn with dashed lines in the object diagram. When the `print()` message is received by the teacher object, it will first try to look up the corresponding member function at the teacher class. Since it

---

[2]Sometimes it may not be desirable to inherit all features of a base class. See Section 4.1 for details.

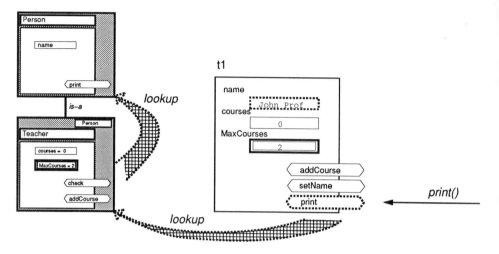

Figure 3.3   Method Lookup for Teacher

does not define a print function, the teacher class will delegate[3]. the lookup to
the person class where `print` will be found. For this example, it will print the
teacher's name as

```
my name is John Prof
```

3.3 Specialization

The second case of subclassing is when a base class is used to define a derived
class that specializes features of the base class. Again, consider zoology and all
animals with four legs: a cat would be a "four-legged" animal. A cat normally
uses all four legs to move forward. Now consider a kangaroo: it also has four
legs; however, it is distinct in that it normally uses only two of its four legs
for transportation. A kangaroo is a specialization of the "four-legged" animal
concept. A kangaroo warrants a new category.

Now consider our sample application concepts: let us redefine the student
class to be derived from class `Person`. The student class does not add any
features; instead, it specializes the `print()` member function. Here, the class
description for `Student` reads:

---

[3]This is where the term "delegation" has its roots within the concepts of object-oriented
programming (see also [Ste87])

```
// Student class declaration
class Student: public Person{
 public:
   Student(char *name):Person(name){};
   void print();
};
```

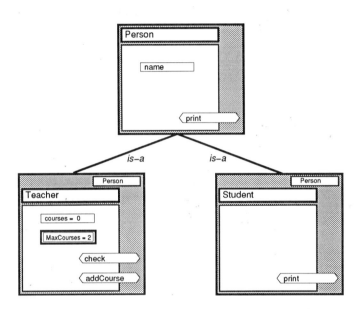

Figure 3.4   Class Hierarchy: Student, Teacher, and Person

Figure 3.4 shows the complete class hierarchy, displaying the person, student and teacher classes in context. The student class inherits the `name` member field and the `print` member function. The `print` function, however, is overwritten in the student class. This allows derived classes to specialize the functionality of their base classes:

```
// Body for class Student
void Student::print() {
   printf("Student: ");
   Person::print();              // explicit call to print function
}                                // of class Person
```

The `print` function of class `Student` internally calls the `print` function of class `Person`. To distinguish the local print function from the inherited print function, the name is preceded by the name of the class and the *scope resolution* operator "`::`".

To illustrate the usage of instances of the student and teacher classes, consider the following main program:

```
main()
{
    Teacher t("John Prof");    // constructor for Person
    Student s("Hugo Meier");   //               is invoked
    t.print();                 // Person's print
    s.print();                 // Student's print
}
```

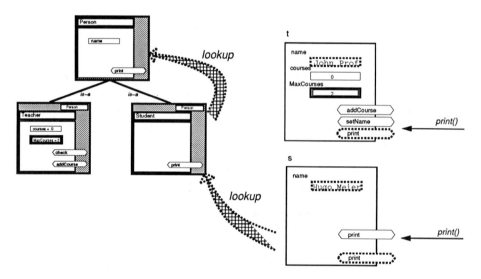

Figure 3.5   Method Lookup

Figure 3.5 shows how the messages are received by the teacher and student objects. The program produces the following output:

```
my name is: John Prof
Student: my name is: Hugo Meier
```

The first line results from the print member function defined for class `Person` and executed by teacher object `t`. The second line is a combination of output from the student's `print` member function and the person's `print`.

The two example classes, `Teacher` and `Student`, illustrate how derived classes extend or specialize their base classes. C++ terminology uses the terms base and derived class. Other languages refer to the same concepts as *subclass* and *superclass*. A subclass is a derived class, while a superclass is a base class. In general, subclasses naturally *inherit* features from their superclasses. The features can be instance variables (member fields) and/or instance methods (member functions).

3.4   A Matter of Type

Classes are essentially implementations of abstract data types. If we have an abstract data type, we may implement it as a class. The specification of an abstract data type defines the behavior of the type, whereas a class description states how the abstract data type is to be realized as software. There is a clear distinction between classes and the abstract data types they implement. For example, the abstract data type *Person* defines the behavior of person objects. The class `Person` describes one implementation of the type *Person* by stating the required instance variables and member functions. Although there is only one person abstract data type with the desired behavior, we could have a number of different classes implementing it, using different instance variables and member functions.

Confusion arises when the notion of subtyping is linked to that of subclassing. A subtype of an abstract data type is itself an abstract data type that has the same behavior as its supertype.

This is not necessarily true for subclasses. A subclass inherits the implementation of the abstract data type that is being implemented from its super class. Yet the type that is implemented by a subclass is, however, not necessarily a subtype of the subclass's superclass. For example, we may want to implement the abstract data type stack as a class that is a subclass of array. Here, the abstract data types, stack and array, are two totally different types that have no relationships to each other. The class stack is defined to be a subclass of array only to reuse its implementation details.

3.5   Method Binding

The binding of messages to methods becomes more interesting with the presence of inheritance. If an object receives a message, it will respond by selecting and executing a method. As we have seen in the last section a method does not need to be one of the local methods declared by the object's class; it can be one of the inherited methods. Again, it is worthwhile to distinguish *static* and *dynamic* binding. With static binding the type information at compile-time is used to bind the message to the method. With dynamic binding, this is done at run-time. Consider the following code segment:

```
main()
{
  Teacher t("John Prof");
  Student s("Hugo Meier");
  Person *array[2] = {&t, &s};    // array holding pointers to
              //  Person, initialized with pointers to t and s
  t.print();
  s.print();
  array[0]->print();
  array[1]->print();
}
```

The program declares two objects, t and s, and a two-slot array that holds two pointers to something of class Person. Since t and s are also person objects, they are fit, or correctly typed, for the array. The array variable illustrates *polymorphism* in object-oriented programming languages. Polymorphism[4] occurs when a program entity, such as a variable, can have multiple roles or types. In our example, the array can hold instances of students, teachers, or persons (and of course, instances of all other possible subclasses of Person and their subclasses, etc.).

With static binding the output is the following:

```
my name is: John Prof
Student: my name is: Hugo Meier
my name is: John Prof
my name is: Hugo Meier
```

The first two invocations of print refer to the print member functions of Teacher and Student. Since the student class has a different implementation for the print method, it prints its version. The second two invocations of print refer to the print member function of class Person. The binding is done statically at compile-time; therefore, the type of the array elements is pointer to class Person, and the member function Person::print is invoked.

With dynamic binding the output would be this:

```
my name is: John Prof
Student: my name is: Hugo Meier
my name is: John Prof
Student: my name is: Hugo Meier
```

[4]The term "polymorphism" is of Greek origin and means "multiple types."

The binding is done dynamically at run-time. At that time, the first element of the array points to a teacher object, and the second element points to a student object. Therefore the appropriate methods can be executed as a response to the print message.

Whether or not a programming language supports dynamic binding (sometimes also called late binding) is in our view, a major criterion for calling that language "object-oriented." C++ supports dynamic binding. Static binding, however, is the default. To express the fact that a member function should be bound dynamically, the member function has to be designated as `virtual`. To achieve dynamic binding in the above example the class declaration has to be modified in the following manner:

```
// Class definition for Person
class Person {
  char* name;
public:
  Person();                  // constructor
  Person(char *n);           //    bodies declared elsewhere
  virtual void print();          // enables dynamic binding
};
```

The keyword `virtual` signals the intention to use dynamic binding for member function `print`. The rest of the class declaration remains the same as in the example above.

3.6   Multiple Inheritance

Inheritance is not limited to a single base or superclass. It is possible and desirable to declare a class as an extension of two or more classes. Again, consider zoology: the Florida panther[5] is an extremely endangered species. The zoological category of Florida panthers is a subcategory of the endangered species in addition to being a subcategory of animals.

Most object-oriented programming languages allow the specification of multiple superclasses for a derived class. For example, consider a class of professors. Professors are researchers who also have a teaching assignment, or vice versa. The professor class is defined as a subclass of both the teacher and researcher class. First, consider the declaration of a researcher class:

```
class Researcher {
  char *expertise;           // field of expertise
public:
```

---

[5]Florida International University is proud to have the Florida panther as its mascot.

```
  Researcher(char *e){          // constructor
    expertise = e;
  }
  void print(){
    printf("I am an expert in: %s\n", expertise);
  }
};
```

With this `Researcher` class and the previously declared `Teacher` class we can declare a new class `Professor` that combines the features of both:

```
class Professor: public Teacher, public Researcher {
  enum nature {teacher, researcher} kind;
public:
                              // combined constructor
  Professor(char *name, char* exp):
    Teacher(name),Researcher(exp){};

  void change(){              // change nature
    if (kind == teacher)
      kind = researcher;
    else
      kind = teacher;
  }
  void print(){               // print according to nature
    Teacher::print();
    if (kind == researcher) {
      printf("and ");
      Researcher::print();
    }
  }
};
```

Figure 3.6 shows the class diagrams for these classes in a class hierarchy. The new class `Professor` inherits all features from the superclasses `Teacher` and `Researcher`. In addition, it defines a private member field `kind`, and a constructor member function. Note how the constructor is defined as a combination of the teacher and researcher superclasses' constructors. The `name` parameter is passed on to the teacher class's constructor (`Teacher`), whereas the `exp` parameter is handed to `Researcher`.

There are also two member functions: `change` and `print`. The `print` function calls either the teacher's or researcher's print method, depending on the value of the `kind` member field. Figure 3.7 shows an instance of a

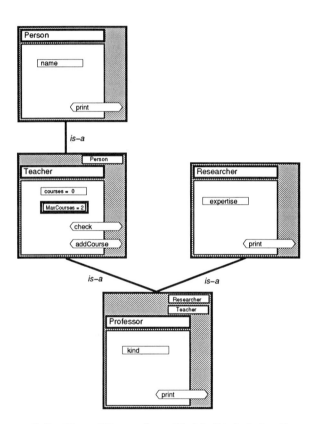

Figure 3.6   Class Hierarchy with Multiple Inheritance

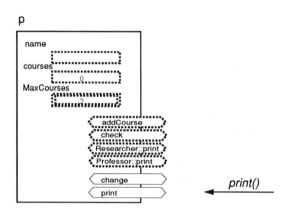

Figure 3.7   Professor Object Receiving a Message

professor. Note, that three print member functions are defined for a professor object. The function defined by the Professor class takes precedence over the inherited ones. To invoke one of the "other" print functions, that print function has to be identified with a scope resolution operation. Here,

```
Teacher::print();
```

refers to the teacher's print function, while

```
Researcher::print();
```

refers to the researcher's print function. Now consider a main program that sends print messages to a professor object:

```
main(){
  Professor p("Albert Einstein","Relativity");

  p.print();     // professor defaults to a teacher
  p.change();    // change to researcher
  p.print();
}
```

When executed the program will output:

```
my name is: Albert Einstein
my name is: Albert Einstein
and I am an expert in: Relativity
```

The first output line stems from the teacher's print function alone. The second and third line are the result of the professor responding to message `print()` by invoking the teacher's and the researcher's print member functions.

Not all object-oriented programming languages allow such a straightforward treatment of ambiguities that arise from multiple inheritance. In C++ multiple inheritance need not be treated as a special case or extension of inheritance. Instead, single inheritance is treated as a limitation of the more general concept.

3.7 Repeated Inheritance

In large class hierarchies it may happen that a base class occurs more than once. It may happen that some superclasses have a common base class. The features that are inherited from this superclass are then repeatedly present in the derived class. For example, consider a new variation of the `Researcher` class: what if it also is a subclass of class `Person`. The modified class description might be

```
class Researcher: public Person {
  char *expertise;              // field of expertise
public:
  Researcher(char *e, char *n):Person(n){       // constructor
    expertise = e;
  }
  void print(){
    printf("I am an expert in: %s\n", expertise);
  }
};
```

Figure 3.8 shows the researcher class as derived from class `Person`. Therefore, class `Person` occurs twice in the class hierarchy. In effect, any instance of professor will have the member fields defined by `Person` twice. If the name is set, it is not clear which name to set. This may result in the following code fragment:

```
main(){
  Professor p("John Prof","something");

  p.print();
}
```

It will attempt to print the name of the professor object. The name is defined as a member field of class `Person`. Since `Professor` inherits twice from class

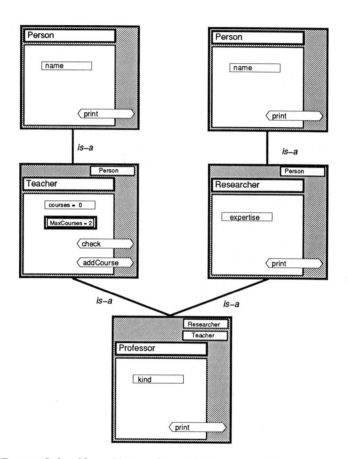

Figure 3.8   Class Hierarchy with Common Base Class

Person, once via superclass Teacher and once via superclass Researcher, the name field occurs twice in a professor object. This results in an ambiguity that the compiler cannot resolve.

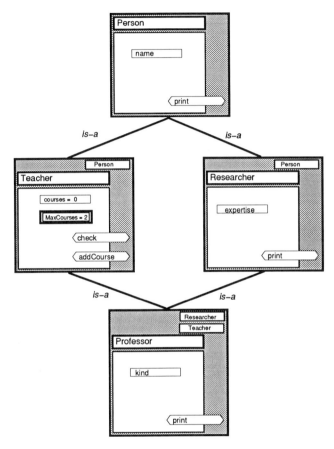

Figure 3.9   Class Hierarchy with Single Common Base Class

Most object-oriented programming languages do not allow the static duplication of a superclass. Whenever a superclass is inherited from repeatedly, its features are not duplicated. In C++ this fact has to be indicated. C++ uses the keyword virtual[6] to denote that the superclass should not be replicated. Both

---

[6]Again, note the inconsistent use of this term in C++.

the `Teacher` and `Professor` classes need to mention the class `Person` as a virtual base class to avoid duplication:

```
class Teacher: public virtual Person { ... };
```

and

```
class Professor: public virtual Person { ... };
```

Figure 3.9 shows the researcher class as derived indirectly from the common superclass `Person`. Now any reference to the member field `name` of a professor object uniquely identifies the professor's name, a feature inherited from the `Person` class.

3.8 Abstract Classes

A class describes the data structure and functionality of its instances. The assumption is that a class will have instances, but not all classes need to have instances. It may be that a class serves as a base class in a class hierarchy to abstract common features of several derived classes. For example, consider the category of "four-legged" animals. Have you ever seen a "four-legged" animal that was just that ? Animals that you will encounter are cats, dogs, kangaroos etc. The category "four-legged animal" describes the common features of these animals. There is, however, no particular "four-legged" animal.

In object-oriented terms, an *abstract class* is a class that serves as a common base class but will not have instances. For example, assume that we want to collect teacher, student, course, and schedule objects of our sample application into a common data structure. Classes `Teacher` and `Student` have a common base class `Person`, so it would be possible to declare

```
Person *collection[10];
```

to define an array to hold 10 pointers to person objects. This array cannot hold courses or schedules, however. The solution is to create a common base class for `Person`, `Course`, and `Schedule`. Figure 3.10 shows the new class hierarchy. Assuming that this superclass is called `Example`, the declaration

```
Example *collection[100];
```

may hold up to 100 example objects, which could be teachers, students, courses or schedules. To benefit from dynamic binding, the `Example` class needs to define all virtual functions that we want to invoke on `Example` objects. The `print` function shown in the class diagram is an example of such a virtual function (it is highlighted in black). Assume that we define a `Collection` class that stores `Example` objects and provides access to them, hiding how objects are actually stored:

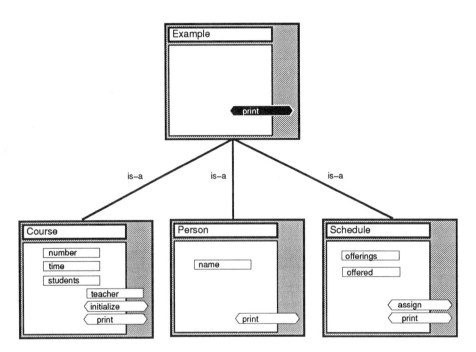

Figure 3.10   Abstract Class Example with Subclasses

```
class Collection {
  Example **list;    // array of pointers to example objects
  int filled;
 public:
  Collection() {
    list = new (Example *[100]);
    filled = 0;
  }
  void add(Example*);
  void print();
};
```

The Collection class keeps an internal list of its elements. It also stores
how many elements fill the collection. The constructor function Collection
allocates enough memory to be able to keep up to 100 elements and initializes
the member field filled to 0. To deposit Example objects into a Collection,
we define an add member function:

```
void Collection::add(Example *element) {
  if (filled < 100)
    list[filled++] = element;
  else
    printf("collection is full \n");
};
```

The member function adds an Example object, which could be a teacher, a
student, a course, or schedule. A second member function, print, might
traverse all elements in a collection and print each of them:

```
void Collection::print() {
  for (int i = 0; i < filled; i++)
    list[i]->print();
};
```

This print member function prints the collection's elements by sending print
messages to each of the elements in the list. The list elements, however, are
typed as Example * (pointer to Example object); therefore it is necessary that
the Example class declares a virtual print function in order to allow dynamic
binding in C++. Its class description is now:

```
class Example {
 public:
  virtual void print(){};
};
```

The body for member function `print` is empty since there is nothing to print for an instance of class `Example`. In fact, it was our intent not to have any instances of the `Example` class. `Example` is an *abstract class*. The derived classes need to declare the appropriate member functions.

Many object-oriented programming languages allow us to enforce these features of an abstract class: it must not have instances and any virtual function it declares needs to be defined by every derived class. In C++ an abstract class is defined in the following way:

```
class Example {
 public:
   virtual void print() = 0;
};
```

The virtual function `print` is assigned the value 0, thus informing the compiler to enforce all derived classes to define a print function. C++ uses the term *pure virtual function* to refer to such a member function. The `Example` class becomes an abstract class. The compiler will also disallow the creation of instances of class `Example`:

```
Example invalidObject;          // error
```

and

```
Example *invalidObject;
invalidObject = new Example;    // error
```

will produce compilation errors.

Other object-oriented programming languages use the term *deferred* to refer to functions that need to be declared in subclasses. A class that declares deferred functions becomes an abstract class.

3.9   Generic Classes

As we have seen in the last section, collections allow the storage of objects. They hide the actual representation of the storage structure, which could store instances of many different classes. Since most object-oriented programming languages are strongly typed, the class of objects that can be stored in a collection has to be fixed when the collection class is defined. Since most object-oriented programming languages provide the class "Object" as a superclass to all classes, the element type of objects stored in a collection is usually "Object." C++ is not among these languages. It does not define a common base class "Object" for all its classes. For elements of different classes to be stored in a collection, they need to agree on a common superclass, e.g., Example, as shown in the last section.

Another possibility is the use of "genericity" [Mey86]. With genericity it is possible to define data structures to hold values of a generic type, or functions to process values of a generic type. Before such data structures or functions are used, the generic type has to be replaced with an existing type. This feature can be used to define a "generic" class. A generic class is a class template that defines and declares everything in a class in terms of a type parameter. A generic class can be transformed into a usable class by replacing the type parameter with a class name. The replacement can be done with an editor, or as done in the programming languages Ada or Eiffel by the compiler.

In its current version C++ does not directly support generic classes. However, it is the intention of the C++ creators to make this feature available in the forthcoming ANSI C++. The Annotated C++ Reference Manual (ARM) [ES90] describes a possible syntax for C++ generic classes. C++ uses the term *class template* to refer to a generic class. A class template differs from a regular class in that it mentions a class parameter to be used in conjunction with the class definition. For example, the collection class can be defined as a class template:

```
template <class T> class Collection {
   T **list;
   int filled;
 public:
   Collection() {
      list = new (T * [100]);
      filled = 0;
   }
   void add(T *);
   void print();
};
```

The Collection class is defined based on a parameter class T. All member fields and member functions are also defined in terms of the parameter. The bodies of the member functions for the Collection class can be defined as follows:

```
template<class T> void Collection<T>::add(T *element) {
   if (filled < 100)
      list[filled++] = element;
   else
      printf("collection is full \n");
}
```

```
template<class T> void Collection<T>::print() {
   for (int i = 0; i < filled; i++)
      list[i]->print();
}
```

As in the example in the last section, this implementation of the collection class assumes that its elements can receive the `print()` message. Collections to hold objects of different classes can be instantiated and accessed with the following statements;

```
Collection<Person> person_collection;
Person p("John");
person_collection.add(&p);
person_collection.print();
```

or

```
Collection<Course> course_collection;
Course c("COP3223");
course_collection.add(&c);
course_collection.print();
```

In both cases, the template class is used to instantiate a collection object. In the first case, its elements are of class `Person`; in the second case, they are of class `Course`. While C++ in its current version does not support these template classes, most of its preprocessors allow the definition of macros to simulate generic classes. Appendix E lists the complete collection class suitable for current C++ compilers.

3.10   Inheritance *versus* Containership

In a class hierarchy classes are usually related by an "*is-a*" relationship. Derived classes extend or specialize base classes and inherit their features. In contrast, consider a "*has-a*" relationship. For example, a cat *has-a* tail. The "cat" category of animals does not inherit features from the "tail" category of animal parts. Instead the "cat" category contains the category of "tail," i.e., a cat instance has a tail.

It is possible to misuse inheritance to represent this containership relation. Especially with multiple inheritance, where it is easy to add another superclass, it is possible to capture "*has-a*" relationships with inheritance.

As an example, consider the `Course` class from our scheduling example. In its previous version, the `Course` class defined member fields for a time slot and a teacher. These features, however, are not common to all courses, they are only common to courses that are scheduled to be taught in a particular semester. Common to all courses would be the course number and course name:

```
class Course {
   char *number;
   char *name;
 public:
   void print();
};
```

This declaration does not define member fields for time slot and teacher. In order to define an appropriate class for a course that is scheduled to be taught in a semester at a specific time we have two choices: (1) the new class could extend the course class with a time slot and a teacher or (2) the new class could contain a course together with a time slot and teacher feature.

The class description for the first case would be

```
class ScheduledCourse: public Course {
   char *time;
 public:
   Teacher *teacher;
   void print() {
     Course::print();
     printf("meeting at %s \n", time);
   }
};
```

Here a ScheduledCourse *is-a* Course. It inherits all features from class Course. For example, a scheduled course object has a name. This feature is inherited from the Course class. The print member function combines the Course print function with a regular printf statement. The printf call prints the time slot at which the course meets.

The class description for the second case would be

```
class ScheduledCourse {
   Course *course;
   char *time;
 public:
   Teacher *teacher;
   void print() {
     course->print();
     printf("meeting at %s \n", time);
   }
};
```

Here a `ScheduledCourse` *has-a* `Course`. There is a member field that refers to a course. Again, there is a `name` field; however, it is within the course object. The `print` function also combines the `Course print` function with a regular `printf` statement. Instead of calling the inherited function, it sends a `print` message to the contained course object.

The question whether inheritance should be used to capture "*has-a*" relationships can generally be answered with no. Class hierarchies should be used to aid in categorizing concepts that specialize and extend each other. If a class hierarchy mixes inheritance and containership, it makes further reuse of its classes harder.

A class hierarchy captures specialization or extension ("*is-a*") relationships among classes. A subclass is a special case or an extension of a superclass. A superclass can also be viewed as a generalization of its derived classes. The "*has-a*" relationship, however, captures an aggregation relationship, where a class "aggregates" or "has" parts. Of course, it is possible to draw part hierarchies, but they need to be considered separately from class hierarchies. Part hierarchies play a role when we design classes. Chapter 12 elaborates on object-oriented design techniques.

3.11 Summary of Chapter

This chapter introduced class hierarchies. Classes that are related with "*is-a*" relationships form a class hierarchy. Subclasses inherit features from superclasses. If only one superclass is allowed, the inheritance is called single. If more than one superclass is allowed, the inheritance is called multiple.

The lookup and binding of messages to methods gets a new dimension with the presence of superclasses. Not only are methods defined by the class of an object, but they may also be inherited from a superclass. Polymorphism is thus extended, and becomes one of the prime features of object-oriented programming.

When inheriting from more than one superclass it is possible to repeatedly inherit features from a common superclass. An abstract class is a class intended only as a superclass; there should not be any instance of it. A generic class allows the specification of a class based on a parameter. Finally, we discussed the difference between the "*is-a*" and "*has-a*" relationships among classes. Inheritance should be limited to the "*is-a*" relationship.

Chapter 4

Encapsulation

Encapsulation is one of the most beneficial concepts in the context of object-oriented programming. Encapsulation combines data structures and functionality into objects. It also hides internal aspects of objects from its users and declares which features of an object are accessible. There are two general types of access to an object: from a client or from an heir. We will describe how C++ manages the different aspects of encapsulation with different variants of its class description syntax.

4.1 What Is Encapsulation ?

One of the primary properties of an object is that it combines data structure and functionality. A software object represents an application entity. It does so by keeping all data pertaining to the application entity bundled together with all the functionality that applies to it. In the terms of a programming language, the code and all related data are packaged together.

In addition to this combination of code and data, we can visualize that an object is inside a capsule. The capsule ensures that the data and code stay together. It also ensures that data and code are not directly visible and accessible. Access to data and code has to be allowed explicitly. The capsule serves as a guard against unauthorized access to an object's internal code and data.

Access to an object is achieved through sending messages. Messages can be used to invoke an object's functionality or to access part of its data. Messages that may access an object are said to be part of the interface to an object. We can visualize the capsule around an object with holes. The holes let only those message pass through that are specified as part of an object's interface. All other messages are just not understood by the object.

Encapsulation is the formal term used to describe the bundling of member fields and functions inside an object. Encapsulation provides information hiding as well as access to selected features of an object.

4.2 Differences in Encapsulation

Since it is a class that describes objects, it is the class that defines what features of an object are visible or not visible The class defines how its instances are encapsulated. Encapsulation provides a capsule around an object that bundles the data fields and functions together. The capsule allows access only to the visible aspects of an object and improves the modularity, quality, and safety of a program.

In general, object-oriented programming languages distinguish two different kinds of access to an object as defined by its class. One kind of access is where another class or a function is a client; i.e., it defines a variable that holds a reference to an object of the class. Another kind of access is where a base class is derived into a subclass. Object-oriented programming languages provide different specification mechanisms and defaults for the different uses.

4.2.1 Client Access

To access any object, it is necessary to know the object's unique identifier, which is usually a variable within some scope. Access to the object is achieved by sending it a message. Through sending a message to an object it is possible to execute one of its member functions or manipulate one of its member fields. The access message is sent by a *sender*. In this context the sender of a message becomes a *client* of the receiver object.

The class of the receiver object defines what messages are understood when received by an instance of the class. The class establishes how permeable the capsule is around the object, and it defines which messages are let through, i.e., which messages form the public interface to an object. All features that are not part of the public interface are hidden inside the class. This allows certain freedom for the designer and programmer of a class. The details of a specific implementation of a feature are hidden from all clients. They can be changed without affecting any clients. The software engineering principle of information hiding is therefore supported directly by object-oriented programming. Object-oriented programs are more likely to be safer and less prone to error from changes.

4.2.2 Subclass Access

A derived class inherits features from its base class. An object has all the features that are defined by its class. In addition, the object inherits features from the superclasses of its class. The base and derived class together specify what features are inherited. In general, the base class may specify which features it makes available to be inherited. Moreover, the derived class may decide which features to inherit from its superclass.

And of course, the derived class may specify which of its inherited features are part of its public interface to clients and subclasses. The concept of encapsulating features relative to subclass access has been introduced to object-oriented programming by newer languages, such as C++ and Eiffel. Smalltalk, for example, does not provide a language feature to control access by subclasses to features of a class.

Encapsulation relative to subclasses has the advantage of ensuring tested behavior of a class, even in a derived class. If a class provides a certain functionality, i.e., a public member function, it is possible to hide the details of its implementation from its subclasses. The subclasses therefore cannot modify the behavior of this functionality; yet, they are free to overwrite the particular public member function, thereby altering the behavior.

For example, consider a class that provides a print function in its public interface. The print function is implemented by sending a `printString` message to a private member field of the class. Assume now that the class is derived into a new subclass. The subclass inherits the print function from its base class. Its designer then chooses to overwrite the member field that receives the `printString` message, sent from within the print function. Now, if this member field contains a reference to an object that cannot respond to the `printString` message, an error will occur. The previously well-tested print function is defunct! If the base class could protect the member field from being overwritten by derived classes, the error would not be possible.

4.3 Specifying Access Rights

C++ is the object-oriented programming language with the richest set of facilities to control access to the features of an object. Throughout the examples, we used the C++ keyword `public` to denote the boundary between the visible and invisible parts of a class. C++ allows even finer control of the visibility of its class features. Table 4.1 shows a skeleton C++ class description. In addition to the keyword `public`, there are two more keywords: `private` and `protected`. They are used to express three different kinds of features for an object. Figure 4.1 shows an object diagram illustrating the three access zones

Table 4.1   General Class Description Layout

```
class ... {
   private:
      ...
   protected:
      ...
   public:
      ...
};
```

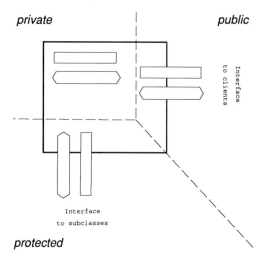

Figure 4.1   Object Diagram with Access Zones

defined by these keywords in an object's class description.

The *private* section contains all private member fields and functions. None of these private features is accessible by clients or subclasses. The *protected* section contains all protected member fields and functions. Protected features are accessible to subclasses. None of these protected features is accessible to clients. The *public* section contains all public member fields and functions. All public features are accessible to clients and subclasses.

Below is an example of a modified person class:

```
class Person {
private:              // beginning of private part
   int age;
protected:            // beginning of protected part
   char *name;
public:               // beginning of public part
   Person(char *n){name = n;};
   void print(){
     if (age < 21)
        printf("I am %d years old, and", age);
     printf("my name is %s\n",name);
   };
};
```

The example shows the use of all three keywords to denote the level of encapsulation for the class. Figure 4.2 shows the new class diagram for the

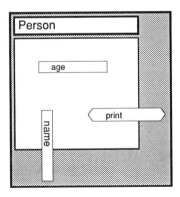

Figure 4.2   Class Diagram for Person

person class. The features following the keyword `private` are hidden inside any instance of class `Person`; features following `public` are accessible to all clients of the class. The keyword `protected` starts a section of features in the class that is accessible to derived classes only.

As an example, consider the following declaration inside a client:

```
Person *p;
```

A person object can be created dynamically since the constructor member function for class `Person` is public:

```
p = Person("John Doe");
```

It is also possible to send a `print` message to person objects:

```
p->print();
```

Object p will understand this message since `print` is a public member function. The following statements, however, are illegal:

```
p->name;        // error, access to protected member
p->age;         // error, access to private member
```

Both statements attempt to access protected and private members of the person object.

Now consider a `Teacher` subclass of `Person`:

```
class Teacher: public Person {
  Collection *courses;
  static int MaxCourses;
 public:
  Teacher(char *name) {
    name = n;
    courses = new Collection;
  };
  void print() {
    Person::print();
    courses->print();
  };
};
```

Inside this class, the public and protected members of class Person are accessible. For example, the constructor function `Teacher` sets the protected inherited member field name. The `print` function calls the public inherited `Person` member function `print`, which prints the name and age of a person. Access to the member field `age` is illegal since it is a private field defined by class `Person`.

4.3.1   Public Inheritance

When a derived class is declared, C++ allows the specification whether the derivation is intended to be public or not. All the examples so far specified that the derivation is public. The class description headlines included the `public` keyword, for example:

```
class Teacher: public Person { ...
```

The teacher class inherits all public and protected features from the person class. In addition, all public features of `Person`, plus all public features of `Teacher`, are accessible to other clients. For example, consider a teacher object:

```
Teacher *t;
```

The question is which are the public features of teacher object t ? The class `Teacher` defines the constructor `Teacher` and the `print` function as public. In addition, it is valid to access t with the `Person` constructor and the `print` function inherited from the `Person` class. Since the inheritance is public, all public features of the base class are public for the derived class.

Without the `public` keyword in the derivation clause, only the public features of `Teacher` are accessible to clients. The keyword `private` may be used to express hidden inheritance:

```
class Teacher: private Person { ...
```

The fact that the teacher class is derived from the person class is hidden. Only the constructor `Teacher` and `print` defined by the `Teacher` class as public are accessible. The statement

```
t->Person::print();      // error
```

is illegal, since `Person::print` is private for class `Teacher`. The fact that `Teacher` is a subclass of `Person` is encapsulated.

4.4   The Trap Door to Encapsulation

C++ has one more feature that controls encapsulation. It allows the definition of friends to a class. A friend of a class has direct access to all private members of a class. Friends can be other classes or functions. This feature is useful for functions that operate on collections of instances of several classes.

For instance, take a function that wants to initialize several teacher objects efficiently. This function may be called `initialize`. The class `Teacher`, as defined in the previous section, defines a private member field `courses` which may hold a collection of objects. The `Teacher` class does not define any access possibility to the course collection, other than the `print` member function that allows printing of all courses in the collection. The `initialize` function needs to initialize the `courses` field with a few courses for each of its teacher objects. This is possible by making the function `initialize` a *friend* of class `Teacher`:

```
class Teacher: public Person {
  friend void initialize();

 // rest of class description

};
```

which allows it to directly access private members of teacher objects:

```
void initialize() {
  Course c[5];
  Teacher *t[5];

  for (int i = 0; i < 5; i++) {
    t[i] = new Teacher;
    t[i]->courses->add(c[i]);
  };
};
```

The function directly accesses the private `courses` member field within the teacher objects. It sends an `add` message to the private field. The private field would normally not be visible. The friend declaration makes the `course` field visible inside the `initialize` function.

It is important to note that the friend mechanism in C++ violates the information hiding property of objects. It gives outside functions access to local member features of an object, and, therefore, should be declared explicitly. This, in turn, is a useful feature in cases where the access rules specified by a class are too prohibitive.

4.5 Summary of Chapter

Encapsulation is a cornerstone of object-oriented programming. It refers to the combination of data and its associated functions inside an object. Encapsulation entails information hiding and giving access to features of an object. The two types of access to an object are access from clients or access from heirs. C++ allows the detailed specification of how clients and heirs may access an object by dividing member features into private, protected, and public parts. A trap door to encapsulation is the declaration of friends. Friends have access to all features of an object without access control.

Chapter 5

An Example Program

Excerpts from a course scheduling application have been used to illustrate the concepts presented in the first four chapters of this book. This chapter presents the complete application, shows the complete class hierarchy of all classes, explains its overall object-oriented organization, and provides all C++ class descriptions plus a main C++ program. This application also shows the existence and use of classes and objects that are provided by supporting libraries.

5.1 The Course Scheduling Application

Suppose that a small university plans to automate its operations. One of the recurring tasks at the university is to schedule courses, teachers, and students every semester. A course, identified by its course number and name, is scheduled for a particular semester with a teacher, and two teaching assistants at a certain time. Students can register for these courses in a specific semester. Teachers can only teach certain courses and have a university-wide limit of how many courses they teach per semester. Teaching assistants are older students, employed by the university to assist professors in teaching a course.

In addition to the task of scheduling courses and registering students, the system must be able to maintain courses, teachers, students, teaching assistants, and schedules for different semesters.

5.2 An Object-Oriented Solution

Objects are the name of the game! The application description mentions quite a few objects. They can usually be detected by selecting the nouns in the text. In our application there are courses, schedules, teachers, students, teaching assistants, and professors. We can capture these objects with classes. Possible classes are course, schedule, teacher, student, teaching assistant, and professor. Some of these classes have common properties. For example, a student has a name, a teacher has a name, a teacher and a teaching assistant have courses to teach, a student and a teaching assistant have courses to take, etc. According to these common properties it is possible to establish "*is-a*" relationships among the classes.

The first task is to establish a class hierarchy that shows the *is-a* relationships among the classes. When establishing a class hierarchy it is advisable to allow a multitude of classes. (One class too many does not hurt!) The class hierarchy represents our interpretation of the concepts that occur in the application. If a class arises that might not be needed immediately, it is still beneficial to name it in the class hierarchy to enhance the accuracy of how the hierarchy reflects the application world. The class may soon be needed in the first revision, update, or enhancement to the system.

Let us first examine the "people" classes. The university considers two basic types of people: employees and students. Employees are teachers, researchers or staff members. Someone who is a teacher and a researcher is a professor. Someone who is a student and a teacher is a teaching assistant. The common superclass for all of them, since all are people, is "Person."

Other classes in this system are the schedule, course, and scheduled course classes. And since we want to maintain collections of instances of all these classes, they are all derived from the abstract class `Example` that serves as base class to store elements in collections. Figure 5.1 shows the class hierarchy of all classes involved in the course scheduling system.

5.3 Supporting Objects

Before we start describing the classes that make up our sample application, we want to introduce some supporting objects that will help the programming task. All object-oriented programming languages provide a library of classes and objects[1] to handle recurring concepts in many applications. In this section we will describe classes of objects that deal with input and output, string handling, and collections.

---

[1] In fact, the number of library classes provided is considered one of the criteria to judge the quality of an object-oriented programming language environment.

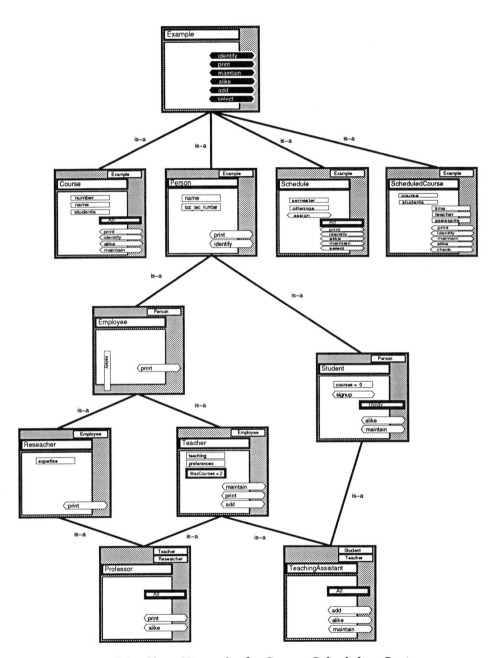

Figure 5.1   Class Hierarchy for Course Scheduling System

5.3.1   Input and Output Objects

Any program wants to input and output data. Traditional programming languages usually provide special statements or library functions for this purpose. C for example, provides the library functions `scanf` and `printf`, among others, to read and write input and output. Since C++ is a superset of C, it also allows the usage of these library functions.

In addition, C++ provides input and output facilities that are object-oriented. Similar to C, C++ views input and output as streams of data. It provides classes that encapsulate the behavior and state of streams. An output stream is modeled by class `ostream`, an input stream is modeled by class `istream`. Since any program has a default input and output stream associated with it — usually the controlling terminal — C++ also provides two predefined objects, `cin` and `cout`, that are instances of the stream classes and can receive messages to cause input and output.

`cout`: **the Output Object**

The output object `cout` understands the message "`<<`". "`<<`" is an operator defined by the class of `cout`, which is `ostream`. The "`<<`" operator is overloaded to accept instances of all C++ predefined types. For example:

```
cout << 10;
```

The output object `cout` receives the message `<<` with parameter `10`. It converts the integer number into two characters, `1` and `0`, and appends them to the output stream. The statement prints

```
10
```

and

```
cout << ''hello world'';
```

prints

```
hello world
```

The "`<<`" operation is defined to return an `ostream` object. In fact, it returns the object it was invoked upon, i.e., the receiver of message "`<<`". Therefore, it is possible to chain multiple "`<<`" operations:

```
cout << ''hello world'' << 10 << ''\n'';
```

which prints

```
hello world 10
```

followed by a new line. C++ also defines an output object called `cerr` that allows printing error messages into a program's error output.

cin: **the Input Object**

The input object cin understands the message ">>". ">>" is an operator defined by the class of cin, which is istream. As the "<<" operator, ">>" is overloaded to accept instances of all C++ predefined types. For example:

```
int i;
cin >> i;
```

will read an integer value from input and assign it to variable i.

5.3.2 String Handling

Most programming languages support the handling of strings. Strings are usually represented as variable-sized arrays of characters. C supports strings as arrays of characters, and it also treats pointers to character arrays special. Since C++ is a superset of C, it also supports them in the same manner.

In addition, most object-oriented programming languages provide a pre-defined class "String" to handle strings in an object-oriented fashion. C++ provides a class "String"[2] that hides the actual representation of a string from its users. The String class provides constructors to initialize strings from C pointers to character arrays. For example:

```
String s("test string");
```

creates an instance of class String holding the string "test string". Operations defined for strings are test for equality (==), assignment (=), test for substring (contains()), string concatenation (+), and many more.

The input and output operators for cin and cout are overloaded to accept string instances as arguments. For example, consider the following simple program:

```
main() {
  String s1("John Doe");
  String s2;

  cout << "my name is " << s1 << "\n";
  cout << "what is your name ? \n";
  cin >> s2;
  if (s1.contains(s2))
    cout << "Hi relative ! \n";
}
```

---

[2]While the "String" class is not part of the standard C++ library, it is provided with some C++ compilers. Appendix C contains a complete implementation of a "String" class suitable for our university example.

which will print

```
my name is John Doe
what is your name ?
```

and wait for input. After typing

```
Doe
```

it will print

```
Hi relative !
```

5.3.3 Collections

Another class frequently found in libraries allows the storage, maintenance and retrieval of sets of objects. These classes are usually called "Collection," "Set," or "Bag." Some libraries provide variations, such as ordered or sequence-able collections, bags, or sets.

Collections allow the storage of objects. They hide the actual representation of the storage structure, which could be arrays, lists, heaps, stacks, etc. Since most object-oriented programming languages are strongly typed, the class of objects that can be stored in a collection has to be fixed when the collection class is defined. Since most object-oriented programming languages provide the class "Object" as a superclass to all classes, the element type of objects stored in a collection is usually "Object." C++ is not among these languages. It does not define a common base class "Object" for all its classes. For elements of different classes to be stored in a collection, they need to agree on a common superclass.

Another possibility is the use of "genericity."[3] With genericity it is possible to define data structures to hold values of a generic type, or functions to process values of a generic type. Before such data structures or functions are used, the generic type has to be replaced with an existing type. This feature can be used to define a "generic" class. A generic class is a class template that defines and declares everything in a class in terms of a type parameter. A generic class can be transformed into a usable class by replacing the type parameter with a class name. The replacement can be done with an editor, or — as done in the programming languages Ada and Eiffel — by the compiler.

Since C++ in its current version does not have a common superclass "Object" nor does it officially support generic classes, we will, for our scheduling application, assume that all its classes are subclasses of class "Example." Table 5.1 shows the class description for the abstract class `Example`. It defines

---

[3]See also Section 3.9.

Table 5.1   Example Class Interface

```
class Example {
 public:
  virtual bool identify(String &) = 0;
  virtual void print() = 0;
  virtual void maintain() = 0;
  virtual Example *alike(String &) = 0;
  virtual bool add(Example *) = 0;
  virtual Example* select() = 0;
};
```

Table 5.2   Collection Class Interface

```
class Collection {
  Example **list;
  int size;
  int filled;
  void add_alike(String &);
  static int GrowIncrement;
public:
  Collection() {
    list = new (Example *[GrowIncrement]);
    size = GrowIncrement;
    filled = 0;
  };
  int get_size() {return filled;};
  void add(Example *);
  Example* search(String &);
  Example* search(Example *);
  void remove(Example *);
  void print();
  void maintain();
  Example* select();
};
```

Table 5.3   Collection Class Body

```
int Collection::GrowIncrement = 5;

void Collection::add(Example *element) {
  if (filled >= size) {
    Example **oldlist = list;
    list = new (Example *[size + GrowIncrement]);
    for (int i = 0; i < size; i++)
      list[i] = oldlist[i];
    size += GrowIncrement;
  };
  list[filled++] = element;
};

Example* Collection::search(String &key) {
  for (int i = 0; i < filled; i++)
    if (list[i]->identify(key))
      return list[i];
  return NULL;
};

Example* Collection::search(Example *key) {
  for (int i = 0; i < filled; i++)
    if (list[i] == key)
      return list[i];
  return NULL;
};

void Collection::remove(Example *element) {
  int j = 0;
  Example **oldlist = list;
  for (int i = 0; i < filled; i++)
    if (oldlist[i] != element)
      list[j++] = oldlist[i];
  filled = j;
};

void Collection::print() {
  if (filled == 0)
    cout << "collection is empty\n";
  else
    for (int i = 0; i < filled; i++)
      list[i]->print();
};
```

Table 5.3   Collection Class Body (continued)

```
void Collection::maintain(){
  String selection, answer;
  Example *sel_example;

  while (TRUE) {
    print();
    cout << "Select an entry or enter 0 to exit: ";
    cin >> selection;
    if (selection == "0") break;
    if ((sel_example = search(selection)) != NULL) {
      sel_example->print();
      cout << "maintain (m) or delete (d) ? ";
      cin >> selection;
      if (selection.contains("d"))
        remove(sel_example);
      else
        sel_example->maintain();
    } else {
      cout << "not found, do you want to create it (y/n) ? ";
      cin >> answer;
      if (answer.contains("y"))
        add_alike(selection);
    };
  };
};

Example* Collection::select() {
  String selection;
  print();
  cout << "enter name: ";
  cin >> selection;
  return(search(selection));
};

void Collection::add_alike(String &name) {
  if (filled == 0)
    cout << "sorry, list is empty, cannot add\n";
  else {
    Example *element = list[0]->alike(name);
    add(element);
  };
};
```

six virtual functions: `identify` uses a string object to determine whether an object has been found; `print` allows the output of information about an object; `maintain` performs change and update operations; `alike` returns an object of the same class as the receiver; `add` adds an `Example` object to the receiver's internal state; and `select` returns an `Example` object. All these functions are declared to be pure virtual and are assigned 0; i.e., all subclasses of `Example` have to define these functions. Since `Example` is an abstract class, no instances will be allowed.

The `Example` class now serves as the vehicle to store elements in a collection. Table 5.2 shows the class interface for the `Collection` class. It defines private member fields to store the `Example` objects (`list`), its size, and its fill status. It also defines a static member field `GrowIncrement` that determines the initial size and increment to grow for the internal private storage structure.

The class interface also describes a public constructor to initialize a newly created collection object. The rest of the class interface declares the function prototypes for the member functions understood by objects of this class. They have to be defined in the class body.

Table 5.3 shows the implementation details of class `Collection`. The first line of the class body sets the static member field `GrowIncrement` to 5. The following lines elaborate the bodies of the member functions of class `Collection`. As an example of how objects are maintained inside a collection, consider the `add` member function. This function is used to add a new element to an existing collection. The element to be added is passed as an argument. The function first checks whether the number of elements stored (`filled`) has reached the current size (`size`) of the collection. If so, it declares a temporary local variable (`oldlist`) to hold the current list of objects in the collection. Then it allocates, using the `new` operation, enough memory to hold the current size of the collection plus the number of elements specified by the `GrowIncrement` class variable. Next, in a loop it copies all elements from the old list (`oldlist`) into the new list (`list`) and increments the size of the collection. Finally, or if the collection was not full beforehand, it stores the `element` in the first open slot of the `list` and increments the fill status (`filled`). From this implementation of the `add` member function we see that the collection uses a semidynamic array of pointers as its internal representation.

A second member function of interest is the `search` function. It searches for an element in the collection based on a `key` argument. The function is overloaded; it can be called with a `String` or `Example` argument. In both cases, the function traverses all elements in the `list`. If the argument was a string, it sends an `identify(key)` message to each element. `Identify` is a virtual function implemented by all objects that can be stored in a collection, since they have to be instances of classes that are subclasses of `Example`. If the argument was an `Example` object, it is compared directly with the element

---

Table 5.4   Person Class Interface

```
class Person: public Example {
  String name;
  String soc_sec_number;
 public:
  Person(){};
  Person(String &n):name(n){};
  void print(){
    cout << "Person: " << name << "\n";
  };
  virtual bool identify(String &);
  virtual void maintain(){};
  virtual bool add(Example *){};
  virtual Example* select(){};
  virtual Example* alike(String &){};
};
```

---

in the `list`. Eventually, one of the elements will be identified and the member function will return that element. If the element is not found, it will return the value `NULL` to indicate failure.

A third member function of interest is `maintain` (see Table 5.3). It maintains the elements in the collection. In a loop it prints all elements of the collection and prompts the user for a selection. If the selection is an element in the collection, the user has the choice to delete or maintain it. Deletion is achieved by calling the `remove` member function. Maintenance is achieved by sending a `maintain` message to the selected element. It is up to the elements in a collection to implement their individual maintenance behavior. If the selection is not yet a member in the collection, the user is asked for permission to create it. A new element is created with a call to the local `add_alike` function which creates a new element of the same class as the other elements in the collection.

In summary, it should be apparent that the classes presented in this section have applications beyond our simple course scheduling application.

5.4   The Person Class Hierarchy

We can now turn to the classes that model the concepts in our course scheduling application. Let us first consider the class `Person` and its derived classes.

Table 5.4 shows the class interface description for class `Person`. This class is a subclass of the abstract class `Example`. `Person` has two private member

---

Table 5.5   Person Class Body

```
bool Person::identify(String &search) {
  if ((name == search) || (soc_sec_number == search))
    return TRUE;
  else
    return FALSE;
};
```

Table 5.6   Employee Class Interface

```
class Employee: public virtual Person {
 protected:
  int salary;
 public:
  Employee(){
    salary = 0;
  };
  void print(){
    cout << "Employee: ";
    Person::print();
  };
};
```

---

fields of class String to hold the name and social security number of a person. It also defines a constructor to initialize a person's name, and a print function to print this information. The virtual functions maintain, add, and select receive empty bodies; i.e., they do nothing when these messages are received. However, class Person defines the identify member function.   Table 5.5 shows how the identify function is implemented. The string argument is compared to the name and soc_sec_number to determine the identity of the person.

Class Employee is a subclass of Person. Table 5.6 shows its class description. Note that Person is a virtual base class to avoid repeated inheritance for further subclasses of Employee. The Employee class defines a protected salary field (a protected field is accessible in derived classes), a public constructor to initialize employee objects, and a print member function. The print member function uses the print member function inherited from class Person to achieve its task.   Table 5.7 shows the Researcher class as a subclass of Employee. It defines a private expertise string and a public print member function.

Table 5.7   Researcher Class Interface

```
class Researcher: public virtual Employee {
  String expertise;
public:
  void print(){
    Person::print();
    cout << "   with expertise: " << expertise;
  };
};
```

Table 5.8   Teacher Class Interface

```
class Teacher: public virtual Employee {
  friend void initialize();
  Collection *teaching;
  Collection *preferences;
  static int MaxCourses;        // course maximum
public:
  Teacher() {
    teaching = new Collection;
    preferences = new Collection;
  };
  void maintain();
  void print(){
    cout << "Teacher: ";
    Employee::print();
  };
  bool add(Example *);
};
```

Table 5.9   Teacher Class Body

```
int Teacher::MaxCourses = 2;

void Teacher::maintain() {
  cout << "can teach these courses: \n";
  preferences->maintain();
};

bool Teacher::add(Example *c) {
  if (teaching->get_size() < Teacher::MaxCourses)
    if (preferences->search(c) != NULL) {
      teaching->add(c);
      return TRUE;
    }
  cout << "teacher cannot teach course\n";
  return FALSE;
}
```

Another subclass of Employee is the Teacher class. Table 5.8 shows its class interface. First, it declares the initialize function to be its *friend*; i.e., it will have access to its private members. The Teacher class also defines two private members, teaching and preferences, which refer to instances of class Collection. They are used to store those courses a teacher prefers to teach and those courses a teacher actually teaches. Note the difference between this new class description and the description of the Teacher class in earlier chapters. Earlier, there was a field courses to hold how many courses are taught by a teacher. Now, there is no need to explicitly store that number since we use a collection to hold all courses that a teacher is teaching. To get how many courses the collection holds, i.e., how many courses a teacher is teaching, we can send a get_size message to the teaching collection (get_size is a member function of class Collection, see Table 5.2).

The class also defines a static member field MaxCourses to limit the number of courses taught by any teacher. In the public section, the Teacher class defines constructors to initialize its name, and the member fields to hold the collections. It also defines more member function prototypes, similar to the previously discussed classes.

Of interest is how the Teacher class implements the maintain and add member functions. Table 5.9 shows the bodies of these functions. The maintain member function defines how a teacher maintains his or her list of preferred courses. The preference member field holds a collection of course

---

Table 5.10   Student Class Interface

```
class Student: public virtual Person {
  Collection *taking;
  void signup();
 public:
  static Collection *Body;
  Student(String &n):Person(n) {;
    taking = new Collection;
    Body->add(this);
  };
  Example *alike(String &name){
    return(new Student(name));
  };
  void maintain();
};
```

---

objects. In the `maintain` function the `Teacher` class delegates the maintenance of these courses to the collection itself. It does so by sending the `maintain` message to the `preference` collection. Consult the listing in Table 5.3 on how a collection implements the maintenance of its elements.

The `add` member function adds a course to the `teaching` collection of courses a teacher is teaching. It does so after it has verified whether the maximum number of courses has not been exceeded and the `preference` collection contains the course; i.e., the teacher has a preference for this course.[4] The course is added by sending the message `add` to the collection field `teaching`. Consult the listing in Table 5.3 on how a collection implements the `add` member function.

`Student` is another subclass of class `Person`. Table 5.10 shows its class interface description. It defines a private member field `taking` to maintain a collection of courses that a student is registered for. The `Student` class declares a static member field `Body` to hold a collection. This collection is intended to contain all students that exist. Remember that static member fields — also known as class variables — are global to all instances of a class. Note that the constructor adds the object `this` to the `Body` collection whenever it is invoked, which is whenever a student object is created. Therefore, the static member field `Student::Body` will contain all student objects.

Table 5.11 shows the member function bodies for class `Student`. First, it ensures that the `Student::Body` is initialized to contain an empty collection at

---

[4]Of course, more checks to validate the assignment of a course to a teacher could be envisioned, e.g., to ensure the courses do not overlap in time, etc. These checks could be inserted into the `add` member function.

Table 5.11   Student Class Body

```
Collection* Student::Body = new Collection;

void Student::maintain() {
  String selection;
  while (TRUE) {
    cout << "register (r) for course or maintain (m) ? ";
    cin >> selection;
    if (selection.contains("r"))
      signup();
    else if (selection.contains("m")) {
      cout << "student is registered for these courses:\n";
      taking->maintain();
    } else
      break;
  };
}

void Student::signup() {
  Example *sel_schedule, *sel_course;
  cout << "select a semester:\n";
  if ((sel_schedule = Schedule::All->select()) != NULL) {
    cout << "select which course:\n";
    if ((sel_course = sel_schedule->select()) != NULL) {
      taking->add(sel_course);
      sel_course->add(this);
    };
  };
}
```

Table 5.12   Professor Class Interface

```
class Professor: public Teacher, public Researcher {
 public:
   static Collection *All;
   Professor(String &n):Person(n){
     All->add(this);
   };
   void print(){
     Teacher::print();
   };
   Example* alike(String &name) {
     return(new Professor(name));
   };
};

Collection* Professor::All = new Collection;
```

the beginning of the program. The member function maintain is implemented
as a loop asking the user whether to register the student for a new course
or to maintain the collection of courses the student is already registered for.
To register a student, it calls the private member function signup.[5] If the
user selects to maintain the list of courses, the student delegates this task by
sending the maintain message to the taking collection (see Table 5.3).

The signup member function selects a semester schedule and one of the
courses in that semester by sending select messages to the collection All
of all schedules, and to the collection of all courses within a schedule. It
then adds the selected course to the taking collection. It also adds the student to the list of students who take the selected courses, by sending an add
message with parameter this to selected course sel_course (method add is
implemented by class ScheduledCourse, see listing in Table 5.20).

The Professor class (Table 5.12) has two base classes: Teacher and
Researcher. It defines a static member field All to maintain a list of all
professor objects. It is filled by the constructor. The class also defines the
alike member function to return another instance of the Professor class.
The alike member function is sent by a collection when it wants to add a new
element of the same class as the other elements already in the collection (see
the implementation of member function add_alike in Table 5.3).

The TeachingAssistant class (Table 5.13) also benefits from multiple in-

---

[5]We could not name this member function register, since register is a reserved word in
C++.

Table 5.13   TeachingAssistant Class Interface

```
class TeachingAssistant: public Teacher, public Student {
 public:
   static Collection *All;
   TeachingAssistant(String &n):Person(n),Student(n){
     All->add(this);
   };
   bool add(Example *);
   Example* alike(String &);
   void maintain();
};
```

---

heritance. It is derived from the Student and Teacher classes. From Student it inherits the features to register for a course and to be part of the student body. From Teacher it inherits the features to have course preference and teaching course collections. There is, however, one problem: it inherits the maintain member function from both the Student and Teacher class.

Table 5.14 shows how the TeachingAssistant class resolves the ambiguity. It overwrites the inherited maintain functions with its own version. In this function, it prompts the user to decide whether to maintain a teaching assistant as a teacher or student. The class body also initializes the All static member field as an empty collection. As in the Professor class, it is filled by the constructor whenever an instance is created. The class body also defines a new version of the add member function. It overwrites what is inherited from class Teacher. The special behavior of this function is that it increments the assistant's salary if a course to be taught is added. To add the course, it explicitly calls the add function of class Teacher. Note that the salary field is inherited from the employee class. This field is accessible, since it is defined as protected, which allows access by subclasses. In our example, a TeachingAssistant receives a "$1000" salary increase for teaching a course.

5.5   Courses and Schedules

The classes that remain to be discussed are Course, Schedule, and the class that models courses being offered in a particular semester: ScheduledCourse. All of them are subclasses of class Example so they can be stored as elements of a collection.

Table 5.15 shows the class interface description of class Course. A course has private strings to hold its name and course number, and a maximum capacity of students. A static member field All holds all instances of courses,

Table 5.14   TeachingAssistant Class Body

```
Collection* TeachingAssistant::All = new Collection;

Example* TeachingAssistant::alike(String &name) {
  return(new TeachingAssistant(name));
};

void TeachingAssistant::maintain() {
  String selection;
  cout << "as teacher (t) or student (s): ";
  cin >> selection;
  if (selection.contains("t"))
    Teacher::maintain();
  else
    Student::maintain();
}

bool TeachingAssistant::add(Example *c) {
  if (Teacher::add(c)) {
    salary += 1000;
    return TRUE;
  } else
    return FALSE;
};
```

Table 5.15   Course Class Interface

```
class Course: public Example {
  String number;
  String name;
  int capacity;
public:
  static Collection *All;
  Course(String &nu, String &na):
        number(nu),name(na),capacity(25) {
    All->add(this);
  };
  void print() {
    cout << "Course: " << number << " - " << name << "\n";
  };
  bool identify(String &);
  Example* alike(String &);
  void maintain();
  bool add(Example *){};
  Example* select(){};
};
```

and it is filled by the constructor and initialized in the class body. Table 5.16 shows the body implementation of class Course. Of interest is the alike member function. Unlike the alike functions for other classes, this function first searches all existing courses for a course with a name as provided by the argument name. Only if the course does not exist is a new course created.

The member function maintain allows changing to the name or capacity of a course. It prompts the user for updates to a course object, effects the change, and calls the print function to display the new status of the course object.

The Schedule class is shown in Table 5.17. Similar to other classes, it defines some private member fields (semester and offerings) and a private member function (assign). It also defines a static member All to collect all schedule instances. The maintain member function (Table 5.18) prompts the user to either call assign to schedule a new course for a semester or send a maintain message to the collection of courses that are offered. The assign member function prompts the user to select a course, a time, a teacher, and two teaching assistants. Then it creates an instance of class ScheduledCourse (see Table 5.19) and sends it the message check to determine whether time, teacher, and assistants can all be scheduled together. If check returns TRUE, the scheduled course instance is added to its collection of offerings.

Table 5.16   Course Class Body

```
Collection* Course::All = new Collection;

Example* Course::alike(String &name) {
  Example *element;
  if ((element = All->search(name)) == NULL) {
    element = new Course(name,"");
  };
  return element;
};

void Course::maintain() {
  String selection;
  while (TRUE) {
    cout << "has capacity: " << capacity << "\n";
    cout << "change capacity (c) or name (n) ? ";
    cin >> selection;
    if (selection.contains("c")) {
      cout << "enter new capacity: ";
      cin >> capacity;
    } else if (selection.contains("n")) {
      cout << "enter new name: ";
      cin >> name;
    } else
      break;
    print();
  };
};

bool Course::identify(String &search) {
  if ((number == search) || (name == search))
    return TRUE;
  else
    return FALSE;
};
```

Table 5.17   Schedule Class Interface

```
class Schedule: public Example {
  String semester;
  Collection *offerings;
  void assign();
public:
  static Collection* All;
  Schedule(String &s):semester(s){
    offerings = new Collection;
    All->add(this);
  };
  void print(){
    cout << "Schedule for: " << semester << "\n";
  };
  bool identify(String &search) {
    return (semester == search);
  };
  Example* alike(String &name) {
    return(new Schedule(name));
  };
  bool add(Example *){};
  void maintain();
  Example *select(){
    return offerings->select();
  };
};
```

Table 5.18   Schedule Class Body

```
Collection* Schedule::All = new Collection;

void Schedule::maintain(){
  String selection;

  while (TRUE) {
    cout << "assign (a) new course or maintain (m) ? ";
    cin >> selection;
    if (selection.contains("a"))
      assign();
    else if (selection.contains("m")) {
      cout << "these courses are offered:\n";
      offerings->maintain();
    } else
      break;
  };
}

void Schedule::assign() {
  Example *selection;
  ScheduledCourse *schedCourse;

  cout << "select a course:\n";
  if ((selection = Course::All->select()) != NULL) {
    schedCourse = new ScheduledCourse(selection);
    cout << "enter time: ";
    cin >> schedCourse->time;
    cout << "select a teacher:\n";
    if ((selection=Professor::All->select()) != NULL) {
      schedCourse->teacher = selection;
      cout << "select first teaching assistant:\n";
      if ((selection=TeachingAssistant::All->select()) != NULL) {
        schedCourse->assistants[0] = selection;
        cout << "select second teaching assistant:\n";
        if ((selection=TeachingAssistant::All->select()) != NULL) {
          schedCourse->assistants[1] = selection;
          if (schedCourse->check())
            offerings->add(schedCourse);
        };
      };
    };
  };
}
```

Table 5.19   ScheduledCourse Class Interface

```
class ScheduledCourse: public Example {
  Course *course;
  Collection *students;
public:
  ScheduledCourse(Example *c){
    course = (Course *) c;
    students = new Collection;
  };
  String time;
  Example *teacher;
  Example *assistants[2];
  void print();
  bool identify(String &s) {
    return (course->identify(s));
  };
  void maintain(){
    course->maintain();
  };
  Example* alike(String &name) {
    return(new ScheduledCourse(course->alike(name)));
  };
  bool check();
  bool add(Example *){};
  Example* select(){};
};
```

Table 5.20 ScheduledCourse Class Body

```
void ScheduledCourse::print(){
  course->print();
  cout << "   meeting at: " << time;
  cout << "\ntaught by: \n";
  teacher->print();
  assistants[0]->print();
  assistants[1]->print();
}

bool ScheduledCourse::check() {
  if (teacher->add(course))
    if (assistants[0]->add(course))
      return (assistants[1]->add(course));
  return FALSE;
}
```

The last class to consider is ScheduledCourse (Table 5.19). It keeps two private member fields: course and students. course refers to the course that is being scheduled, and students maintains a collection of who takes the course. The constructor accepts a pointer to a course object as argument to initialize the course field. Notable member functions are maintain, which uses the Course classes' maintain function, and alike, which retrieves an alike course before it creates and returns a new ScheduledCourse object.

Finally, Table 5.20 shows the implementation of member functions print and check for class ScheduledCourse. print outputs the complete information known about a scheduled course by sending appropriate print messages to the member fields. check adds a particular course to the teacher, the first and second assistant, and returns its success.

5.6 Creating Instances

The classes described in the last sections do not by themselves implement a solution to our application problem. A main program is needed to create instances of these classes and to start sending messages to them.

The main task of this application is to schedule courses for semesters and to register students for them. To achieve this, there needs to exist a set of professors, courses, teaching assistants, and students.

Table 5.21 shows the function initialize that is called from the main program to create sets of professors, courses, assistants, and schedules. It does

Table 5.21   Initialization Function

```
void initialize() {

  int i;

// create professors

  Professor *prof[4];
  for (i = 0; i < 4; i++) {
    prof[i] = new Professor(String("Teacher-") + dec(i+1));
  };

// create courses

  Course *course[4];
  for (i = 0; i< 4; i++) {
    course[i] = new Course(String("COP") + dec(i+1),
                           String("Course-") + dec(i+1));
  };

// create teaching assistants

  TeachingAssistant *ta[4];
  for (i = 0; i < 4; i++) {
    ta[i] = new TeachingAssistant(String("Assistant-") + dec(i+1));
  };
```

Table 5.21   Initialization Function (continued)

```
// add course preferences

  prof[0]->preferences->add(course[0]);
  prof[0]->preferences->add(course[1]);
  prof[0]->preferences->add(course[2]);
  prof[1]->preferences->add(course[0]);
  prof[2]->preferences->add(course[1]);
  prof[2]->preferences->add(course[3]);
  prof[3]->preferences->add(course[1]);

  ta[0]->preferences->add(course[0]);
  ta[0]->preferences->add(course[1]);
  ta[0]->preferences->add(course[2]);
  ta[1]->preferences->add(course[0]);
  ta[2]->preferences->add(course[1]);
  ta[2]->preferences->add(course[3]);
  ta[3]->preferences->add(course[1]);

// create two schedules

  Schedule *sched[2];
  sched[0] = new Schedule("Spring91");
  sched[1] = new Schedule("Fall91");

// create Students

  Student *student[4];
  for (i = 0; i < 4; i++) {
    student[i] = new Student(String("Student-") + dec(i+1));
  };

}
```

so by calling the appropriate constructors. Also, the function adds courses to the professors' and assistants' lists of preferred courses. It has access to the private `preferences` member field of class `Teacher`, since it is a *friend*.

The main program is shown in Table 5.22. After calling the `initialize` function it presents a menu of choices to the user in a loop. The user may select to maintain professors, courses, teaching assistants or schedules, or to register students. Based on the selection made by the user, the `main` program sends `maintain` to one of the static member fields of the appropriate class.

For example, consider a user who wishes to examine and possibly update the crowd of professors maintained in our system. The user selects "1" from the menu of choices. The `main` program receives this `selection` and sends the `maintain` message to object `Professor::All`, which is a static member field of class professor. It contains a collection of all professor objects that have already been created (so far, the `initialize` function has created a few professor objects to get us started). `Professor::All` is of class `Collection`, which defines a `maintain` method (see Table 5.3).

Table 5.23 shows a session to maintain professors. After the initial menu of choices, it shows the list of professors that are known. They are listed by the `maintain` message as received by collection `Professor::All`. Within the `maintain` method, the listing is achieved by executing the local function `print`, or in object-oriented terms: "sending the message `print` to itself."

As we have discussed earlier, the `Collection`'s print function sends print messages to all elements in the collection. In the case of the `Professor::All` collection, the elements are professor objects. They receive `print` messages and respond (see Table 5.12) by invoking the `Teacher` class's `print` function and prepending the string "Teacher: " to the output. The `Teacher`'s print delegates printing further to the `Employee` class (see Table 5.8), which delegates it to the `Person` class (see Table 5.6), and finally prints the professor's name (see Table 5.4). For the first professor object in the collection this results in:

```
Teacher: Employee: Person: Teacher-1
```

All professor objects are listed. The `maintain` function now asks the user to make a selection from the list. The user enters a professor's name, here `Teacher-2`. The selection is used to search the collection. Again, like printing, searching a collection is achieved by traversing all elements in the collection (see Table 5.3). Each element in the collection receives an `identify` message. The argument passed with the message is the selection string provided by the user. Therefore, the professor objects in the `Professor::All` collection receive the message:

```
identify("Teacher-2")
```

Table 5.22   Main Program

```
main() {
  initialize();                    // setup a number of objects

  while(TRUE) {

    int selection;

    cout << "Welcome, these are the available services:\n";
    cout << "  1 Maintain Professors\n";
    cout << "  2 Maintain Courses\n";
    cout << "  3 Maintain Teaching Assistants\n";
    cout << "  4 Maintain Schedule\n";
    cout << "  5 Register Students\n";
    cout << "Enter selection number or 0 to exit: ";
    cin >> selection;

    if (selection == 0)
      break;
    else if (selection == 1)
      Professor::All->maintain();
    else if (selection == 2)
      Course::All->maintain();
    else if (selection == 3)
      TeachingAssistant::All->maintain();
    else if (selection == 4)
      Schedule::All->maintain();
    else if (selection == 5)
      Student::Body->maintain();
  };
  cout << "Bye -- thanks for using the scheduling system\n";
}
```

Table 5.23   Program Run: Maintaining Professors

```
Welcome, these are the available services:
  1 Maintain Professors
  2 Maintain Courses
  3 Maintain Teaching Assistants
  4 Maintain Schedule
  5 Register Students
Enter selection number or 0 to exit: 1
Teacher: Employee: Person: Teacher-1
Teacher: Employee: Person: Teacher-2
Teacher: Employee: Person: Teacher-3
Teacher: Employee: Person: Teacher-4
Select an entry or enter 0 to exit: Teacher-2
Teacher: Employee: Person: Teacher-2
maintain (m) or delete (d) ? m
can teach these courses:
Course: COP1 - Course-1
Select an entry or enter 0 to exit: COP3
not found, do you want to create it ? y
Course: COP1 - Course-1
Course: COP3 - Course-3
Select an entry or enter 0 to exit: 0
Teacher: Employee: Person: Teacher-1
Teacher: Employee: Person: Teacher-2
Teacher: Employee: Person: Teacher-3
Teacher: Employee: Person: Teacher-4
Select an entry or enter 0 to exit: 0
```

Table 5.24   Program Run: Maintaining Courses

```
Welcome, these are the available services:
  1 Maintain Professors
  2 Maintain Courses
  3 Maintain Teaching Assistants
  4 Maintain Schedule
  5 Register Students
Enter selection number or 0 to exit: 2
Course: COP1 - Course-1
Course: COP2 - Course-2
Course: COP3 - Course-3
Course: COP4 - Course-4
Select an entry or enter 0 to exit: COP4
Course: COP4 - Course-4
maintain (m) or delete (d) ? m
has capacity: 25
do you want to change: capacity (c) or name (n) it ? c
enter new capacity: 35
Course: COP4 - Course-4
has capacity: 35
do you want to change: capacity (c) or name (n) it ? 0
Course: COP1 - Course-1
Course: COP2 - Course-2
Course: COP3 - Course-3
Course: COP4 - Course-4
Select an entry or enter 0 to exit: 0
```

Table 5.25   Program Run: Maintaining Teaching Assistants

```
Welcome, these are the available services:
  1 Maintain Professors
  2 Maintain Courses
  3 Maintain Teaching Assistants
  4 Maintain Schedule
  5 Register Students
Enter selection number or 0 to exit: 3
Teacher: Employee: Person: Assistant-1
Teacher: Employee: Person: Assistant-2
Teacher: Employee: Person: Assistant-3
Teacher: Employee: Person: Assistant-4
Select an entry or enter 0 to exit: Assistant-2
Teacher: Employee: Person: Assistant-2
maintain (m) or delete (d) ? m
as teacher (t) or student (s): t
can teach these courses:
Course: COP1 - Course-1
Select an entry or enter 0 to exit: COP4
not found, do you want to create it ? y
Course: COP1 - Course-1
Course: COP4 - Course-4
Select an entry or enter 0 to exit: 0
Teacher: Employee: Person: Assistant-1
Teacher: Employee: Person: Assistant-2
Teacher: Employee: Person: Assistant-3
Teacher: Employee: Person: Assistant-4
Select an entry or enter 0 to exit: 0
```

which they need to answer with true or false. But class Professor does not implement a identify method. We need to consider the class hierarchy to find which of Professor's superclasses implements identify (we are now tracing the compiler's actions). Figure 5.1 shows the complete class diagrams for all classes in our application. Class Person implements method identify. Table 5.4 shows how identify is implemented. It will return TRUE if either the name or soc_sec_number of the receiving person object matches the search string.

The second professor object in the Professor::All collection is found in this way. The maintain function asks the user whether he wants to maintain or delete the selected professor object. To delete the object, it would call the local remove function. In our example run, the user wishes to maintain, which results in a maintain message being sent to the selected professor object.

The maintain method is implemented by the Teacher class. It maintains the list of a teacher's course preferences by sending it a maintain message in turn. Since preferences contains a collection, we (and the compiler) find the implementation of maintain in the Collection class (see Table 5.3). It lists its elements — now the elements are course objects — and asks the user for a selection. Note that earlier the maintain function listed professor objects, and now it lists course objects. This is an example of polymorphism. In our example run, the user selects COP3, which is not an element of the current collection. The user is therefore prompted whether he wishes to add this course to the list of course preferences for the current professor object. The course is then added with the local add_alike method. A collection adds a new element by sending the alike message to one of its elements to retrieve a properly typed element. In our case, a course object receives the alike message (see Table 5.15) and proceeds as follows: it searches the Course::All collection for a course with the same name; if one exists, it is returned, else a new course object is created and returned.

Back in the add_alike function (see Table 5.3), this element is added to the collection, and the maintain function proceeds to prompt the user for more selections. The user indicates that he is done by entering "0", which causes a return to the maintain function of class Teacher. This in turn returns to its caller, the maintain function operating on the collection of all professors, Professor::All. Again, the user selects "0" and we are done with the task of maintaining professors.

Table 5.24 shows a session to maintain courses. Table 5.25 shows a session to maintain teaching assistants. Table 5.26 shows a session to maintain schedules. And finally, Table 5.27 shows a session to register students. It is left as an exercise to the reader to trace the execution of these program runs.

Let us now consider the main program again. It does not seem to adhere to the same object-oriented style as the other functions defined for the classes. The main function continues old-fashioned programming style with its case

Table 5.26   Program Run: Maintaining Schedules

```
Welcome, these are the available services:
  1 Maintain Professors
  2 Maintain Courses
  3 Maintain Teaching Assistants
  4 Maintain Schedule
  5 Register Students
Enter selection number or 0 to exit: 4
Schedule for: Spring91
Schedule for: Fall91
Select an entry or enter 0 to exit: Fall91
Schedule for: Fall91
maintain (m) or delete (d) ? m
assign (a) new course or maintain (m) ? a
select a course:
Course: COP1 - Course-1
Course: COP2 - Course-2
Course: COP3 - Course-3
Course: COP4 - Course-4
enter name: COP1
enter time: MW1030-1200
select a teacher:
Teacher: Employee: Person: Teacher-1
Teacher: Employee: Person: Teacher-2
Teacher: Employee: Person: Teacher-3
Teacher: Employee: Person: Teacher-4
enter name: Teacher-1
select first teaching assistant:
Teacher: Employee: Person: Assistant-1
Teacher: Employee: Person: Assistant-2
Teacher: Employee: Person: Assistant-3
Teacher: Employee: Person: Assistant-4
enter name: Assistant-1
select second teaching assistant:
Teacher: Employee: Person: Assistant-1
Teacher: Employee: Person: Assistant-2
Teacher: Employee: Person: Assistant-3
Teacher: Employee: Person: Assistant-4
enter name: Assistant-2
```

Table 5.26   Program Run: Maintaining Schedules (continued)

```
assign (a) new course or maintain (m) ? 0
Schedule for: Spring91
Schedule for: Fall91
Select an entry or enter 0 to exit: Fall91
Schedule for: Fall91
maintain (m) or delete (d) ? m
assign (a) new course or maintain (m) ? m
these courses are offered:
Course: COP1 - Course-1
   meeting at: MW1030-1200
taught by:
Teacher: Employee: Person: Teacher-1
Teacher: Employee: Person: Assistant-1
Teacher: Employee: Person: Assistant-2
Select an entry or enter 0 to exit: 0
assign (a) new course or maintain (m) ? 0
Schedule for: Spring91
Schedule for: Fall91
Select an entry or enter 0 to exit: 0
```

---

selection. Can we use dynamic binding to simplify the selecting of maintain functions?

The answer is yes, of course. Consider the following modification to the collection class: adding a new string member field that reflects the nature or purpose of the collection. Of course, we need not change the original Collection class; instead, we create a subclass. The new class, PurposeCollection, derived from class Collection is shown in Table 5.28. It defines a public member field purpose to hold a string, and declares a constructor to initialize it.

We now change the declaration and initialization of the static member fields All and Body in the Professor, Course, TeachingAssistant, Schedule, and Student class to create instances of the new PurposeCollection class:

```
PurposeCollection* Professor::All =
        new PurposeCollection("Maintain Professors");
PurposeCollection* Course::All =
        new PurposeCollection("Maintain Courses");
PurposeCollection* TeachingAssistant::All =
        new PurposeCollection("Maintain Teaching Assistants");
PurposeCollection* Schedule::All =
        new PurposeCollection("Maintain Schedules");
```

Table 5.27   Program Run: Registering Students

```
Welcome, these are the available services:
  1 Maintain Professors
  2 Maintain Courses
  3 Maintain Teaching Assistants
  4 Maintain Schedule
  5 Register Students
Enter selection number or 0 to exit: 5
Teacher: Employee: Person: Assistant-1
Teacher: Employee: Person: Assistant-2
Teacher: Employee: Person: Assistant-3
Teacher: Employee: Person: Assistant-4
Person: Student-1
Person: Student-2
Person: Student-3
Person: Student-4
Select an entry or enter 0 to exit: Student-1
Person: Student-1
maintain (m) or delete (d) ? m
register (r) for course or maintain (m) ? r
select a semester:
Schedule for: Spring91
Schedule for: Fall91
enter name: Fall91
select which course:
Course: COP1 - Course-1
   meeting at: MW1030-1200
taught by:
Teacher: Employee: Person: Teacher-1
Teacher: Employee: Person: Assistant-1
Teacher: Employee: Person: Assistant-2
enter name: COP1
register (r) for course or maintain (m) ? 0
```

Table 5.27   Program Run: Registering Students (continued)

```
Teacher: Employee: Person: Assistant-1
Teacher: Employee: Person: Assistant-2
Teacher: Employee: Person: Assistant-3
Teacher: Employee: Person: Assistant-4
Person: Student-1
Person: Student-2
Person: Student-3
Person: Student-4
Select an entry or enter 0 to exit: Assistant-4
Teacher: Employee: Person: Assistant-4
maintain (m) or delete (d) ? m
as teacher (t) or student (s) s
register (r) for course or maintain (m) ? r
select a semester:
Schedule for: Spring91
Schedule for: Fall91
enter name: Fall91
select which course:
Course: COP1 - Course-1
   meeting at: MW1030-1200
taught by:
Teacher: Employee: Person: Teacher-1
Teacher: Employee: Person: Assistant-1
Teacher: Employee: Person: Assistant-2
enter name: COP1
register (r) for course or maintain (m) ? 0
Teacher: Employee: Person: Assistant-1
Teacher: Employee: Person: Assistant-2
Teacher: Employee: Person: Assistant-3
Teacher: Employee: Person: Assistant-4
Person: Student-1
Person: Student-2
Person: Student-3
Person: Student-4
Select an entry or enter 0 to exit: 0
```

Table 5.28   PurposeCollection Class Interface

```
class PurposeCollection: public Collection {
 public:
   String purpose;
   PurposeCollection(String &n): purpose(n) {};
};
```

```
PurposeCollection* Student::Body =
        new PurposeCollection("Register Students");
```

Now it is possible to greatly simplify the main program. Table 5.29 shows the new version of the main program. The program defines an array of PurposeCollection objects that is initialized with the above modified static member fields. This array greatly simplifies the loop. Inside the loop, the program retrieves the menu text to print from the public purpose field of the collections. The user is prompted for a selection that is used as an index into the worklist array to select the correct collection to maintain.

Notice that the worklist variable holds a list of objects. Elsewhere in our application we used the Collection class to help store and maintain lists of objects. So why not do the same here? It should be apparent that we can convert the worklist list into a collection and use the maintain function to maintain it. As an exercise the reader may want to derive a new subclass from Collection, whose instances could be used instead of the worklist array. Its elements would be Collection objects themselves. Its maintain function would be similar to the body of our main program. The new main program would be simplified to a single maintain message being sent to a single instance of this new collection.

We hope that the example showed how an object-oriented application is composed from classes, and how these classes are brought into life, i.e., how instances are created from them. The instances are the actors that achieve the overall mission of the program by interacting with messages. Also notice the frequent code reuse that we have achieved. The center of the application is the maintain method defined for class Collection. It is used for the many collections that make up this application.

Table 5.29   Better Version of Main Program

```
main() {
  initialize();                  // setup a number of objects

  PurposeCollection *worklist[5] = {
        Professor::All, Course::All, TeachingAssistant::All,
        Schedule::All, Student::Body};

  while(TRUE) {

    int selection;
    cout << "Welcome, these are the available services";
    for (int i = 0; i < 5; i++)
      cout << "  " << i << " " << worklist[i]->purpose << "\n";
    cout << "Enter selection number or 0 to exit: ";
    cin >> selection;

    if ((selection > 0) && (selection < 6))
      worklist[i]->maintain();
    else
      break;
  };
  cout << "Bye -- thanks for using the scheduling system\n";
}
```

5.7   Summary of Chapter

In this chapter we presented a complete object-oriented application that implements a simple course-scheduling system for a university. The example showed the use of existing classes taken from libraries, as well as the declaration of a moderate class hierarchy. The classes, while created for this specific application, can be placed in a class library and reused by future enhancements to the system, or by applications that use similar concepts.

Chapter 6

Object-Oriented Programming Languages

This chapter surveys the major object-oriented programming languages. It begins with an overview of the features that are expected in these languages and then discusses Smalltalk, Objective-C, Eiffel, and an object-oriented version of Pascal in detail. Each of these languages has its own distinct style of syntax and its own interpretation and implementation of the basic concepts. For each language, examples illustrate the basic and special features. The examples are drawn from the course scheduling application discussed in Chapter 5.

6.1   Elements of Object Orientation

Throughout the first part of this book, C++ was the tool to illustrate the concepts of object-oriented programming. C++ is a complete object-oriented programming language, because it sufficiently implements all major features and because it is the most widely used object-oriented language. In this chapter we will discuss the other major object-oriented programming languages. From the pool of possible languages, we have chosen to discuss Smalltalk, Objective-C, Eiffel, and an object-oriented version of Pascal (i.e., TurboPascal), because we think they represent four distinct sectors in the field of object-oriented languages. They are also the four languages that, in addition to C++, are already widely accepted or are gaining wide acceptance.

   To set the backstage for the survey it is useful to reiterate the key concepts that need to be supported by object-oriented programming languages: an object-oriented programming language must be *object* and *class based*, and it must support *inheritance* and *polymorphism*. We will also comment on existing class libraries, and whether a language comes with or fits into, an object-oriented environment, and whether it qualifies for what we call: "Object Heaven."

6.1.1 Object-Based

The underlying model for an object-oriented programming language is the "object." Just as in the everyday world, an object is an identifiable something with a boundary. The object encapsulates data and method elements. Data elements store an object's state. Method elements allow an object to perform its behavior. The methods of an object share the object's data. What methods and data elements are visible outside an object is very important. Computation is achieved by messages that are sent to an object. An object executes one of its methods as a result of receiving a message. A message states "what" should be done by an object, whereas a method expresses "how" it will be done. A message is "bound" to a method either statically or dynamically.

An object-oriented application is a set of objects that work together to achieve an overall goal. In the discussion of object-oriented programming languages we will see how each language treats objects, the sending of messages, the binding of messages to methods, and what measures of encapsulation it allows.

6.1.2 Class-Based

Object-oriented programming languages describe objects with classes. A class is a description of similar objects. The class defines the data and method elements of individual objects. Programming languages need to allow the creation of objects from their classes. The class should also provide the memory management, relieving the programmer from this task. While most object-oriented programming languages provide some kind of memory management, they treat the allocation and deallocation of memory space for an object differently. While there is the consensus that memory is allocated for an object when it is created, and that the object maintains its own space according to its behavior, there are two schools of thought to handle the deallocation of object space. In one, it is the programmer's responsibility to dispose of memory that is occupied by obsolete objects, whereas in the other, it is the programming environment — a watch dog — that takes care of disposing of obsolete objects. The second variety uses a garbage collector as its watch dog, which routinely checks all objects to determine whether any are obsolete, can be disposed of, and its memory freed.

It is also important that the class becomes the structuring entity for all programs. The class description acts as the module that allows the separation of programs into smaller portions.

In our look at object-oriented programming languages we will focus on how they use classes and their facilities to structure a program and handle memory management.

6.1.3 Inheritance

The most important feature supported by object-oriented programming languages is inheritance: the ability to derive new classes from existing ones. Inheritance allows a programmer to draw from and extend large amounts of existing program code. Inheritance is the object-oriented concept that contributes most to the productivity increase attained with object-oriented programming languages.

Classes and their subclasses form class hierarchies, which capture the "is-a" relationships among them. An instance of derived class is also an instance of all its superclasses.

While object-oriented languages all implement inheritance, they vary in how they treat multiple and repeated inheritance, and how they handle the access and redefinition of features in a subclass that are defined by a superclass.

6.1.4 Polymorphism

Polymorphism is another key concept. Conceptually, it is based on the assumption that the type (or class) of a variable need not match the type (or class) of the object that the variable refers to. While an object cannot by itself be polymorphic, a variable which is after all only a marker or temporary helper to refer to an object can have multiple types: a variable declared to be of a certain class may refer to objects of that class, or objects of any subclass. Strictly speaking, the class of a variable declares the minimum requirements for objects it may hold. Since any object of a subclass fulfills the minimum class requirements, i.e., they "are"[1] instances of that superclass, they are correctly typed.

Polymorphism allows the specification of algorithms at higher or more abstract levels. The typical example is an algorithm to list all elements in a list. With polymorphism the algorithm can be expressed at an abstract level: "traverse the list and send a print message to each element." That the list may be filled (at run-time) with a variety of objects from different classes can be neglected, as long as they all implement a "print" method. We will look at how the different languages facilitate or hinder the use of polymorphism.

---

[1] "are" as plural of "is-a"

6.1.5 Object Heaven

While the previous four criteria suffice to classify a programming language as object-oriented, there are a few features found in object-oriented programming languages that stimulate enthusiasm in the *truly* object-oriented programmer.

The primary feature to qualify for object heaven is the "total" object-oriented look that a programming language can take toward itself.[2] Since object orientation is such a powerful modeling tool, why not apply it to the language itself? Elements of the programming language itself can be modeled in object-oriented terms: a class can be viewed as an object, since it describes how its instances are structured and behave; a class hierarchy can be viewed as an object. If classes are objects, it will be possible to send messages to classes. Class constructors and initialization methods can be viewed as messages that can be received by classes.

A second feature that may qualify a language for object heaven is whether it comes with, or is part of, a programming environment that is object-oriented. An example is the object-oriented input and output features provided by most object-oriented programming languages: they provide input and output objects that can receive messages to affect the input or output of data. The wealth and size of the class library provided with a language also plays a major role.

6.2 Smalltalk

In the early 1970s, Alan Kay and Adele Goldberg developed the Smalltalk system at the Software Concepts Group of the Xerox Palo Alto Research Center. While not the first object-oriented programming language,[3] Smalltalk became the leading force that originated the object-oriented era in computing.

The first publicly available version of Smalltalk was released in 1983 as Smalltalk-80. It was initially available only on powerful graphical workstations. Because Smalltalk is embedded into a complete interactive programming environment it requires significant memory, computing, and graphics capabilities. Since its initial introduction, the boom in personal workstations and the development of compacter Smalltalk versions have lessened the hardware requirements and made it widely available. The current version of Smalltalk, Object-Works for Smalltalk-80, and Smalltalk/V are available for small personal computers up to the most advanced graphical workstations.

In addition to these two commercial versions of Smalltalk, there are also two versions available that reside in public domain: Little Smalltalk [Bud85],

---

[2]Programming languages that can be modeled in their own terms are known as *reflective*.

[3]Simula was developed in the late 1960s. Simula is the first object-oriented programming language.

which implements the language only and provides a text-based user interface, and GNU Smalltalk, which is based on the X11 window system.

When using the term "Smalltalk," one actually refers to the Smalltalk programming environment. It has three components: the basic Smalltalk language, a collection of classes that are used to implement the complete Smalltalk system, and the actual programming environment that enables a programmer to input, test, and run Smalltalk applications.

6.2.1 Smalltalk, the Language

The basic building block of a Smalltalk program is the class. The class holds the description of instance variables and methods. "Method" is the Smalltalk term for "member function." As in C++, the methods contain the code that defines how an object responds to a message. The basic form of a Smalltalk statement is a "message send":

```
receiver message: argument
```

It expresses that a message is sent to a receiver with an argument. Messages can be unary, such as

```
receiver message
```

or may have multiple arguments labeled with key words, such as

```
receiver message: firstArgument and: second Argument
```

which sends a message with two arguments to the receiver. Local variables can be defined within a method. Smalltalk does not support strong typing. To declare a variable, it is merely listed between two vertical bars at the beginning of a method. For example:

```
| person |
```

defines a variable called `person`.

Other basic elements in the Smalltalk language are the assignment operation, expressed as ":=", and the statement sequence, expressed as ".". Since, like in C++, methods are functions, they can return their result following the "^" operator. To send a message to the current object, Smalltalk provides the keyword "self." Smalltalk allows the grouping of statements without executing them immediately. A sequence of statements delimited by brackets is called a block. For example:

```
[ a := 0. b := a + 2 ]
```

defines a block. The key concept is that a block of statements is itself an object. It can be assigned to a variable:

```
| block |
block := [ a:= 0. b := a+2]
```

A block contains a sequence of statements that can be evaluated at a later time. The message "value" is understood by block objects, upon which the statements are evaluated and the result of the last statement in the block is returned. For example:

```
block value
```

will result in the integer object "2".

Blocks are used in Smalltalk to implement the basic control structures. For example, the "it-then-else" clause is implemented as an "if True: if False:" message sent to a Boolean object as receiver. The message carries two block objects as arguments. As an illustration consider the following "if" statement:

```
( a > b ) ifTrue: [ c := 0 ] ifFalse: [ c := 1 ]
```

This statement is executed as follows: object "a" receives message ">" with argument object "b" and executes its method ">". The ">" returns the Boolean object "true" or "false" depending on outcome of the comparison. If "true" is returned it will receive the message "ifTrue: ifFalse:". The method "ifTrue: ifFalse:" for the "true" object evaluates the first argument block and returns its result. It completely ignores the second argument block. If the "false" object receives the message it ignores the first argument and evaluates and returns the second argument.

Smalltalk implements loops in a similar fashion. "While" loops, for example, express repeated execution of statements by sending a parameter block to a receiver block:

```
[ i < 1000 ] whileTrue: [ i: = i + 1 ]
```

This statement increments variable "i" until it reaches the value "1000".

Smalltalk is a completely dynamic language. Methods are looked up when an object receives a message. Static binding is not an option in Smalltalk.

Methods are part of a class definition. The class definition names a class, defines its superclass, its class variables, instance variables, class methods, and instance methods. The following table relates these terms to their C++ equivalents:

Table 6.1   Student Class Description

```
Person subclass: #Student
    instanceVariableNames: 'taking'
    classVariableNames: 'Body'

!Student class methods!

new: aString
 |s|
    s := self new.
    s initialize: aString.
    ^s.

!Student instance methods!

initialize: aString
    name := aString.
    taking := Collection new.
    Body add: self.

print
    Transcript show: 'Student:'.
    super print.
```

Smalltalk	C++
class	class
superclass	base class
subclass	derived class
class variable	static member field
instance variable	member field
class method	static member function
instance method	member function

Table 6.1 shows the class description of class "Student" as a subclass of class "Person." The definition is phrased as "adding a subclass Student to the class Person." Note that the class definition mentions only names of the instance and class variables. The new "Student" class is a subclass of class "Person." In Smalltalk, it is not possible to define a class that is not a subclass of another class. At the very least, a class needs to be a subclass of class "Object," which serves as the common root for the complete Smalltalk class hierarchy. Class "Object" defines the class method "new" that allows the creation of instances. In the case of class "Student," an instance is created

with the statement:

```
| s |
 s := Student new.
```

which creates object "s" as an uninitialized student object. The "Student" class declares a class method to allow the creation of custom student objects. Table 6.1 shows class method "new: a string." It calls the message "new" to create a new instance which then receives the "initialize" message. Table 6.1 also shows the "initialize" method. The "name" instance variable is set to hold a new collection and the "self" object is added to the "Body" of all students.

Smalltalk has very simple rules that govern the access to instance variables and methods of an object. In general, all instance variables are private and all instance methods are public. One way to give a client access to an instance variable is to define a unary instance method with the same name that returns the instance variable. In Smalltalk it is not possible to hide an instance method. In a subclass all features of all superclasses are accessible. Smalltalk does not provide for encapsulation toward heirs of a class.

Table 6.1 shows the declaration of a "print" method. "Transcript" is a predefined global variable that allows string output into a standard window on the Smalltalk screen. Its "show" method implements the simplest form of output in Smalltalk. The second statement in the "print" method,

```
super print
```

is equivalent to

```
this->Person::print();
```

in C++. The intent of the statement is to send the print message to itself, i.e., the current object, but as though it were an instance of class "Person." The statement:

```
self print
```

would cause infinite recursion. Smalltalk does not provide a scope resolution operation. It uses the reserved word "super" to refer to the current object, but at the next higher level in the class hierarchy. In the example, the message "print" sent to receiver "super" will execute the "print" method of class "Person," which prints the name of the student.

Smalltalk supports inheritance like all other object-oriented programming languages. It does not allow stand-alone classes. It is not possible to define a class without a superclass. The root of the Smalltalk class hierarchy is class "Object." The "Object" class implements the basic memory management methods that are shared by all classes.

Smalltalk does not support multiple inheritance.[4] This limits Smalltalk's modeling power somewhat. Consider the "TeachingAssistant" and "Professor" classes from our course scheduling application example. To implement them in Smalltalk, all the features inherited from one superclass will have to be duplicated: a needless effort. Since multiple inheritance is not supported, repeated inheritance is not an issue in Smalltalk.

Smalltalk does not support strong typing. Thus it naturally supports polymorphism. It allows specifying code at an abstract level without an immediate check whether or not it can be executed correctly. Therefore, while the direct support of polymorphism is one of Smalltalk's strongest traits, it also results in a definite weakness. Most errors in a typical Smalltalk program occur at run-time. Since a method is looked up at run-time, one of the typical error messages is "message not understood."

6.2.2 Object Heaven

Smalltalk is said to be a "pure" object-oriented language: "Everything in Smalltalk is an object." This statement is not completely true. Within the Smalltalk language there is a clear distinction between a class and its instances: the objects. The reason one is tempted to declare everything in Smalltalk as an object is that in the Smalltalk programming environment "everything" is represented as an object, and all computation is achieved by sending messages to objects.

In the programming environment classes are represented as instances of a "class description" class, and all objects know what class they belong to. This feature is implemented by including a reference to the class object into every object's data structure. For example, consider the "alike" member function declared for instances of class "Student" in the C++ version of our example application. Its intent was to return a new instance that was of the same class as the receiver. In Smalltalk, there is no need to define this method. The following statement will achieve the same result:

```
s class new: 'hugo'
```

It returns a new instance of the same class as object "s," already initialized to have the name "hugo." Another example is Smalltalk's syntax to define a new class. In Smalltalk, a new class is created by sending the message:

```
subclass: instanceVariableNames: classVariableNames:
```

to a class. The new class is added as a subclass of the receiver.

---

[4]Earlier versions of Smalltalk-80 allowed the specification of multiple superclasses when defining a new class [BI82]. This feature, however, was never well supported, and was finally dropped in the latest version of ObjectWorks for Smalltalk-80.

Table 6.2   Collection Class Description

```
Collection subclass: #OurCollection
  instanceVariableNames: ' '
  classVariableNames: ' '

! OurCollection instance methods !
print
  self do: [:each | each print].
```

6.2.3   The Smalltalk Class Hierarchy

The Smalltalk programming environment includes a large library of several hundred classes. To manage the large list of classes, Smalltalk groups them into categories. Categories of classes implement many basic data structures: collections, sets, bags, dictionaries. In addition, there are predefined classes to accomplish input and output and to help develop user interface components. Examples are classes such as Point, Rectangle, Display Medium, Form, View, Controller.

As an example consider the class "Collection." It allows creation of instances that may hold any number of objects. The type of elements in a collection is not restricted. There is no need for a generic class, since in Smalltalk all classes are subclasses of the common superclass "Object." The class collection implements methods to "add" elements to a collection. Another interesting method is "do." It can be involved with a block argument. The collection executes the block for each element in the collection.

The collection class could be used in our course scheduling application. Since our idea of a collection might differ from what Smalltalk already implements, we will define a subclass "OurCollection" that extends the predefined "Collection" class. Table 6.2 shows its Smalltalk class description.

6.2.4   The Smalltalk Programming Environment

Smalltalk as a programming language is almost inseparable from its programming environment. Almost any tool that a programmer can conceive to develop programs with is part of this environment. The central tool is the class browser that is used to define and modify class descriptions. Other tools are the debugger, inspector, workspace, and the change management tool.

All elements of the Smalltalk environment are part of an *image*. An image contains all objects needed to support a Smalltalk session of a simple user. Figure 6.1 shows a screen hardcopy. The screen contains a browser, a

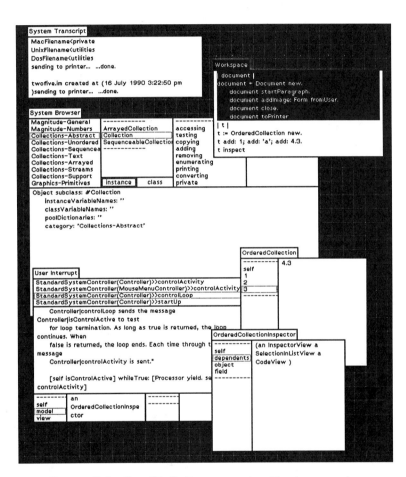

Figure 6.1   Smalltalk Programming Environment

workspace, an inspector, and a debugger window.

The Smalltalk browser serves as the sole maintenance and editing tool for classes. The top portion allows the selection of a class and its methods. The lower portion is an editing window to input class descriptions and method bodies. Smalltalk does not provide a separate compilation tool. Instead, after code has been entered or changed in the editing window, compilation is part of the "save" operation. Normally, for typically small methods, the compilation time is barely noticeable.

A Smalltalk workspace allows the execution of Smalltalk code pieces. Local variables can be declared, objects can be created, and messages can be sent. The workspace in Figure 6.1 shows a student object being created and inspected. Any Smalltalk object understands the "inspect" message. It invokes the Smalltalk inspector, which displays and allows manipulation of an object's state.

The Smalltalk debugger is usually invoked when an error has occurred. It displays the stack of messages that are active at the moment of the interruption. Some of the functions that the debugger provides are to step through methods, change values of instance variables, and even change and recompile methods.

The browser contains all classes that are known in an image. It especially contains all system classes. For example, the class browser itself is an instance of class "Class Browser." This class is listed in the class Browser. All other elements of the Smalltalk system are also available: workspaces, inspectors, and debuggers are all instances of existing classes. In addition, classes that support them are also available: all their superclasses can be browsed with the class browser. The abundance of predefined classes is one of the major reasons why Smalltalk is so well suited for rapid prototyping. Almost any conceivable application can be derived (i.e., subclassed) from the existing classes, at least for a prototype version.

Another advantage of the large class library is that it implements a common style of invocation. All windows behave in a similar fashion, menus pop up in a unique style, menu settings are uniform, etc. A Smalltalk user can easily adapt to a new application, since it will have a similar look and feel as the overall Smalltalk environment.

The Smalltalk browser gives access to all classes; even the predefined class can be manipulated. While this openness has advantages for the experienced Smalltalk programmer, a novice might inadvertently change a critical system component. For instance, suppose the user changes the implementation of "+" for integer numbers to perform subtraction instead of addition. Upon compilation of this change in the Smalltalk browser the system will fail immediately. Too many computations in the Smalltalk run-time system rely on adding integer numbers, since for each message "+" sent to an integer, Smalltalk will look up the now incorrect method. It is most likely that even the method lookup will fail, because it involves some integer addition.

Smalltalk has very few safeguards against such misuse of the browser. One safeguard is that a user is only manipulating the classes in his own image, so damage is limited to a single user. Another safeguard is the change management browser, which can list all code changes that were made to any class. It allows selectively backing out changes that a user did not intend.

The Smalltalk environment contains a garbage collector. While allocation of space for new objects is handled when objects are created, the programmer need not explicitly release it. The garbage collector, a continuous process running in the background, checks for objects that are obsolete. An object becomes obsolete when no other object contains a reference to it. Space occupied by obsolete objects is freed by the garbage collector.

6.2.5 Smalltalk Summary

Smalltalk distinguishes itself from other object-oriented programming languages with its complete object-oriented organization throughout. It also provides the richest and most mature programming environment. Smalltalk is built on simple and clear concepts. Encapsulation, for example, is achieved by hiding all instance variables and exposing all instance methods. C++, in contrast, supports a host of encapsulation measures, which, while being powerful, are confusing at first.

Smalltalk is the most dynamic programming language. With its untyped variables and method arguments, combined with dynamic binding of messages to methods, it allows a programmer broad flexibility in designing classes, their variables and methods.

Smalltalk is best suited to teach object-oriented programming. A novice, however, especially if he is an experienced programmer of conventional languages, will find it hard to master the Smalltalk approach. The biggest step is to write the first Smalltalk program. After that, programming productivity will rapidly increase.

Smalltalk is a very good prototyping environment. Because of its wealth of predefined classes new applications can be quickly designed and prototyped. Execution speed, however, is a negative factor, due to Smalltalk's dynamic nature.

Another drawback of Smalltalk is that it is a single-user system. Whatever a programmer creates and modifies is done to his image only. While tools are available to allow groups to share the development of a system, it is hard to coordinate all changes to all classes because of Smalltalk's openness.

Overall, Smalltalk is the language of choice for the object-oriented programming enthusiast. It clearly puts him into "Object Heaven."

6.3 Objective-C

Objective-C is another interesting entry in the landscape of object-oriented programming languages. Objective-C, like C++, extends the C programming language with object-oriented concepts. The language is featured in Brad Cox's landmark book on "Object-Oriented Programming" [Cox86]. In his book, Cox relates the concept of "class" to that of an "integrated circuit (IC)." As in hardware, where engineers design a new product with "off-the-shelf" components, "classes" can serve a similar purpose in building software products. "Off-the-shelf" classes — named software ICs — could dramatically increase software productivity.

Objective-C is built around the idea of software ICs. It extends C with a notion of class. Classes are defined with an instance description that is separate from its implementation. Objective-C extends C in a Smalltalk style. Its terms and basic concepts show a strong Smalltalk influence. As with Smalltalk, Objective-C comes with a large standard class library that allows the rapid construction of new applications from predefined components.

In the following sections we will examine the basic language constructs, the predefined classes, and the tools provided in the Objective-C programming environment.

6.3.1 Objective-C, the Language

Objective-C is based on C. It extends C with notions of "class" and "message sending," and a new basic type, the "object identifier."

A class is declared in two separate parts: the interface and the implementation. The interface part of a class is delimited by @interface and @end statements. The class interface declares the instance variables, class and instance methods. Class methods are called "factory" methods in Objective-C as a metaphoric reference to a class as the factory of objects. Objective-C does not support class variables. The class interface also specifies the single superclass, Objective-C does not support multiple inheritance.[5]   Table 6.3 shows a class interface for class "Student" as a subclass of "Person." Class methods start with the "+" character and instance methods start with "-". The method definitions show the competing influences of C and Smalltalk. While a method name is constructed in Smalltalk style, the arguments are typed in C style. Objective-C offers a slight extension to Smalltalk's limited measures of encapsulation: all methods are public; instance variables are private by default, but can be made public by including the "@public" directive.

---

[5]In the current version of the Objective-C compiler multiple inheritance is not supported.

Table 6.3   Student Class Interface

```
#import "person.h"
#import "Collection.h"

@interface Student: Person {
  OrdCltn *taking;
}

// Student factory methods

+ new: (char *) aString;

// Student instance methods

- init: (char *) aString;
- print;
@end
```

The second object-oriented extension to C is the introduction of a message-sending syntax. In Objective-C, message sending is similar to Smalltalk. A complete "message sending" expression is enclosed in brackets:

```
[receiver message: argument]
[receiver message: first and: second]
```

These expressions can occur within regular C expressions in Objective-C, which yields a distinct programming style:

```
if ([teacher add: course]) {
  print ("teacher can add course\n");
  return TRUE;
else
  return FALSE;
}
```

Note, that while Objective-C uses Smalltalk message sending style, it reverts to regular C for its control structures. From Smalltalk it also copied the use of predefined variables "self" and "super" to refer to the current object in a method. As in Smalltalk, "super" allows starting the search for a message in a superclass.

The third extension to C is the introduction of a new basic type: the object identifier ("id"). Variables of type "id" can refer to objects of any type. Objective-C supports the same level of dynamic binding as Smalltalk. When an object receives a message at run-time, it is its class that determines which method is executed in response.

Table 6.4 shows the implementation for class "Student." It declares a global variable to hold the "StudentBody" collection as a substitute for the "Body" class variable found in the C++ and Smalltalk implementations of class "Student." The implementation part of the "Student" class contains the bodies for the methods declared in the class interface. Consider the "init" instance method. It sets the "name" field inherited from class "Person," initializes "taking" to hold an instance of an ordered collection, and adds the current student object ("self") to the "StudentBody" collection of all students. The "print" method uses the standard C "printf" function to output "Student:" before sending "print" to itself. The "print" method search will be started in the "Student" class' superclass "Person," where it might be defined as

```
- print {
  printf("my name is %s\n", name);
}
```

Table 6.5 shows a simple main program that creates three student objects. Since all student objects are automatically entered into the "StudentBody" collection, it is possible to print all in a single statement. While Objective-C does not support statement blocks or a "do:" method for collections, it does allow treating treat message names, also known as "selectors," as first class program entities. The last statement in the main program tells the "Student Body" collection to send the "print" message to all its elements. The resulting output is

```
Student: my name is John
Student: my name is Mike
Student: my name is Hasi
```

6.3.2   The Objective-C Class Library

Like Smalltalk, Objective-C comes with a large number of predefined classes. The classes are organized into two main libraries: the foundation class library "ICPak101" and the graphics class library "ICPak201."

The foundation library contains classes to capture basic data structures such as arrays, trees, lists, stacks, and several kinds of collections. The "Student" class example uses the ordered collection class "OrdCltn" to store all student objects. In addition, there are classes to handle object-oriented input and output and other recurring programming tasks.

The graphics library provides classes to allow the development of graphical user interfaces. It supports windows, menus, scrollbars, buttons, notifiers,

Table 6.4   Student Class Body

```
#import "student.h"

id StudentBody;

@implementation Student

// Student factory methods

+ new: (char *) aString {
   id temp;
   temp = [ self new ];
   [ temp init: aString ];
   return temp;
}

// Student instance methods

- init: (char *) aString {
   name = aString;
   taking = [ OrdCltn new ];
   [ StudentBody add: self ];
}

- print {
   printf("Student: ");
   [ super print ];
}

@end
```

Table 6.5   Objective-C Main Program

```
#import "student.h"

extern id StudentBody;

main (int argc, char* argv[]) {
id p,q,r;

StudentBody = [ OrdCltn new ];

p = [Student new: "John"];
q = [Student new: "Mike"];
r = [Student new: "Hasi"];

[StudentBody elementsPerform: @selector(print)];
}
```

---

and other facilities that can be easily built into applications. The graphics classes are built on top of a window system. Among others, for example, Objective-C supports the X11 window system.

6.3.3   The Objective-C Programming Environment

Objective-C provides a compiler, a class browser, and tracing and debugging facilities in its programming environment. The browser has the same look and feel as applications built with the graphics library. The browser allows the user to traverse complete class hierarchies quickly.

A useful debugging facility provided by Objective-C is message tracing. Enabling message tracing generates a record for every message sent, showing the receiver of the message, the message name, its arguments, and the message sender. Objective-C also allows tracing the allocation and deallocation of objects.

Objective-C provides basic functionalities to manage object space. Space for an object is allocated when an object is created with the "new" message. Once an object becomes obsolete, it is up to the programmer to free its associated storage by sending it a "free" message.

6.3.4   Objective-C Summary

Objective-C provides a truly object-oriented extension to C. It combines some of the advantages of C, such as a large base of C programmers and large amounts of C code, with the conceptual elegance of Smalltalk's approach to object-orientation. The combination of C and Smalltalk concepts, however, might create confusion. For example, to access an object's public instance variable, one writes:

```
object->publicVariable
```

whereas to access an object's public instance method, one writes:

```
[object publicMethod]
```

Nevertheless, Objective-C also benefits from its dual heritage. Like Smalltalk, it retains information about classes at run-time. For example, class "Object" implements the class method "instancesRespondTo:", which, given a selector (message name) as argument, returns whether the class (or any superclass) implements the message. In effect, the method determines whether instances of the class can respond to the particular message.

Overall, Objective-C fulfills all criteria to be truly object-oriented. While class variables and multiple inheritance are missing, its Smalltalk heritage almost qualifies it for "Object Heaven."

6.4 Eiffel

Eiffel is a newer entry in the set of object-oriented programming languages. It is featured in Bertrand Meyer's book "Object-Oriented Software Construction" [Mey88]. Eiffel is not a language hybrid as are C++ or Objective-C. It was developed to fully support all object-oriented concepts with a strong emphasis on the support of current software engineering principles. The basic style of Eiffel has a Pascal flavor and it has few, yet elegant and powerful features. Eiffel goes beyond implementing all object-oriented features, in that it also provides powerful features such as run-time assertion checks and an exception-handling mechanism. The Eiffel programming environment provides a large library of predefined classes and several useful tools for program development.

6.4.1 Eiffel, the Language

The sole structuring criterion in an Eiffel program is the "class." A class is a single unit and is not separated into an interface and an implementation part. An Eiffel class defines the basic ingredients of its instance objects: instance variables, instance methods and a class method. Instance variables are also called "attributes"; instance methods are also called "routines"; and attributes

---

Table 6.6   Student Class Description

```
Class Student
   export
      print;
   inherit
      Person
         rename print as personprint;
   feature
      io: STDFILES;
      Create (n: STRING) is
      do
        personname := n;
      end;
      print is
      do
        io.putstring("Student: ");
        personprint;
      end
end;
```

---

and routines are collectively referred to as "features." Eiffel allows the definition of a single class method only. Its name is "Create." It can be defined to accept different arguments. Eiffel does not support class variables.

Table 6.6 shows the Eiffel class description for "Student." The "Student" class is defined as a subclass of "Person." It defines the "create" and "print" methods. Eiffel has a very strict rule to support encapsulation: every feature of a class is private unless explicitly listed in an "export" clause. In the example, the "Student" class exports the "print" feature. Clients of class "Student" have access to the "print" routine. This binding of the private features also applies to heirs, or descendants, of a class. For example, for the "Student" class's "create" routine to set the "personname" attribute, which is defined by and inherited from the "Person" class, it has to be explicitly exported by the class "Person."

Eiffel has a unique way to resolve ambiguities when accessing features that are multiply defined in a class hierarchy. In our example class hierarchy, both "Person" and "Student" define a "print" routine. To access the "print" routine of class "Person" within "Student," it has to be renamed. Table 6.6 shows that "print" is renamed as "personprint" within the "inherit" clause.

Eiffel supports multiple inheritance. Any ambiguities resulting from multiply defined features in a superclass have to be resolved when the derived class is defined. For example, Eiffel allows the definition of the "TeachingAssistant" class from our sample application as a subclass of both "Student" and "Teacher." Features that occur in both superclasses, such as the "maintain" routines, have to be renamed. Assuming they were renamed into "teacher-maintain" and "studentmaintain," the "maintain" routine for class "Teaching-Assistant" will be

```
maintain is
do
    io.putstring_nl("maintain as student or teacher?")
    io.readchar;
    if io.lastchar = 's' then
        studentmaintain;
    else
        teachermaintain;
    end
end
```

The routine prompts the user as to which way he wants to maintain the teaching assistant, and calls the appropriate routine. Since Eiffel supports multiple inheritance, repeated inheritance may occur. Eiffel will not repeat a superclass that is inherited from more than once. It ensures that all features from that superclass occur only once in the ancestor class.

Eiffel supports full dynamic binding and polymorphism. It also supports strong typing. Eiffel behaves as if all features were "virtual." Nevertheless, it does not pay a general performance penalty, since it only includes the run-time lookups of methods into the compiled code if a method is actually redefined in a subclass. In Eiffel a feature can be labeled as "deferred," which declares it in the class, but advises the compiler that it needs to be defined by all subclasses. If a class contains "deferred" features, then in effect it becomes an abstract class.

In addition to the purely object-oriented concepts, Eiffel allows the definition of generic class. A generic class is a class that is defined in terms of a type parameter. For instance, consider the class "Array." An array stores elements of a certain type. In Eiffel the generic class "Array" can be defined with a generic type parameter:

```
class Array [T]
```

An array's features are defined in terms of variable "T". An instance of an array can be created for different types. For example:

```
a1: Array [INTEGER];
a2: Array [Person];
```

"a1" holds an array, which may contain certain integer objects. "a2" holds an array, which may contain certain person objects.

Eiffel supports "type declaration by association," which allows declaration of variables of the same type as another object. For instance, this capability simplifies the "alike" function defined by all possible elements in a collection in our sample application. In Eiffel, "alike" could be defined by the "Example" class:

```
alike (n: String): like Current is
    other: like Current
do
    other.create(n);
    Result:= other;
end;
```

"Current" is the Eiffel equivalent for "self" or "this." It refers to the current object that received the "alike" message. The return type of function "alike" and the local variable "other" are declared to be of the same type as "Current": if it is a "Student" object, "other" will be of type "Student"; if it is a "Course" object, "other" will be of type "Course", etc. "Other" is initialized with the "Create" message and returned by assigning it to the "Result" of the function.

Eiffel enables programmers to express formal properties of classes and their instances by specifying assertions. Eiffel supports three kinds of assertions: (1) "Precondition" is an assertion that is evaluated before a routine is called. It expresses a true statement about the values stored in an object. (2) "Postcondition" expresses a condition that has to be guaranteed upon exit of a routine. (3) "Invariant" is a condition that must be satisfied by all instances of a class at all times. The Eiffel run-time environment ensures that all assertions are maintained during a program run . These assertions greatly improve the quality of software produced with Eiffel.

6.4.2   The Eiffel Class Library

The Eiffel programming environment provides a large library of predefined classes. The predefined classes range from kernel, support, and data structure classes to simple graphics support for points, rectangular classes, and advanced graphic classes. The advanced graphics library supports the X11 window system. They enable an Eiffel programmer to easily build a sophisticated user interface.

6.4.3   The Eiffel Programming Environment

The Eiffel compiler, a class browser, an editor, and the "flat" and "short" tools comprise the Eiffel programming environment.

The Eiffel compiler has a built-in automatic recompilation feature. It recompiles only those classes that are affected by a change. The class browser allows the examination of classes in the context of their sub- and superclasses. It can visualize the relationships that exist among classes. The Eiffel editor, actually an Eiffel version of the "Cepage" editor, knows the Eiffel syntax and helps to enter syntax-correct Eiffel programs.

The documentation tool "short" produces a summary of a class showing only the interface as available to clients. The "flat" tool produces a class that is equivalent to the original but without any inheritance clauses. All inherited features are reproduced from the superclasses. The "flat" feature allows delivery of stand-alone classes that do not need any support from a class hierarchy.

Memory management in Eiffel is provided by the programming environment. Object space is allocated when objects are created. Eiffel provides automatic garbage collection. It checks when an object becomes obsolete and frees its associated space. Eiffel also supports an exception-handling mechanism.

6.4.4   Eiffel Summary

Eiffel is a very powerful programming language. Not only does it support the complete spectrum of object orientation, but it also supports software engineering concepts such as pre-/post conditions and invariants for classes. While Eiffel does not allow treating a class as an object, it does provide an abundance of other features that make it an excellent language to build, support, and maintain large software projects. Eiffel achieves all this with a surprisingly clean and compact set of language constructs.

6.5   Object-Oriented Pascal

Object-oriented versions of Pascal are the newest entries in the object-oriented programming language market place. While Object Pascal has been available for some time for Apple computers, only recently have object-oriented versions become available for the IBM personal computer market. TurboPascal from Borland International and QuickPascal from Microsoft extend Pascal with most of the object-oriented concepts. In the following sections we will base our discussion on the latest version of TurboPascal.

Table 6.7   Student Class Description

```
type
   Student = object (Person)
      taking: array[1..5] of Course;
      constructor init(n: String);
      procedure print;
   end;

constructor Student.init(n: String);
begin
   name:= n;
end;

procedure Student.print;
begin
   write('Student:  ');
   Person.print;
end;
```

6.5.1   TurboPascal, the Language

TurboPascal supports the basic concepts of object, class, method, message, and inheritance. A class is defined similar to a conventional user-defined record type. The keyword "record" is replaced by "object." The "object" type description contains the declaration of instance variables and instance methods. Table 6.7 shows the class description for class "Student." "Student" is a subclass of "Person." It inherits the field "name" of type "String" from class "Person." The "object" description lists only the header declarations of instance methods. In the example, constructor "init" and procedure "print" and declared. The actual definition of the method bodies includes the appropriate class name.

As the example shows, TurboPascal supports instance variables, instance methods, and constructors. Similar to C++, it also allows the declaration of destructors. Among the object-oriented features that TurboPascal does not support are multiple inheritance, class variables, and class methods. It does support dynamic binding in C++ fashion: the keyword "virtual" is used to label methods that are to be bound dynamically.

A serious omission in TurboPascal is that it fails to support the data binding aspect of encapsulation. All instance variables in an object are freely accessible. This defeats one of the major advantages of object-oriented programming, which encapsulates and protects data and all its associated procedures and functions.

6.5.2 The TurboPascal Programming Environment

TurboPascal comes as an integrated programming environment with an editor, compiler, debugger, and run-time environment. Notable is the online help that explains even language-dependent topics in an instant. Although TurboPascal does not provide a substantial class library, many programming examples are provided.

6.5.3 Object-Oriented Pascal Summary

Object-oriented Pascal takes a definite step toward introducing object-oriented concepts to the Pascal domain. Current implementations, however, stop short in providing some essential features. The missing features will no doubt be added in the near future, considering the dynamic nature of the personal computer market. Object-oriented Pascal makes a significant contribution to object-oriented programming in general by providing a learning path for many Pascal programmers.

6.6 Summary of Chapter

This chapter surveyed the major and important object-oriented programming languages. Each of the languages: Smalltalk, Objective-C, Eiffel, Object-Oriented Pascal, and of course C++, make a distinct contribution to the object-oriented landscape.

Smalltalk is the most dynamic language and has a pure object-based programming environment. Objective-C brings some of the Smalltalk advantages into the C programming world. Eiffel is a powerful, completely object-oriented and self-sufficient programming language. It goes beyond the other languages in its support of software design aspects, as well as run-time support with garbage collection and exception handling. Object-oriented Pascal's positive contribution is that it opens a learning path for many Pascal trained programmers. Finally, C++, seemingly the language of choice for most object-oriented programmers, while supporting all object-oriented concepts, excels in the area of encapsulation. Its capabilities to control access to the members of a class are not rivaled by any of the other languages.

Part II

Object-Oriented Environment

Chapter 7

The Object-Oriented Advantage

How useful is object-oriented programming ?

The second part of this book is starting out with a discussion of software engineering principles, such as abstraction and modularity, information hiding and encapsulation, and their potential to increase software productivity and reuse. The chapter explains how object-oriented concepts improve the software engineering process. Several examples illustrate the improvement in quality and productivity.

7.1   Introduction

Object, class, and inheritance are the key elements of object-orientation. While Part I of this book introduced, discussed, and illustrated these elements and their details on their own merit, Part II of this book covers programming issues. This second part illustrates how and why these concepts can be applied to all aspects of programming. The first chapter in this part deals with the usefulness of object-oriented programming in general.

Object-oriented programming is a special form of programming. Programming is the task of instructing a computer to perform a task. The task is usually related to some application problem and solves a particular aspect of it. The program — the result of programming — represents a model of that task. Programming in general is the task of modeling an application problem. The application problems that programmers attempt to model have become more and more complex as the computing power available from modern hardware has increased. The modeling task became increasingly harder, to the point were a "software crisis" was proclaimed [Bro87], citing the mismatch of complexity-handling capabilities of programming concepts and the complexity of modern software endeavors. Luckily, since the early days of programming, the tools provided to the programmer, in terms of capabilities and expressiveness of the modeling tool (the programming language), have been modernized perpetually. Object-oriented programming is just the latest step on the ladder of tools that help the programmer to accomplish the programming task.

Object-oriented programming brings the concepts of knowledge representation to programming. Abstraction and modularity, information hiding and encapsulation, categorization and reusability are actively supported by object-orientation. In the following sections, we will explain these concepts and discuss their benefits to improve the modeling aspect of programming. Together, these concepts lead to better engineered software.

7.2 Abstraction and Modularity

Object is the recurring term in object-oriented programming. One might view an object-oriented program as a set of objects that compute and interact to complete the task that the program is modeling. Upon writing an object-oriented program, one realizes that objects are not most important, but that "classes" are. Instead of describing individual objects, objects are described in groups. The class is the description of a set of objects that are similar. The concept of "class" signifies how object-oriented programming supports abstraction and modularity.

Abstraction is defined as "extracting essential properties of a concept." Abstraction allows us to neglect the specific details of something, for example a teacher, and consider the more general concept or category. For example, consider the concept "Teacher." From all specific teachers who might exist, one extracts the essential properties that are common to all teachers and uses them to describe the general "Teacher" concept. "Teacher" becomes an abstraction. Essential to a teacher might be his or her teaching specialty, or the fact that he or she teaches courses. Any specific teacher would have a specific teaching specialty and specific courses to teach.

Abstraction is supported in any traditional programming language. Data structures and types are an example. They allow the abstraction of structural aspects of data organization. Procedures and functions are another example. They allow the abstraction of behavioral aspects.

Object-oriented programming allows the combination of the two abstraction kinds. If data and procedural abstraction are combined, they form an "Abstract Data Type." The "Teacher" concept, for example, can form an abstract data type. Consider a possible data structure for a teacher: a teacher has a name, a list of courses he or she can teach (based on his or her specialty), and a list of courses he or she is teaching in a particular semester. The data structure is the data abstraction part of the abstract data type. The procedural aspects of a teacher encompass the behavior of teachers: the teacher is able to maintain the list of courses he or she prefers to teach and is actually teaching. The behavior is defined with procedures, which make up the procedural abstraction part of the abstract data type.

Abstract data types are supported by object-oriented programming languages. C++ uses classes to implement abstract data types. A class "Teacher" (see Table 5.8 and 5.9) implements such an abstract data type in the context of our course scheduling example.

This "class" programming language construct not only supports abstraction, but it also supports the concept of modularity. Ever since complex problems were faced by humans, it was recognized that they are easier to solve and manage as collections of smaller units (modules) — *divide et impera* !

Object-oriented programs provide a natural way to modularize an application. The class serves as the unit for a module. In our example, the "Teacher" class represents a single module of the university course scheduling application example.

The "class" as an implementation of an abstract data type enables an object-oriented program to represent knowledge found in the application domain much more closely than was possible in conventional programming languages. Another object-oriented concept, inheritance, further enhances the knowledge representation capabilities of an object-oriented program. Categories, and hierarchies of related categories and concepts, can be easily captured with a class hierarchy of related classes, where classes inherit features from their superclasses. Figure 5.1 shows the somewhat complex class hierarchy for the course scheduling example discussed in Chapter 5. Each subclass shares the code of its superclass. Considering the height of the hierarchy, image the amount of code that is shared by the classes at the leaves of the class hierarchy. Sharing implies reusing of code and results in a dramatic increase in programming productivity.

Together, abstraction and modularity greatly increase the modeling power of an object-oriented program and increase the productivity of the software designer and programmer.

7.3   Information Hiding and Encapsulation

If one compares the notion of class with a coin, and abstraction is one side of the coin, then "information hiding" is the other side of the coin. Information hiding is defined as "hiding the nonessential properties of a concept." Information hiding deals with the specific details of something. These details were neglected by abstraction. While in abstraction, we mentioned that a teacher is able to maintain the courses he or she prefers to teach; in information hiding, we are concerned with the concrete details of how the courses are represented and how their maintenance is achieved for specific teachers.

C++ and other object-oriented programming languages use the class construct to implement information hiding. What aspects of a class are hidden depends on how the language supports measures of encapsulation. Encapsulation governs the boundary between abstraction and information hiding. Encapsulation is achieved by maintaining access control to the features defined by a class.

The benefit for the programmer comes from this separation of accessible and inaccessible aspects of class. It allows the separation of the class creation process into a specification and an implementation phase. The specification can typically be done by the software designer, while the implementation is done by the programmer. The software designer is freed from implementing specific detail, and the programmer may choose and vary his implementation details as long as it conforms to the specification.

Another benefit from the possible separation of specification and implementation is that it allows multiple implementations for a single specification. This allows for experimentation with different versions, and also for factoring out device or platform specific details of a system. The specification represents a general solution that can be filled in by a specific implementation. Chapter 11 will elaborate further on how to take advantage of this property in the context of object-oriented user interfaces.

It may not be immediately apparent, but "late" or "dynamic" binding is also a way to further enhance the separation of abstract (visible) and hidden properties of a concept. "Dynamic" binding provides this separation at the object level: an object receives a message at run-time and binds it to the method body defined by its class. Since the class of the object is not predetermined at compile-time (or when the source code is edited), the programmer gains another level of flexibility: the generality of a program or algorithm can therefore be improved. As an example, consider the "maintain" member function for class "Teacher" (see Table 5.9). It achieves its behavior by sending a "maintain" message to the collection of "preferences" courses. How the elements of the collection are maintained (see Table 5.3) depends on the actual class of its elements. That is only determined at run-time, since "maintain" is defined as a virtual member function that allows "dynamic" binding. The "maintain" member function exhibits a high degree of generality and elegance.

7.4 Reusability

Object-oriented programming eases the management problems of complex systems in software. The better management and knowledge representation facilities of object-oriented concepts provide the bulk of programmer productivity increases that are expected from this technology.

The standard mode of object-oriented programming is to seek out prior solutions to the application problem at hand: instead of programming from scratch — or reinventing the wheel — it is possible to start from default beginnings. This requires that more emphasis is placed on providing reusable classes that are well tested and documented. Whenever a new class is created it is important that it be as general as possible, i.e., provides the highest level of abstraction and the highest degree of information hiding. Of course, it is also important that the class itself is well described and documented, as well as its public features.

Tools need to be provided to help a programmer seek out prior solutions. A new generation of computer-aided software engineering tools needs to come of age, that allow the browsing of class hierarchies and show and illustrate the relationships and interdependencies among its classes.

7.4.1 A Word of Caution

Reusability is sometimes touted as the major advantage of object-oriented programming. While this is true in most cases, especially within a large complex application, it is not true in general. The most reuse occurs within a closely knit class hierarchy. Subclasses inherit from their superclasses, and in a substantial class hierarchy it is easy to see that the "leaf" classes share much code with other classes in the hierarchy.

While it is possible and easy to reuse, or share, code within one application, there are some hurdles to reusability across applications, or in future programming endeavors. Apart from standard recurring abstract data types, such as input/output, lists, bags, collections, strings, etc. (see also Chapter 9), application-specific abstract data types are harder to reuse.

For example, consider our course-scheduling application example. It uses a "Collection" class, a standard abstract data type found in virtually any library of classes. It will be reused many times. It is usually well documented and its implementation is trusted. The "Collection" class is a good example of efficient code reuse.

On the other hand, consider the "Person" class. It appears to implement a general "Person" abstract data type and is suited to be reused in another application. If it was a simple stand-alone "Person" class, it would be easy to use or subclass it in another application. However, this is not the case. "Person" is a subclass of class "Example" and superclass to several other classes. It defines two virtual functions, itself provides very little substance for them, for the purpose of these special subclasses. Most likely, in another application, new subclasses will need some specific behavior and would like to add more virtual functions. Therefore the original "Person" class needs to be changed, possibly conflicting with the original class hierarchy context.

Object-oriented programming languages that rely solely on dynamic binding, i.e., every function is virtual, do not have this limitation and allow more flexibility in reusing classes in different contexts. However, there is still the danger of changing a class afterward in such a way that the original application is corrupted.

7.5 Summary of Chapter

This chapter investigated the benefits that can be gained from object-oriented programming. Abstraction, modularity, information hiding, encapsulation, and reusability were illustrated. The class and subclassing constructs of object-oriented programming languages lend themselves to increases in programmer productivity.

Chapter 8

Elements of Object-Oriented Systems

Especially in object-oriented programming, programming starts from a base of existing elements. These elements form a base system for all programs. In an object-oriented environment the base is twofold: (1) there are existing classes to handle recurring data structures and algorithms, and (2) there is (or should be) an existing overall object-oriented organization. Typical elements of an object-oriented organization are a user interface and a database component. This chapter illustrates how to approach the programming task in such an object-oriented environment.

8.1 Introduction

As the name "object-oriented" implies, the main components of an object-oriented system are the objects. An object-oriented system is a collection of objects. Each object is a small part of the application that the overall system implements. The nature and behavior of the overall system is achieved by the collective nature and behavior of the objects. Each object implements a small part of the overall nature and behavior. It represents these as its data structure and functionality.

Objects work together with the other objects by sending and receiving messages. The sending and receiving of messages is a form of communication, much like any real world system or organization would use communication to further its goals.

As messages are passed among objects, they lead to the behavior of objects. As messages are received by objects, objects respond by executing part of their functionality. Each object knows how to react to the messages that it receives.

165

The nature and behavior of an object is described by a class. An object does not exist by itself: any object is an instance of a class. The class describes its data structure and functionality. And the class itself is not a stand-alone unit; it is related to other classes and is part of class hierarchies.

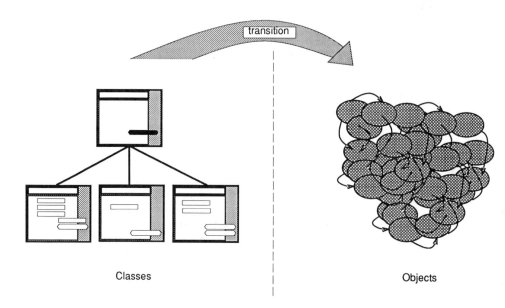

Classes   Objects

Figure 8.1   Classes and Objects

Figure 8.1 shows the duality within an object-oriented system. While objects achieve the actual computation, their behavior is defined by classes. The objects matter at "run-time". The classes matter at "programming-time." An "instantiation" act marks the transition from "programming-" to "run-time", creating instances from classes and starting the computation.

To discuss an object-oriented system, we need to examine three aspects:

1. the modeling of an application with classes and class hierarchies;

2. the execution model and environment of an application; and

3. how an application is solved, i.e., how the transition from classes to objects is achieved.

The next three sections will discuss and illustrate each aspect in detail.

8.2 Programming with Classes

An object-oriented program mostly consists of class declarations. The class is the description tool that the programmer uses to model aspects of the application to be implemented. The class supports and embodies the software engineering principles of abstraction, information hiding, and encapsulation.

Whenever an application concept is to be modeled with a class, the programmer (or class designer) is faced with three choices:

1. to create a new class with the sole purpose of modeling the specific application concept;

2. to search existing classes for one that matches the needs of the application concept; or

3. to search for an existing class that does not match the need but serves as a superclass for a new class.

Given the general goal of increasing programming productivity, it is obvious that choices two and three are the best solutions. It therefore becomes one of the primary programming tasks to seek out classes that can be reused in new applications. These classes can be found in class libraries. In general, common class libraries contain two kinds of classes:

1. general purpose classes, and

2. classes that serve a specific purpose within the programming environment.

8.2.1 General Purpose Classes

Anybody who has written computer programs has noticed the recurrence of certain data structures and algorithms. Almost any program will deal with and maintain sets or arrays of elements. It is therefore not unexpected that most object-oriented class libraries provide classes such as "stack," "tree," "collection," etc., that encapsulate the storage and manipulation of more than one element of a certain type.

The course scheduling application example in Chapter 5 showed how a "Collection" class can be used and reused many times in various circumstances. Another class used in that example was "String." It will occur in almost any application. Of course, it can also serve as superclass. For example, consider an application that handles various kinds of command messages. The command messages are basically strings; however, they also carry a type: messages can be advisory or mandatory in nature. Instead of declaring a stand-alone class, we can define class "MessageString" as a subclass of class "String." It inherits all public and protected features from class "String" and adds a public field "nature" and a function "print." The class interface might be defined as

```
class MessageString: public String {
    public:
        enum {advisory, mandatory} nature;
        void print();
};
```

Another set of existing classes was also illustrated in the course scheduling example: the stream classes that encapsulate the input and output stream functionalities of C++ programs. Chapter 9 will elaborate further on libraries of classes that are available for reuse.

8.2.2 Classes for a Purpose

Another "breed" of classes that is commonly found in object-oriented systems does not necessarily serve to capture data structures and functionalities, but serves to structure the overall organization of an object-oriented application. The purpose of these classes is governed by the "where" within an application framework they occur. The objects can be grouped according to their use. The main objects are those that achieve the behavior of an application: they are the *computation* objects and are described by *computation* classes. The computation objects communicate with database objects and user interface objects. The database objects are special in that they *persist*; i.e., they exist beyond the single run of an application invocation. User interface objects visualize the computation and persistent objects; they interact with the user and are called the *interactive* objects of an application.

Figure 8.2 shows the overall organization of an object-oriented application. The arrows shown from objects to objects illustrate the messages that are sent and received among objects. Objects communicate among their group, i.e., within the persistent objects, within the computation objects, or within the interactive objects. They also communicate among the groups.

For example, consider a more elaborate implementation of the course scheduling application that uses an object-oriented database (see also Chapter 11) and provides a graphical user interface (see also Chapter 10). The course, student and teacher objects persist in the database; they are part of the computation and become interactive as part of a user interface.

Of course, in a specific object-oriented programming environment, we expect to find suitable classes that can serve as superclasses to application-specific classes. These classes would encapsulate the persistent, computa-

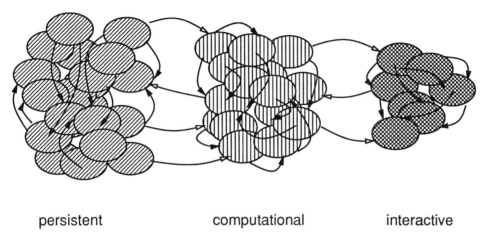

persistent   computational   interactive

Figure 8.2   A World Full of Objects

tional, and interactive framework and thus simplify the structure and organization of new programs.

8.3   Programming with Objects

While the last section focused on classes, and classes describe an object-oriented application, it is still the objects that achieve the application task. It is therefore important to also consider the object level of an application.

Figure 8.2 illustrated the organization of an object-oriented application. While there can be classes that take advantage of the separation of structure and functionality, the separation gives rise to special objects that may occur and preexist in a specific environment.

For example, consider the stream input and output objects of C++. "cin" is a preexisting object, an instance of the input stream class; "cout" is a preexisting instance of the output stream class in any C++ program. "cin" and "cout" can also be viewed as examples of persistent objects: they represent standard input and output connections in all C++ programs. The use of these objects somewhat constitutes an object-level reuse of existing code.

In a more complex programming environment we expect more preexisting objects. For example, as part of a graphical user interface, we expect objects that refer to the i/o media, such as the "root" window, the keyboard, or mouse

---

Table 8.1   Part Class

```
class Part {
 public:
   virtual void print()=0;
};
```

---

sensors. In a database context we may expect a root object that allows the traversal of all database objects from a single anchor.

Other elements of the programming environment may also occur as objects. In Smalltalk-80, for example, it is possible to refer to a "compiler" object that can recompile methods during run-time. Other examples are debugger or inspector objects that allow the observation of the state of objects or the complete program at run-time. Smalltalk-80 (see Section 6.2) offers more examples of how objects capture part of the run-time environment of an application.

8.4   Program Organization

The final step in producing an object-oriented application is to achieve the transition from the class to the object level.   This is usually achieved by the main program. The main program creates[1] objects, initializes them, and "throws the first stone," i.e., initiates computation by sending messages to the primary objects. The objects respond by executing their functionality and changing their data values as defined by their classes. These objects may also create more objects and start communicating with them.

As an illustration, let us consider a simple application that models the production and consumption of cars. The concepts to be modeled are consumer, factory, car. The consumer buys cars produced by a factory. Cars are to be manufactured in a factory. On our example, we want to keep track of the number of cars being produced by a specific factory. Cars are bought by car owners. They "consume" cars and should also keep track of the number of cars consumed.

The classes that we need to handle this application are, so far, "Factory," "CarOwner," and the subject of production and consumption, the "Car." At this stage of the program design we notice that a factory is actually a special case of a "Producer" concept. We check our available class libraries for a suitable class and find a "Producer" class.[2] The "Producer" class produces

---

[1]or loads, if persistent objects are to be retrieved from an object-oriented database.

[2]If such a class is not found, it needs to be created and made available for future reuse.

Table 8.2   Car Class

```
class Car: public Part {
  Factory *make;
 public:
  Car(Factory *m):make(m){};
  void print(){
    cout << "a car from ";
    make->print();
  }
};
```

Table 8.3   Counter Class

```
class Counter {
    int count;
 public:
   Counter():count(0){};
   void increment(){ count++;}
   void report(){
     cout << count << " is the count" << endl;
   }
};
```

"Part" objects; therefore, we conclude that the new class "Car" can be derived from it.

Table 8.1 shows the "Part" class. "Part" is an abstract class; it requires a virtual function "print" for all its subclasses.   Class "Car" (Table 8.2) defines a private member field "make," referring to the factory it originated from. The field is initialized with the "Car" constructor and printed in the "print" public member function.

The "Producer" class (Table 8.4) is a subclass of class "Counter" (Table 8.3). The "Counter" class encapsulates a counting feature to enable the "Producer" to keep track of how many parts are being produced. The "produce" member function increments the counter and calls "next" to get the next part. Again, "next" is a virtual function that is fully defined in class "Factory" (Table 8.5) and returns a new instance of class "Car."   The "Factory" class also defines a "make" string that refers to the brand of cars being manufactured. It is set with the constructor.

The "Consumer" class (Table 8.6) serves a purpose for the "CarOwner" class

Table 8.4   Producer Class

```
class Producer: public Counter {
  virtual Part* next()=0;
 public:
  Part* produce(){
     increment();
     return next();
  }
};
```

Table 8.5   Factory Class

```
class Factory: public Producer {
  String make;
  Part* next(){
    return new Car(this);
  }
 public:
  Factory(String m):make(m){};
  void print(){
    cout << "a factory making " << make << endl;
  }
};
```

Table 8.6   Consumer Class

```
class Consumer: public Counter {
 public:
   void consume(Part *p){
     increment();
     cout << "consuming ";
     p->print();
   }
};
```

Table 8.7 CarOwner Class

```
class CarOwner: public Consumer {
   int many;
   Factory &preference;
   void buy(){
     consume(preference.produce());
   }
 public:
   CarOwner(Factory &p):preference(p){many=2;}
   void live(){
     for (int i=0; i<many; i++)
       buy();
   }
};
```

Table 8.8 Main Program

```
main(){
    Factory gm("Pontiac");
    CarOwner me(gm);

    me.live();
    me.report();
    gm.report();
}
```

similar to that served by the "Producer" class for the "Factory" class. The "Consumer" class provides a "consume" procedure that increments a counter (also inherited from the "Counter" class).   Table 8.7 shows the "CarOwner" class. It defines two private fields: "many" to denote the number of cars to buy, and "preference" to hold a reference to the car owner's favorite car manufacturer. These two fields are set in the constructor function. "Buy" is a private member function that achieves the consumption of cars. "CarOwner" also defines a public member function "live" that invokes the private "buy" function "many" times.

Altogether, seven classes describe this simple car-buying application. The class-level task is completed. What is missing is the transition to the object level. The main program, shown in Table 8.8, achieves this transition. It instantiates two objects: an instance "gm" of class "Factory," and an instance "me" of class "CarOwner." It then sends the message "live" to object "me." This message starts the computation in our sample application.

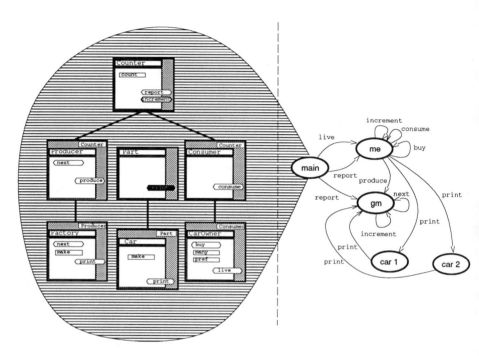

Figure 8.3   The Start of Communication

Figure 8.3 shows the class level and object level of the application. The left part shows the classes and their hierarchy. The right part shows the objects and the messages that are sent at run-time. The main program originates the first message: it sends "live" to object "me," an instance of class "CarOwner." The object "me" receives the message and responds by sending "buy" to itself, which sends "consume" and "increment" all to itself. Object "me" also sends a "produce" message to the "gm" factory object. The "gm" object responds by incrementing its counter and producing a new car object with the "next" message sent to itself. A pointer to the new car object is returned to the "me" object, which uses the pointer to send a "print" message to the car object. The car object then prints (in part by sending another "print" message to its manufacturer):

```
consuming a car from a factory making Pontiac
```

The whole process is then repeated for the production and consumption of a second car. And at last the main program sends "report" messages to the "me" and "gm" objects, which respond with printing the number of consumed and produced cars.

While the example implements a very simple application, it still shows the relative importance of the design effort put toward an efficient class hierarchy. The main program is reduced to making the transition from the class to the object level and to initiate computation.

8.5 Summary of Chapter

In this chapter we presented a metaphorical view of an object-oriented program as an active collection of communicating objects that work toward a common goal. The objects are described by their classes that are part of class hierarchies. It is the classes that make up the core of an object-oriented program, but it is still the objects that achieve the actual behavior. The main program is reduced to an initiator function to create and initialize instances of classes and to start the computation.

Chapter 9

Data Structures and Algorithms

Almost any object-oriented programming language provides a library of existing classes that are available to programmers to use directly or to subclass into application-specific classes. The most common classes for handling of predefined types (numbers, strings, Booleans, etc.), sets (array, collection, bag, etc.), input and output are illustrated with examples in C++. The chapter also provides an overview of some available class libraries for C++.

9.1 Introduction

Data structures and algorithms have always been at the core of computer science. It is considered a science or art to be able to capture recurring structures and functionalities efficiently. Many books have been written about this topic and how to best exploit the current state of computer programming languages to solve and implement common structures and functionalities.

The newest level in programming language evolution — object-oriented programming — directly addresses this concern: to capture data structures and algorithms. At the heart of object-oriented programming is the "class," the programming language construct that serves as a repository for common data structures and their associated procedures. The structure and functionality encapsulated by a class is reused in an object-oriented program by creating instances of a class, or by using the class as a base of a hierarchy of subclasses. This capability to reuse classes, i.e., to capture and reuse data structures and algorithms, is the most promising aspect of object-oriented technology.

Smalltalk-80 — the model object-oriented programming language — not only introduced the necessary object-oriented language constructs, but it was the many classes that are part of its programming environment that contributed largely to its success and the emerging of object orientation. The

177

Smalltalk-80 programming environment comes with a large class library: It contains classes to capture magnitudes, such as numbers, date, or time, or various kinds of collections (arrays, dictionaries, sets, etc.). It also provides classes to partially implement graphical user interfaces, input and output to files, access to operating system services, and even a scanner, a parser, a compiler, and a debugger. The wealth of its class library was a convincing argument for the benefits of object orientation. The large and useful class library contains solutions or partial implementations for almost any programming endeavor. The introduction of this library made the concepts of object-oriented programming fashionable, because it show-cased the productivity increases gained from reuse of classes. Initially, Smalltalk-80 was considered a great "rapid prototyping" tool, since it was so easy and fast to put together a new application. It has since been recognized that the gains from class libraries are not limited to rapid prototyping, but can be achieved in all areas of programming.

Other object-oriented programming languages have since been introduced or rediscovered.[1] It is not surprising that they are sometimes judged not only on the merit of their support of object-oriented concepts, but also by the size of the libraries of classes that are available for the language. Any object-oriented programming language in our knowledge provides a class library, even in its most basic version. And for all these languages larger and more complicated class libraries are available commercially or otherwise.

This chapter is dedicated to a survey of what to expect in such a class library. For the organization of this chapter we follow the usual categories of classes found in standard class libraries, such as the Smalltalk-80 class library. Examples in C++ illustrate the classes and their use. Section 9.2 covers magnitudes, Section 9.3 covers strings and string handling, Section 9.4 covers common input and output classes, and Section 9.5 covers sets and collections. Section 9.6 provides an overview of some larger class libraries available for the C++ programming language.

9.2 Magnitudes

Magnitudes are a common subject to abstraction. They are frequently found as classes in class libraries. As magnitudes we understand numbers of various kinds. Examples are integer, floating point, or complex numbers, random numbers, times and dates. Some of these abstract concepts can be found in traditional programming environments. For example, the types "integer," "float," or "real" can be found in almost all programming languages. Even

---

[1]This is the case for Simula, the original object-oriented programming language.

some operating systems provide data structures for "time" and "date."

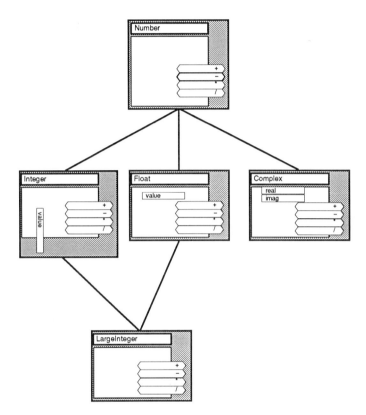

Figure 9.1   The Number Class Hierarchy

In an object-oriented programming language we expect to find the corresponding classes that model these magnitudes. We also expect to find these magnitudes related to each other in class hierarchies. C++, for example, has predefined types "int," "float," and "double." However, these are not classes in C++; they are just predefined types. It may seem that "int" is a C++ class — it hides an implementation data structure and allows access through public operations, such as arithmetic, etc. — but it is not possible to define a subclass of "int." If we want "int" to be part of a class hierarchy, we need to reimplement an "int" class as base class of others. Of course, the "int" class could itself be derived from another class.

Table 9.1   The Integer Class

```
class Integer: public Number {
 protected:
   int value;
 public:
   Integer(): value(0) {};
   Integer(int i): value(i) {};
   Integer operator+ (Integer other) {
     return * new Integer(value + other.value);
   }
   Integer operator- (Integer other) {
     return * new Integer(value - other.value);
   }
   Integer operator* (Integer other) {
     return * new Integer(value * other.value);
   }
   Integer operator/ (Integer other) {
     return * new Integer(value / other.value);
   }
   operator int() {
     return value;
   }
};
```

Figure 9.1 shows a possible class hierarchy. The "Integer" class is derived from class "Number." "Number" factors out the commonalities among the "Integer" and "Float" classes, another derived class. The "Number" class declares virtual functions for arithmetic, etc. These functions are filled in by the "Integer" and "Float" classes. The "Integer" class (see Table 9.1) can be implemented in a very simple way. It hides the representation of "Integer": here the integer value is represented as a member field of type "int". The constructors for "Integer" allow the initialization of the protected "value" member field. In this simple example of an "Integer" class we also provide operator functions to allow simple integer arithmetic. The "Integer" class can be used to create "Integer" objects, such as

```
Integer i;
Integer other(128);
```

Integer objects can be part of arithmetic expressions, such as:

```
i + other
other * i
```

To facilitate the use of this class in conjunction with regular "int" variables and function parameters, it is useful to also declare an automatic conversion function. The operator function "int" provides this: it returns an "int" value.

Another derived class of "Number" in Figure 9.1 is class "Float." It encapsulates the representation and operations usually performed for floating-point numbers. The advantage of defining "Integer" and "Float" as classes is that they themselves can serve as base classes for more detailed or enhanced classes. An example might be a class "Budget" that is derived from class "Float." It might be defined for the sole purpose of making an application program that deals with budget figures more readable, without adding or specializing any features of class "Float."

As another example, consider a class "LargeInteger" that might be useful to capture very large whole numbers for numerical applications. Most compilers represent integers with 16 or 32 bits, which limits their range to about -2^{15} to 2^{15} or -2^{31} to 2^{31}. Figure 9.1 shows a "LargeInteger" class derived from both the "Integer" and "Float" class. Our simple-minded idea to implement large integers is to use the representation of floating-point numbers to capture large integers.

A more useful subclass of class "Number" is a "Complex" number class (see Figure 9.1). It encapsulates the representation and functionality of complex numbers. Table 9.2 shows the class interface for such as class. "Complex" numbers are represented as a "real" floating-point number coupled with an "imag" floating-point part for the imaginary portion of the complex number. A

Table 9.2   The Complex Class Interface

```
class Complex: public Number {
  float real;
  float imag;
 public:
  Complex();
  Complex(float,float);
  Complex operator+ (Complex);
  Complex operator- (Complex);
  Complex operator* (Complex);
  Complex operator/ (Complex);
};
```

Table 9.3   The Time Class Interface

```
class Time: public Integer {
 public:
  Time();
  Time(int);
  void now();
  void print();
};
```

---

constructor allows the initialization of the private member fields. The class also defines public operator member functions to allow complex number arithmetic. For example, uses of this class are

```
Complex c1(1.3,2.0), c2(4.3,1.0), c3;
c3 = c1 + c2;
c1 = c3 * c2;
```

"Time" and "Date" are yet two more magnitude abstractions that are found in most class libraries. The "Time" class allows abstracting the notion of keeping time. Time can be represented as the number of time units since some reference point. That is why it is possible to derive a "Time" class from the "Integer" class. Depending on how much time we want to represent (for example, we might want to represent time as the number of microseconds since January 1, 1900), it might be necessary to derive the "Time" class from the "LargeInteger" class.

Figure 9.2 depicts "Time" as a subclass of class "Integer." Table 9.3 shows the class interface. The constructor allows the initialization of the time count.

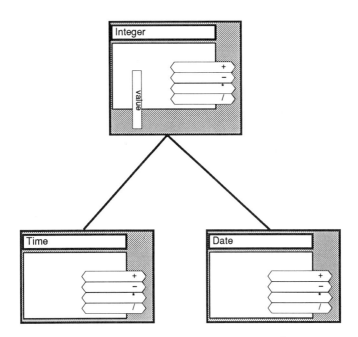

Figure 9.2 The Integer Class Hierarchy

Note that class "Integer" declared its member field "value" as protected; therefore, it is accessible in this subclass. The member function "now()" sets the time to the current time; the function "print()" prints a readable representation of the time to the standard output. Other member functions to access seconds, minutes, or hours of a time object can be easily envisioned and added to the class. Member functions to manipulate time objects, e.g., to add or subtract, are inherited from the "Integer" class.

Another class dealing with time, but with a larger granularity, is the class "Date." Similar to class "Time," class "Date" can be derived from class "Integer," or if need be from class "LargeInteger."[2] Of course, another alternative would be to consider "Date" as a subclass of "Time," or better yet to combine the two classes into a "DateTime" class that uses a single representation that can be interpreted as a date or as a time interchangeably.

Random numbers are another incarnation of magnitudes. Simulation applications use random numbers extensively. Due to the heritage of object-oriented programming most libraries provide classes that capture various random distributions. Each possible distribution of random numbers is encapsulated in a class. For example, consider a class for a "uniform" distribution. Its class interface would specify a member function that for each call returns a new sample value according to a uniform distribution. Other kinds of distribution follow the same protocol; each answers to a message "next" with a new sample value according to the characteristics of the distribution.

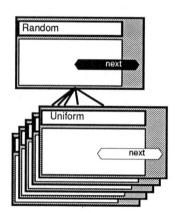

Figure 9.3   The Random Class Hierarchy

---

[2]In case your application needs to represent dates that are very, very far into the future or past.

Table 9.4   The Random Class Interface

```
class Random {
 public:
   virtual double next() = 0;
};
```

Table 9.5   The Uniform Class Interface

```
class Uniform: public Random {
 public:
   double next() {
      // calculate and return
      // next sample value according
      // to uniform distribution
      // ...
   }
};
```

It is therefore easy to create a base class for all random number classes. The class defines a single virtual function "next" which returns the next sample value. Figure 9.3 shows a class hierarchy of "Random" number generators. The root of the class hierarchy, class "Random," is an abstract class; i.e., no instances are intended. It shows the virtual function "next." "Random" is the base for classes "Uniform," "Normal," "Poisson," "Geometric," and "Binomial." Table 9.4 shows the class declaration for class "Random." We chose "double" as the return type of the "next()" member function in order to be most general.[3]   Table 9.5 lists the outline of a derived class "Uniform" that implements the "next" member function. The other random number classes are implemented in a similar fashion.

The "Random" numbers class hierarchy allows its flexible use in a possible application. Consider this code fragment:

```
void simulation_run(Random);

main() {
   Uniform u;
   simulation_run(u);
```

---

[3]Note that "next" is set to "=0" as a pure virtual function, enforcing "Random" as an abstract class.

```
    Normal n;
    simulation_run(n);
}
```

We assume an existing function "`simulation_run()`" that implements a simulation application completely but for the specific random number distribution to be used. In the code fragment we call this function first with an instance of class "Uniform" to run the simulation with a uniform distribution of random numbers. Inside the function, the "Uniform" instance receives the "`next()`" message, which it answers with a new sample value. Of course, the simulation can be run with other distributions, as the second example shows, where "`simulation_run()`" is called with an instance of a "Normal" distribution class.

In summary, the aforementioned magnitudes of model numbers, time, and random numbers exemplify how object-oriented programming supports the capture and reuse of recurring data structures and algorithms.

9.3   String Handling

Much of the information processed within common applications can be represented as strings, that is, as sequences of characters. Most programming languages deal with strings as arrays of characters. It is the nature of strings that they are seldom of a fixed length. They are therefore hard to handle, or to capture in a general way, in languages that do not support dynamic size arrays. In C++, as in C, strings can be declared with the "`char *`" type, which allows treating them as arrays of characters with no predetermined size, but also places the burden of memory allocation and management on the shoulders of the programmer.[4]

As we have already mentioned in Section 5.3.2, it is therefore a splendid opportunity for any object-oriented class library to contain a "String" class. The class can encapsulate the representation of strings and provide the functionality to allocate and manage strings and the memory they use.

Table 9.6 shows the class interface of a "String" class. It defines two private, hidden member fields: "len" of type integer to hold the actual size of the string, and "str" of type "`char *`" to point to the memory allocated for the string. The class interface further declares the constructors and public member functions. The member functions provide the operations available for "String" objects.

Table 9.7 shows the class body for class "String." There are two constructors. The first declares an empty string, the second determines the length of

---

[4]This is also a frequent source of errors in a C or C++ program.

Table 9.6   The String Class Interface

```
class String {
      enum bool {false, true};
      int len;
      char *str ;
   public:
      String();
      String(char *s);
      String& operator=(String);
      bool operator==(String);
      bool contains(String);
      String& operator+(String);
      operator char*();
};
```

the argument string "s" and allocates the necessary memory, which is then used to receive the argument string via a class to the "strcpy()" function.

Table 9.7 also shows the implementation of the assignment operation. The assignment operation must be defined for class "String" since the default "=" operation only performs a member-wise copy of the argument's member fields. The assignment operator function ("operator=") is defined to determine the size of the string contained by the argument "String" object. Note, that the access to field "s.str" is valid, since, although "str" is a private field of object "s", the access takes place within the scope of class "String" and is therefore allowed. With this assignment operation defined, this code segment performs correctly:

```
String s, t("other");
s = t;
```

Another interesting operation for class "String," declared in the class interface (see Table 9.6) and defined in the class body (see Table 9.7), is "operator char*". It allows type casting for objects of class "String" into "char *" variables. For example,

```
String s("test");
printf("%s", (char *) s);
```

while "s" is an instance of class "String," and would therefore be of incompatible type for the "%s" format directive. The explicit type cast "(char *)" converts it: how the conversion is achieved is defined in the implementation of "operator char*".

Table 9.7   The String Class Body

```
String::String(){
    len = 0;
    str = NULL;
}

String::String(char *s){
    len = strlen(s);
    str = new char[len + 1];
    strcpy(str,s);
}

String& String::operator=(String s) {
    delete [len + 1] str;
    len = strlen(s.str);
    str = new char[len + 1];
    strcpy(str,s.str);
    return *this;
}

bool String::operator==(String s) {
    return (bool) !strcmp(s.str,str);
}

bool String::contains(String s) {
    if (strstr(str,s.str))
        return true;
    else
        return false;
}

String& String::operator+(String s) {
    int all = len + strlen(s.str);
    char *both = new char [all + 1];
    strcpy(both,str);
    strcat(both,s.str);
    return *new String(both);
}

String::operator char*() {
    return str;
}
```

The reverse type conversion, from "char *" to "String" is already defined, since the class "String" defines a constructor "String(char *)" that accepts "char*" arguments. C++ uses the constructor to perform automatic type conversion if necessary, as in the following code segment:

```
String s;
s = "test string";
```

Here, the "char *" literal "test string" is passed to a "String" constructor, which creates a temporary string object. The temporary string is then assigned to the "s" string object.

Another notable operator member function, which illustrates not only C++'s object-orientation but also how it enhances traditional C programming, is the concatenation operator "+". Supplied with a string instance parameter, it concatenates the receiver with the parameter string. Table 9.7 shows its implementation: it uses the C "strcpy" and "strcat" library functions. The return type of "operator" is to be a reference to a "String" object. This allows to treat the return value as a first-class object, even as a left-hand side of an assignment. For example, these statements are all allowed and make sense in C++:

```
String s, t("test"), o ("other");
s = t + o;
if ( t + o ).contains(o) )
   printf("so true");
```

These statements also use the member function "contains()" that determines whether the argument is contained in the receiver.

Even this statement is correct, albeit not necessarily useful:

```
( t + o ) = "other string";
```

Here, "t + o" returns a temporary string object that is the target of an assignment operation. The use of a "reference" return type makes this functionality possible.

Strings are a very useful abstraction. The class "String" can be found in almost any object-oriented class library. The "String" class can also serve as a base class of its own class hierarchy. Subclasses may extend "String" to model other concepts, for example regular expressions, or different kinds of messages.

9.4   Input and Output

The communication of data to and from a program is another area of programming where common abstractions have evolved. The notion of reading and writing input and output can be found in all programming languages. Concepts such as standard input and output files, sequential and direct file access, even i/o to unusual media have been captured with data structures and algorithms.

Therefore, we do expect to find classes and objects in an object-oriented programming environment that allow the reuse of these existing concepts and their implementation. In the following sections we will focus on the AT&T stream i/o library that is common to most implementations of C++. The more general concepts of interfacing with object-oriented programs will be covered in Chapter 10 (User Interfaces) and Chapter 11 (Databases).

The AT&T stream i/o library perceives input and output as sequences of characters. It defines two classes that capture most of the structural and functional properties that occur in dealing with i/o: the class "istream" for input and the class "ostream" for output. The two classes are able to handle buffered input and output to the standard default files associated with a C++ program. The classes define a multitude of operations and member functions. See Table 9.8 for a listing of most public "istream" member functions. For example, "istream" defines the "extraction" operation ">>": it is overloaded to operate on most predefined types of C++, and allows type-correct input and assignment to variables. The other member functions of "istream" are reminiscent of the input functions defined in the C standard input library. The member function "read," for example, can be used to read a number of characters from an input stream. Note that "read" is a regular member function, whereas ">>" is defined as an operator function (it is still a member function, though).

Figure 9.9 shows the public member functions of class "ostream." Most notable is the "insertion" operation "<<". It is overloaded to allow type-correct output for most of C++'s predefined types. The functions, e.g., "flush," "put," or "write," provide similar functionality to the C standard output library. The member function "write," for example, can be used to write a number of characters to an output stream. Again, note that "write" is a regular member function, whereas "<<" is defined as an operator member function.

The classes "istream" and "ostream" are defined as subclasses of class "ios." Class "ios" defines the commonalities of input and output streams. Its public member functions are shown in Table 9.10. The functions deal with the global state of i/o and allow the setting and inquiry of flags and defaults.

C++ provides predefined instances of these classes that allow input and output to standard places: "cin" captures standard input, "cout" standard output, and "cerr" standard error output (unbuffered). Different C++ compilers provide more such instances to allow easy access to debug files and log files, and even to printer and device ports.

Most operations in the stream input and output library are overloaded to

Table 9.8   Public Member Functions of "istream"

istream	stream input class
>>	extraction operation, overloaded for all predefined C++ types
ipfx	input prefix function, called by extraction operations before actual input
isfx	input suffix function, called by extraction operations after actual input
seekg	direct access function, sets position of get pointer in input stream
tellg	direct access function, returns current position of get pointer in input stream
get	input function, gets next character in input stream
getline	input function, gets next line from input stream
peek	input function, returns next character in input stream without advancing get pointer
ignore	input function, advances get pointer by ignoring characters in input stream
read	input function, reads sequence of characters from input stream
gcount	status function, returns number of characters read in last extraction operation
putback	undo function, pushes a character back into the input stream
sync	status function, establishes consistency between internal data structures of input stream and external source of characters

Table 9.9   Public Member Functions of "ostream"

ostream   stream output class

<<	insertion operation, overloaded for all predefined C++ types
opfx	output prefix operation, called by insertion operation before actual output
osfx	output suffix operation, called by insertion operation after actual output
flush	status function, forces all characters in internal data structures to be actually written to the real output
seekp	direct access function, sets position of put pointer in output stream
tellp	direct access function, returns current position of put pointer in output stream
put	output function, appends a character to the output stream
write	output function, appends a sequence of characters to the output stream

accept arguments of different types. Most of them are also defined to return the stream object that they were invoked for (or, in object-oriented terms: they return the receiver of the message). This definition allows concise i/o statements, for example:

```
int i = 10;
char *s = "text";
cout << i << " and " << text;
```

Moreover, it is common practice to overload these operations with arguments of classes that are newly defined. For example, it is possible to overload the insertion operation ">>" to accept instances of class "String." This allows such statements as

```
String s;
cin >> s;
cout << "String content: " << s;
```

The necessary additional declarations for the "String" class are shown in Table 9.11. It shows the declaration of two "friend" member functions: "operator>>" and "operator<<" for arguments that are "String" references.   Table 9.12 shows the implementation of these functions as part of the body of class "String." Both functions use the "<<" and ">>" operations to input and output characters into the "str" private member field of a string. This access is possible, since they are defined as "friends" of class "String."

Table 9.10   Public Member Functions of "ios"

ios	stream i/o abstract base class
!	error status operation, returns true if state of stream has "bad" or "fail" bit set
rdstate	error status function, returns the current error state of the stream
eof	error status function, returns true if state of stream has "eof" bit set
fail	error status function, returns true if state of stream has "bad" or "fail" bit set
bad	error status function, returns true if state of stream has "bad" bit set
good	error status function, returns true if no bit is set in error state
clear	error status function, clears all bits in error state
sflags	status function, returns or sets the format flags
setf	status function, sets the format flags for padding and justification
unsetf	status function, unsets the format flags
width	format function, sets the field width for next insertion or extraction operation
fill	format function, sets the fill character to be used in padding of output fields
precision	format function, controls number of significant decimals to be used for floating point input and output
rdbuf	control function, return buffer that is associated with stream
sync_with_stdio	control function, synchronizes stream i/o with standard C i/o
tie	control function, associates streams for coordinated synchronization and flushing

Table 9.11   The String Class Interface

```
class String {
    enum bool {false, true};
    int len;
    char *str ;
  public:
    String();
    String(char *s);
    String& operator=(String);
    bool operator==(String);
    bool contains(String);
    String& operator+(String);
    operator char*();
    friend istream& operator>>(istream&, String&);
    friend ostream& operator<<(ostream&, String&);
};
```

Table 9.12   The String Class Body

```
ostream& operator<<(ostream& o, String& s) {
    o << s.str;
    return o;
}

istream& operator>>(istream& i, String& s) {
    i >> s.str;
    return i;
}
```

The "istream" and "ostream" classes define input and output to standard files. They also serve as base classes for classes that extend input and output to regular files. These classes, "ifstream" for input and "ofstream" for output, inherit the respective operations from their base classes. In addition, they declare operations to open and close files. Files can be opened in two ways:

1. By using the explicit "open" member function: it requires a "char *" argument to denote the filename of the file to be opened. For example,

```
ifstream file;
file.open("input.dat");
```

associates the file "input.dat" with the "file" instance of class "ifstream" and opens it for input.

2. By using a constructor that accepts a "char *" argument. The argument is interpreted as the filename and the associated file opened. The following statement achieves the same effect as the two lines above:

```
ifstream file("input.dat");
```

Of course, the "ofstream" class implements the same functionality. And similarly, files can be closed explicitly or are closed by the destructor defined for these classes.

As an extended example of the usefulness and flexibility of the stream classes, let us define a new class "Buffer." The "Buffer" class is intended to implement a character buffer concept. Characters can be deposited into it and retrieved again, it can serve as a buffer that stores characters sequentially. Table 9.13 shows the class interface for class "Buffer." It declares a private member field "buf" to refer to the characters stored in the buffer. It also declares a static member field "size" that determines the maximum size of any buffer. The public member field "current" maintains the current fill status of the buffer; the constructor allocates the maximum size of memory for the buffer; the destructor takes care to free it again; and there are two functions "put" and "get" to deposit or retrieve characters from the buffer. The interesting aspect of the class interface is that it declares two "friend" functions: "operator>>" and "operator<<".

Table 9.14 shows the implementation of these two operator functions. One reads from an input stream while possible, and the other writes all characters in the buffer to an output stream. Table 9.14 also shows the initialization of the static member field "size" to the constant "MAXSIZE."[5] With these definitions it is now possible to instantiate and use buffer objects. For example,

---

[5]The definitions of "put" and "get" are missing, since they are not significant for our example.

Table 9.13   The Buffer Class Interface

```
class Buffer {
  char *buf;
  static int size;
 public:
  int current;
  Buffer() {
    current = 0;
    buf = new char [size];
  }
  ~Buffer(){
    delete [size] buf;
  }
  put(char);
  get(char &);
  friend ostream& operator<<(ostream&, Buffer&);
  friend istream& operator>>(istream&, Buffer&);
};
```

Table 9.14   The Buffer Class Body

```
int Buffer::size = MAXSIZE;

istream& operator>>(istream& i, Buffer& b){
  while (i.get(b.buf[b.current++]));
  return i;
}

ostream& operator<<(ostream& o, Buffer& b){
  for (int i=0; i<b.current; o.put(b.buf[i++]));
  return o;
}
```

```
                    Table 9.15   A Simple Copy Utility
main(int argc, char* argv[]) {

   if (argc < 3) {
      cout << "usage: copy source-file target-file\n";
      return (1);
   }

   Buffer b;

   ifstream ifile(argv[1]);
   ofstream ofile(argv[2]);

   cout << "Copying " << argv[1] << " into " << argv[2] << endl;
   ifile >> b;
   ofile << b;
   cout << b.current << " bytes copied\n";
}
```

```
Buffer b;
cin >> b;
cout << b;
```

will echo all characters that are entered at standard input into standard output. The ">>" and "<<" operators have been overloaded to accept buffer instances. But of course, it is also possible to read and write buffer instances from and to other file streams.

Table 9.15 shows a simple implementation of a file copy utility. The program opens two files: òne as input and one as output file. It then invokes the ">>" operation on a buffer instance to "extract" data from the input file into the buffer. The input file is an instance of class "ifstream"; it receives the operation ">>". The application is type correct, since "ifstream" is derived from "istream"; i.e., it is a subclass of "istream." All characters in the input file are read into the buffer. The characters in the buffer are then written out to the output file by applying the operator "<<" to the output file stream. Again, since "ofile" is an instance of "ofstream," which is derived from "ostream," the application is correct and all characters in the buffer are transferred to the "ofile" file. As a result, a simple but useful "copy" utility has been programmed without changing the "stream" or "Buffer" classes.

Figure 9.4 shows part of the class hierarchy found in the AT&T stream

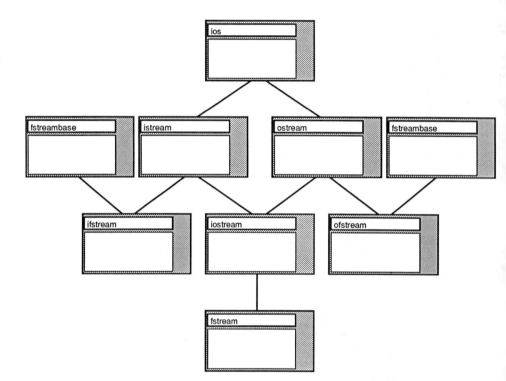

Figure 9.4   The Stream Class Hierarchy

input and output library.[6] In addition to the classes that we discussed so far, it shows a class "iostream" that combines the input facilities of "istream" with the output facilities of "ostream." It allows simultaneous input and output, and also serves as base class for the "fstream" class that allows input and output to the same file.

In addition to the functions described in this section, the AT&T stream library allows manipulation of the exact formatting of input and output to handle things such as number precision. It also provides classes to perform in-core string formatting similar to the "sprintf" and "sscanf" functions in the C standard i/o library.

9.5   Collectibles

Another example of sets of useful classes that have proven useful are those that deal with sets or collections themselves. These classes allow several or many objects to be stored in a structure and to be accessed and manipulated. The need to be able to store multiple entities in a structure has been present ever since there was programming. Most programming languages support this need by providing mechanisms to define arrays or vectors of single or even multiple dimensions.

Again, as argued in the previous section, the tools provided in these languages fall short in their usefulness compared to object-oriented programming because they are hard to extend, specialize, or reuse.

Object-oriented class libraries provide classes to allow the gathering of objects and to allow their manipulation and access. As we have seen in the previous sections, these classes hide the implementation details and provide abstract features that help a logical organization of programs around these classes.

Smalltalk–80 provides a rich hierarchy of classes that handle collections. Figure 9.5 shows its "Collection" class hierarchy. The root of the hierarchy is class "Collection," an abstract class whose purpose is to factor out the commonalities of its subclasses. A notable member of the class hierarchy is class "Set": it is very close to the most general collection. It collects its elements and does not impose a specific ordering or access criteria on them. A set does not store duplicate elements true to a mathematical "set." Its subclass "Dictionary" differs from "Set" in that it stores key-value pairs as its elements.

A "Bag" is similar to a "Set," except that it allows duplicates of elements and also notes their count. A "Mapped Collection" is a collection that uses a map to determine the ordering of its elements.

---

[6]The class "fstreambase" is shown twice to simplify the layout of the figure. It is technically also a subclass of the "ios" class.

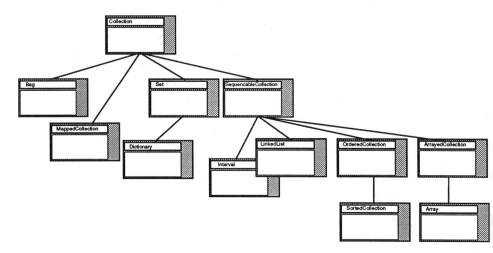

Figure 9.5   The Smalltalk-80 Collection Class Hierarchy

A "Sequenceable Collection" is an abstract class that serves as a superclass for classes that capture collections that can be sequenced. An "Interval" is a finite sequence of elements that can be used in algorithms that require stepping. A "Linked List" is a collection where each element points to the next. An "Ordered Collection" provides an integer index for each of its elements. It differs from class "Array" in that elements can be added and removed freely. Its subclass "Sorted Collection" keeps a sorting criterion for its elements that is used when elements are added. The class "Arrayed Collection" is abstract and superclass to class "Array," which allows the maintenance of the relative position of its elements.

Smalltalk-80, unlike C++, requires a closed class hierarchy: all Smalltalk-80 classes are — directly or indirectly — derived from class "Object." That allows a relatively easy approach to how the elements of a collection should be typed. In Smalltalk-80, all instances stored in collections are at least instances of class Object, and since all classes are subclasses of Object, this is always the case.

Other object–oriented programming languages do not offer this convenience. For example, recall the C++ "Collection" class described in Chapter 5. C++ demands a concrete type be given to the elements. The least restrictive type possible in C++ , "void *" , does not allow any functions to be applied to it. In Chapter 5, we had to define an "Example" class to serve as a superclass for all classes whose instances were to be stored in such a "Collection."

Another solution to the problem is — rather than to provide complete classes in a class library — to provide templates of class descriptions that are complete but for the exact type of the elements to be stored. This concept is called "genericity" which allows the definition of "generic classes" that are completely described but for a parameter. The upcoming ANSI standards for C++ include a mechanism to define class templates or generic classes (see also Appendix E for an example of how class templates can be simulated in current C++).

9.6   Class Libraries

The first five sections of this chapter illustrated the usefulness of classes and class libraries and gave examples of frequently found classes. This section will give an overview of which classes can be found in some common class libraries.

Before we go to specific class libraries, it is important to point out a class that occurs in most class libraries: most class libraries have a root class that does not necessarily capture the most essential data structure and its associated data structures. Instead, the root class encapsulates features that implement common assumptions or defaults used throughout the class library. Such a class, usually called "Object," implements common memory allocation and allocation schemes, object interdependencies, debugging facilities, simple store and retrieval operations, etc.

Some object–oriented programming environments, notably Smalltalk–80, require all classes to be directly or indirectly derived from a "root" class. Such programming environments are usually termed "closed." If multiple inheritance is not supported, then a "closed" policy makes it impossible to use more than one class hierarchy.

C++, on the other hand, is not a "closed" language, and it supports multiple inheritance, making it very flexible in respect to using classes from class libraries. In the following subsections we give an overview of two C++ libraries that are available publicly.

9.6.1   The NIH Class Library

The National Institutes of Health originated the most widely known class library for C++ [GOP90].

It is loosely modeled after the Smalltalk–80 class library. Tables 9.16, 9.17, 9.18, and 9.19 show the classes that are part of the NIH library. Table 9.17 shows the "Object" class, the root of the NIH class hierarchy, and its immediate subclasses. Notable is class "Class" which implements a property

---

Table 9.16   The NIH Class Library (top level)

NIHCL: Library Static Member Variables and Functions

Object: Root of the NIH Class Library Inheritance Tree

OIOifd: File Descriptor Object I/O "readFrom()" Formatting

OIOin: Abstract Class for Object I/O "readFrom()" Formatting

OIOofd: File Descriptor Object I/O "storeOn()" Formatting

OIOout: Abstract Class for Object I/O "storeOn()" Formatting

ReadFromTbl: Tables used by Object I/O "readFrom()"

StoreOnTbl: Tables used by Object I/O "storeOn()"

---

of all instances of NIC classes: it allows any instance to know its class. This feature is reminiscent of Smalltalk–80 where classes are treated as objects themselves and can be considered during computation.

Table 9.18 shows the "Collection" class and its derivations. The subclasses implement various kinds of collection structures as explained earlier in this chapter.

Table 9.19 shows the "Vector" class and its subclasses. "Vector", like "Collection" and "Object," is an abstract class and cannot be instantiated. Other interesting subclasses are "Process," "Schedules," and "Semaphore," (Table 9.17) which show that object-oriented programming has found its way into the operating system world of programming.

9.6.2   The GNU C++ Library

The Free Software Foundation originated another library of C++ classes.

It contains classes that are similar in nature to the classes described in the earlier sections of this chapter and to the NIH class library. Most notable, it also contains an implementation of a stream library. This stream library, however, differs from the AT&T stream library. Table 9.20 summarizes the classes that are part of "libg++", the GNU C++ class library.

Table 9.17   The NIH Class Library (Object subclasses)

Object: Root of the NIH Class Library Inheritance Tree

Bitset: Set of Small Integers (like Pascal's type SET)

Class: Class Descriptor

Collection: Abstract Class for Collections

Date: Gregorian Calendar Date

FDSet: Set of File Descriptors

Float: Floating Point Number

Fraction: Rational Arithmetic

Integer: Integer Number Object

Iterator: Collection Iterator

Link: Abstract Class for LinkedList Links

    LinkOb: Link Containing Object Pointer

    Process: Co-routine Process Object

        HeapProc: Process with Stack in Free Store

        StackProc: Process with Stack on "main()" Stack

LookupKey: Abstract Class for Dictionary Associations

    Assoc: Association of Object Pointers

    AssocInt: Association of Object Pointer with Integer

Nil: The Nil Object

Point: X-Y Coordinate Pair

Random: Random Number Generator

Range: Range of Integers

Rectangle: Rectangle Object

Scheduler: Co-routine Process Scheduler

Semaphore: Process Synchronization

SharedQueue: Shared Queue of Objects

String: Character String

    Regex: Regular Expression

Time: Time of Day

Vector: Abstract Class for Vectors

Table 9.18   The NIH Class Library (Collection classes)

Collection: Abstract Class for Collections

> **Arraychar:** Byte Array
>
> **ArrayOb:** Array of Object Pointers
>
> **Bag:** Unordered Collection of Objects
>
> **SeqCltn:** Abstract Class for Ordered, Indexed Collections
>> **Heap:** Min-Max Heap of Object Pointers
>> **LinkedList:** Singly-Linked List
>> **OrderedCltn:** Ordered Collection of Object Pointers
>>> **SortedCltn:** Sorted Collection
>>>> **KeySortCltn:** Keyed Sorted Collection
>> **Stack:** Stack of Object Pointers
>
> **Set:** Unordered Collection of Non-Duplicate Objects
>> **Dictionary:** Set of Associations
>>> **IdentDict:** Dictionary Keyed by Object Address
>> **IdentSet:** Set Keyed by Object Address

Table 9.19   The NIH Class Library (Vector classes)

Vector: Abstract Class for Vectors

> **BitVec:** Bit Vector
>
> **ByteVec:** Byte Vector
>
> **ShortVec:** Short Integer Vector
>
> **IntVec:** Integer Vector
>
> **LongVec:** Long Integer Vector
>
> **FloatVec:** Floating Point Vector
>
> **DoubleVec:** Double-Precision Floating Point Vector

Table 9.20   The GNU C++ Class Library

AllocRing: circular list, whose elements contain references to other objects

Bag: abstract class for bags: unbounded potentially duplicate elements

>   **CHBag:** unordered bags, implemented with chained hash tables
>
>   **OSLBag:** ordered bags, implemented with linked lists
>
>   **OXPBag:** ordered bags, implemented with class Plex
>
>   **SLBag:** unordered bags, implemented with linked lists
>
>   **SplayBag:** ordered bags, implemented with splay trees
>
>   **VHBag:** unordered bags, implemented with hash tables
>
>   **XPBag:** unordered bags, implemented with class Plex

BitSet: provides bit manipulation with "set" semantics

BitString: provides bit manipulation in "string" or "vector" semantics

>   related classes: BitPattern, BitSetBit, BitStrBit, BitSubString

Complex: provides complex number arithmetic

CursesWindow: repacking of the "curses" C library for window-like i/o to character-based terminals

Deque: abstract class for double ended queues

>   **DLDeque:** dynamic size queue, implemented with linked lists
>
>   **XPDeque:** dynamic size queue, implemented with class PLex

File: basic i/o class for sequential files: supports functions to open physical files, basic i/o methods, file and buffer control, and methods for maintaining logical and physical file status.

>   **PlotFile:** plot file class: supports the UNIX plotfile format.
>
>   **SFile:** structured file class: supports processing of fixed record length binary data.

Fix: fixed bit representation, interpreted as real number in [-1,+1] range

Fix16: fixed bit representation (16 bits), interpreted as real number in [-1,+1] range

Fix24: fixed bit representation (24 bits), interpreted as real number in [-1,+1] range

Fix32: fixed bit representation (32 bits), interpreted as real number in [-1,+1] range

Fix48: fixed bit representation (48 bits), interpreted as real number in [-1,+1] range

Table 9.20   The GNU C++ Class Library (cont.)

GetOpt: access to UNIX style command line options

Integer: provides multiple precision integer arithmetic

List: provides for manipulation of homogeneous lists

DLList: doubly-linked list

SLList: singly linked list

Map: abstract class for maps: support associative array operations

>   **AVLMap:** ordered maps, implemented with threaded AVL trees
>   **CHMap:** unordered maps, implemented with chained hash tables
>   **RAVLMap:** ranked AVLMaps
>   **SplayMap:** ordered maps, implemented with splay trees
>   **VHMap:** unordered maps, implemented with hash tables

Obstack: stack of objects

Plex: "natural" array: provides arbitrary indices, may grow and shrink

>   **FPlex:** can only shrink within declared bounds
>   **MPlex:** may grow or shrink, allows deletion and restoration of elements
>   **RPlex:** may grow and shrink without bounds

PQ: abstract class for priority queues

>   **PHPQ:** pairing heap priority queue
>   **SplayPQ:** splay tree priority queue
>   **XPPQ:** binary heap priority queue, implemented with class Plex

Queue: abstract class for queues

>   **SLQueue:** dynamic size queue, implemented with linked lists
>   **VQueue:** fixed size queue, implemented with arrays
>   **XPQueue:** dynamic size queue, implemented with class Plex

RNG: random number generator

>   **MLCG:** multiplicative linear congruential generator
>   **ACG:** linear congruential generator

Table 9.20 The GNU C++ Class Library (cont.)

Random: random numbers

>   **Binominal:** binomial distribution
>
>   **DiscreteUniform:** discrete uniform distribution
>
>   **Erlang:** Erlang distribution
>
>   **Geometric:** discrete geometric distribution
>
>   **HyperGeometric:** hypergeometric distribution
>
>   **NegativeExponential:** negative exponential distribution
>
>   **Normal:** normal distribution
>
>>   **LogNormal:** LogNormal logarithmic normal distribution
>
>   **Poisson:** poisson distribution
>
>   **RandomInterval:**
>
>   **RandomRange:**
>
>   **Uniform:** uniform distribution
>
>   **Weibull:** weibull distribution

RandomInteger: provides uniformly distributed random integers

Rational: provides multiple precision rational number arithmetic

Regex: supports regular expression searching, comparing and matching

Set: abstract class for sets

>   **AVLSet:** ordered set, implemented with AVL trees
>
>   **BSTSet:** ordered set, implemented with binary search trees
>
>   **CHSet:** unordered set, implemented with chained hash tables
>
>   **OSLSet:** ordered set, implemented with linked lists
>
>   **OXPSet:** ordered set, implemented with class Plex
>
>   **SLSet:** unordered set, implemented with linked lists
>
>   **SplaySet:** ordered set, implemented with splay trees
>
>   **VHSet:** unordered set, implemented with hash tables
>
>   **VOHSet:** unordered set, implemented with unordered hash tables
>
>   **XPSet:** unordered set, implemented with class Plex

Table 9.20   The GNU C++ Class Library (cont.)

SampleStatistic: provides accumulation of samples

SampleHistogram: provides collection of samples

Stack: abstract class for stacks

SLStack: dynamic size stack, implemented with linked lists
VStack: fixed size stack, implemented with arrays
XPStack: dynamic size stack, implemented with class Plex

String: supports string processing

SubString: supports substring extraction and modification

istream: provides input from standard input

ostream: provides output to standard output

streambuf: buffer mechanism for streams

filebuf: buffer associated with file

Vec: provides vector type structure and services

AVec: vector with arithmetic operations
AVLVec: AVLVec

9.7 Summary of Chapter

This chapter focused on the use of classes to capture common data structures and their associated functionalities. We illustrated classes that treated magnitudes, strings, streams, and collectibles. We also gave an overview of some of the widely used and freely available C++ class libraries: the National Institutes of Health class library and the Free Software Foundation GNU library.

The extent and use of class libraries are the cornerstone of the argument that object-oriented programming will greatly increase productivity in programming. An issue that still needs to be resolved is to allow mixing of classes from different class libraries. While the goal at hand is to mix classes that are described in the same programming language, the ideal goal is to allow the interoperability of classes and their instances that stem from different programming languages.

Chapter 10

Object-Oriented User Interfaces

The typical overall organization of an object-oriented user interface is shown and its layered relationship with the application is explained. Typical classes and their hierarchies in the presentation (output), input, and control components are illustrated, such as classes for graphical objects: windows, menus, icons, mouses, keyboards. The chapter explains how object-oriented concepts improve user interfaces: (1) by allowing flexible construction and dynamic behavior in a uniform programming framework, (2) by producing reusable and extensible components, and (3) by achieving multiple levels of device and platform independence. The Smalltalk MVC paradigm and the C++ InterViews toolkit are described.

10.1 Introduction

Ever since computers were able to process information, there has been a need to interact with them. Humans use computers to solve application problems. As applications become more and more complex, it is even harder for humans to efficiently communicate with the computer. Increasingly, more and more software is dedicated to the human-computer aspect of applications. This chapter tells how object-oriented programming is improving the design and implementation of user interfaces.

Human-computer interaction has advanced rapidly, keeping pace with the newest hardware developments. It was the development of advanced graphical displays and advanced input devices that transformed user interfaces from a mere text base to the current standard of graphical user interfaces. The new media allow new styles of interaction that are more elaborate and more complex, but also more expressive. The increased expressiveness enhances the bandwidth of information transferral between human and computer, and vice versa.

Modern graphical user interfaces aim to be more efficient than text-based user interfaces. The features provided by graphical user interfaces usually fall into two categories: *task oriented* or *direct manipulation*.

In a *task oriented* feature, the user interface presents a selection of tasks to the user. The user can select a task and is guided through all steps necessary for the completion of the task by the user interface. For example, consider a file and directory interface. The task choices presented to the user are to copy, rename, or delete a file in a directory. The tasks are displayed to the user as a panel of buttons that appears on the display screen. To start a task the user moves his pointing device (i.e., mouse) to a button (e.g., the delete button) and presses a mouse button. The user interface reacts by displaying a subwindow listing all files in the directory and prompting the user for a selection. The user selects a file (i.e., by pointing at it), which causes the file to be deleted. The task is then completed and the user can select a new task from the panel of choices.

Another style of user interface is called *direct manipulation*. Here the user is presented with graphical images of the entities that belong to the application. The user interface provides a set of generic operations that can be applied to the displayed entities. For the example illustrated above, all files in a directory would be presented graphically (e.g., as icons) on the display screen. One of the generic operations, the delete operation, can be achieved by directly manipulating the file icons. In addition to the file icons there is a special icon displayed on the screen symbolizing a waste basket. The delete operation is achieved by selecting the desired file (i.e., by pointing with the mouse and pressing a mouse button) and dragging it to the waste basket. The user interface interprets this action and deletes the file. The delete operation is achieved by directly manipulating a file object.

Both styles of user interfaces achieve the same result with different means. One would assume that one of the styles should be used by a specific user interface. However, there is no general agreement whether one or the other style should be enforced. Most user interfaces today have elements of both styles.

As the above discussion illustrated, user interfaces are becoming elaborate components of many applications. Instead of the traditional "input-processing-output" cycle of old-style application programs, modern application programs have a user interface component that is structured according to — and specifically for — the capabilities of the associated user interface media and the style of interaction. These user interface components are very complex. Luckily, advances in software technology have accompanied hardware advances.

Object-oriented programming in general improves the quality of design and implementation of any application. Therefore we expect to see the same benefits and advantages when object-oriented technology is applied to user interfaces. Object-oriented programming represents entities in an application as *objects*: in an object-oriented user interface we expect to see mouse, window, menu, etc., objects. Object-oriented programming lets objects interact by *sending messages* among them: in an object-oriented user interface we expect to see messages being sent among windows, mouse, and menu objects. Object-oriented programs specify objects with *classes* and allow *subclasses*, thus improving the modularity and level of reuse in applications: in an object-oriented user interface we expect to see windows, mouse, and menu classes that are parts of class hierarchies.

Object-oriented user interface technology has been touted as a major step in increasing the productivity in designing and programming modern direct-manipulation user interfaces, e.g. [FGKK88], because of the clear decomposition of structure and functionality. Several user interface programming environments (e.g. Smalltalk-80, the X window system with its various toolkits, such as InterViews [LVC89]) that follow the "Seeheim User Interface Model"[Gre85] are in use and have demonstrated a gain in user interface quality, as well as in programmer productivity.

This chapter gives an overview of the state of the art in object orientation of user interfaces. In the next section we will discuss their general organization, framework, and advantages. In Section 3, we will illustrate the use of object-orientation to develop device-independent user interface applications. Section 4 presents the idea of building and maintaining libraries of reusable classes for user interfaces. Section 5 discusses user interface paradigms, where a certain style and framework is imposed on all user interfaces built within a single programming environment. The chapter concludes with some of the author's ideas for improving the user interface design process.

10.2   Object Orientation

An object-oriented system can be viewed as a collection of objects. Each object implements a small part of the overall behavior of the complete application or system. As we have illustrated in Chapter 8, objects can be grouped according to their use. The main objects are those that achieve the behavior of an application: they are the *computation* objects. The computation objects communicate with database objects and user interface objects. The database objects are special in that they *persist*; i.e., they exist beyond the single run of an application invocation. User interface objects visualize the computation and persistent objects; they interact with the user and are called the *interactive* objects of an application.

When building object-oriented user interfaces one needs to be aware of the overall object organization of an application. To design and implement a user interface component, the designer needs to specify what communication can occur among the objects. Communication occurs among *interactive* objects, but also between *interactive* and *computation* objects. The possible messages that can be sent and received and their sequence is called a *protocol*. Objects in a complex object-oriented application need to follow a certain protocol. The protocol is different for different applications, depending on the style and framework that is followed. Section 5 will elaborate further on this concept and give examples of specific programming environments and their protocols.

Of course, an object-oriented program does not directly describe objects; it describes classes of objects. A class allows a level of encapsulation. Objects have features that describe its behavioral or structural aspects. Features can be encapsulated; that is, access to them can be limited and controlled. The class describes the encapsulation aspects of its instances. Since classes hide certain implementation aspects, it is possible to make a specific implementation device-dependent. Programs that use these classes can be shielded from implementation detail. Section 3 describes this concept of providing class specifications to impose a device-independent layer in user interface development.

The third characteristic feature of object-oriented user interfaces stems from the use of class hierarchies to capture relationships among classes. Classes can have subclasses, which in turn have subclasses. These class hierarchies serve as repositories of reusable and extendible components for recurring and common tasks in a user interface. Section 4 illustrates some of the common classes found in a typical programming environment.

10.3   Device Independence

A common concern of user-interface builders is to stay away from device-dependent features. The variety of available graphical devices and the speed with which they change their functionality, become improved or obsolete, dictates that user interface components be as device independent as possible.

Object-oriented programming technology provides an answer. A class describes objects. The description is done at two levels. One level describes the general features of instances of the class. These features are accessible and visible. The second level describes the internal features of instances of the class. These features determine how the externally visible and accessible features are implemented.

Classes describe common elements in a user interface. The "window" class for example, captures a graphical window displayed with a border, title bar,

Table 10.1   C++ Window Class

```
class Window {
 private:
   Point coordinates;
   DisplayObject content;
 public:
   display();
   move(Point);
};
```

background, and content on a display screen. The class specifies the visible features and hides the implementation-specific details. Table 10.1 shows the C++ class description of a window class.   In C++, public features are accessible, private features are hidden. Table 10.1 shows the "move" and "display" functions as public features. An application that uses a window makes use of these features without depending on implementation details. The implementation details are hidden in the private features. They might implement the "move" or "display" function by manipulation of the private "coordinates" or "content" features, which will depend on the specific device the application is targeted for. To port the application to different devices, only a small, well-defined part of the overall application — the private features of the window (and similar) classes — have to be modified.

Classes can provide a layer of device-independent features that enhance the portability of an application. Typical classes found in an object-oriented programming environment capture the features of windows, menus, locators, keyboards, and other input devices.

10.4 Reusable Components

Classes that capture the input and output characteristics of user interface components are designed with two objectives in mind. The first objective is to capture the component-specific functionality and to make it available to the user interface. The second objective is to capture the functionalities in the most general way possible. Classes that provide a general service can be reused in more than one context.

Examples of such classes were mentioned in the last section: window, menu, mouse, etc. Classes such as these can be reused in two ways. First, another application can reuse the class directly. For example, it can create instances of the window class. Second, another application can refine the class by specifying a subclass. For example, it can define more specific menu classes to support pop-up, pull-down, and pull-right menus. The reused menu class and the new pop-up, pull-down, and pull-right menu classes build a class hierarchy. Most programming environments provide class hierarchies of reusable classes.

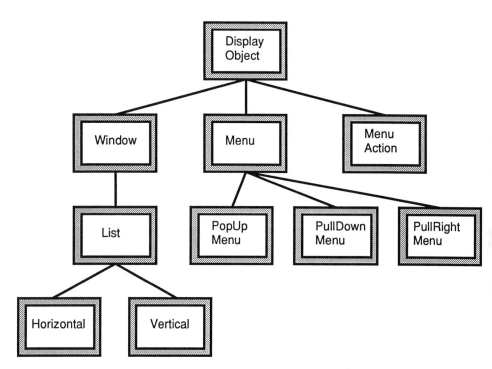

Figure 10.1   User Interface Class Hierarchy

Figure 10.1 shows a class hierarchy of some typical classes for graphical user interfaces. The hierarchy has a single root, the class "DisplayObject," which captures the features common to all objects in an interactive application (e.g., location). Class "Window" is one of its subclasses and is also superclass to a "List" class, which allows the display of listable elements in a window. The listable elements are instances of class "Displayobject," allowing the listing of any other object in this hierarchy. Subclasses of "List" further specify whether elements are listed vertically or horizontally. Other classes in the class hierarchy capture different kinds of menus. Notable is the "Menu-Action" class, which models an entry in a menu: it has features for a selection

text, a selection criterion, and a response to the selection. This class makes
the implementation of menus simple: menus are collections of menu actions.
Menu actions can also be used to implement various kinds of buttons and
switches.

The class hierarchy shown in Figure 10.1 is just a small example of what
can be found in a typical object-oriented programming environment. The next
section will further describe examples of complex class hierarchies.

10.5 User Interface Paradigms

While class hierarchies allow us to capture and classify features and functionalities necessary for object-oriented user interfaces, they need to make assumptions and enforce conventions about how user interfaces are constructed
in a specific environment. The protocol of messages that are sent among objects in the user interface, and to and from computational objects, impose a
specific framework or architecture. To assemble a complete interactive system,
it is necessary to predetermine in what sequence specific objects receive user
input, affect a change to the state of the application, and cause updates to
the screen presentation. This sequence, the protocol, has a level of complexity that depends on the complexity of the desired interactive and application
behavior. The level of complexity increases rapidly for even simple interactive
applications.

For example, consider a simple application that presents a graphical display of some application objects. Assume that the objects displayed represent
entities (entries) in a folder. The entries symbolize different kinds of data: they
can be files, pictures, or folders themselves. Figure 10.2 shows a sample display. The application allows the user to select entries displayed on the screen
and to invoke operations for them. The operations are specific to the entries.
For example, a file entry can be deleted or edited; a picture entry can be viewed;
and a folder entry can be opened, which will start up the same application for
the folder entry displaying the entries within.

During the design of this interactive application, we define the following
classes: "Window" contains all entries for a folder; "FileHolder" contains a
reference to a file and a menu that describes the possible operations on the
file; "PictureHolder" contains a reference to a bitmap describing the picture and
a menu describing the possible operations on a picture; and "FolderHolder," it
contains a reference to another folder object and a menu with its operations.
The "FileHolder," "PictureHolder," and "FolderHolder" classes are subclasses of
a general "DisplayObject" class (similar to the one mentioned in the previous
section) that handles general display and location features and functions.

The "Window" class acts as the control object. It has access to the input

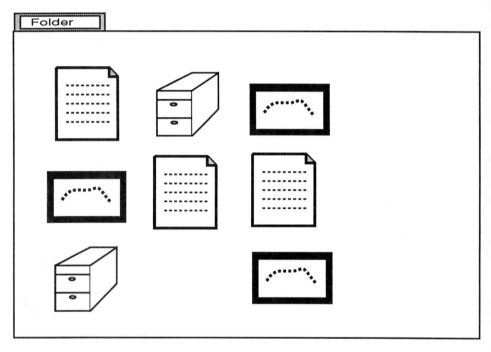

Figure 10.2   Folder Interface Example

Table 10.2   Control Function for Window Class

```
Window::control() {

  while(true) {          // loop forever
                         // display all entries
    for (int i=0; i<size; i++)
      entries[i]->display();
                         // if mouse select button is pressed
    if (mouse->select())
                         // detect which object is selected
      for (int i=0; i<size; i++)
        if (entries[i]->contains(mouse->location))
          current=entries[i];
                         // if mouse menu button is pressed
                         // then ask current object to
                         // popu-up its menu
    if (mouse->buttonpush())
      current->menu();
  }
}
```

and output media. In this example, input is achieved by selecting an entry in the folder with the mouse, and selecting an entry-specific operation from its menu. Output is achieved by displaying the individual entries on the screen with the entry-specific display functions. The window control algorithm (see Table 10.2) is very simple: in a loop, the function displays all entries, checks whether the user selected an entry, and invokes the entry menu of the currently selected entry. The function operates on two local variables: "entries," an array of pointers to entry objects, and "current," a pointer to the currently selected entry. The function assumes that the "mouse" object understands the messages "select( )," "location," and "buttonpush," and that an entry understands "display( )," "contains( )" and "menu( )" messages.

While the control algorithm seems simple, it implements a certain protocol of messages that has to be followed by all participating components in this interface. Existing paradigms for object-oriented user interfaces similarly implement and enforce a precise protocol of sending and receiving messages. In the following two subsections, we outline the Smalltalk-80 MVC paradigm and the InterViews/X11 toolkit. Both systems are good examples for more advanced object-oriented user interfaces.

10.5.1   The Smalltalk-80 Model-View-Controller Paradigm

Any interface within the Smalltalk-80 programming environment consists of three major components [GR83]:

1. Model: a collection of objects representing the application domain of the user interface.

2. View: a collection of objects that are presented to the user on the display screen.

3. Controller: a collection of objects that control the flow of information to and from the user of the application.

Together the three components form an "MVC" triple.   The controller ("C") handles the user input and communicates with the model ("M") and view ("V"). Communication among them is achieved with message sending.   Messages received by a component result in the invocation of object-specific procedures. Figure 10.3 illustrates the components and their relationships. For example,

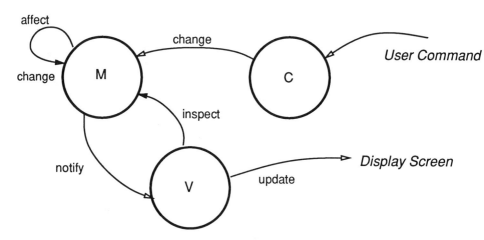

Figure 10.3   Smalltalk-80 MVC Paradigm

consider that a user issues a command to change data. The controller receives and handles the input — the command — from the user. It then sends a message to the model to affect the user's request for a change. As a response, the model executes a procedure that changes some of its aspects, and then notifies the view that it has changed. The view, in response, inquires as to the current state of the model and updates or redisplays its presentation on the screen.

Figure 10.4   Dialog Example

Any user interface within the Smalltalk-80 programming environment is built as a triple of model, view, and controller. As a simple example, consider a graphical user interface that prompts the user for a string answer. Figure 10.4 shows a possible screen appearance of such a user interface. The appearance on the screen is actually the presentation part of the user interface; its input is controlled by a control component and related to an application or model object. Even this simple user interface falls under the MVC paradigm. The following Smalltalk-80 code fragment was used to produce it:

```
| model view |
model := ValueHolder new.
view := DialogView model: model.
view indent: 8;
    addVerticalSpace: 4;
    addTextLabel: 'Are we having fun ?';
    addVerticalSpace: 4;
    addTextFieldOn: model
    initially: 'of course';
    addVerticalSpace: 4.
view open
```

The "model" is created as an instance of the "ValueHolder" class. "ValueHolders" provide the service to hold a specific value and are suitable as models in an MVC triple. The "view" is created as an instance of the "DialogView" class. Note that when the "view" is created, it is immediately associated with the "model." There is no need to create and associate a controller, since a "DialogView" comes with a default controller — a "DialogController" instance. The third and following (but for the last) statements in the code instruct the "view" how to format the presentation appearance on the display screen. The last statement in the code initiates interaction: it sends the "open" message to the "view," which then activates its controller to produce a complete and running interface.

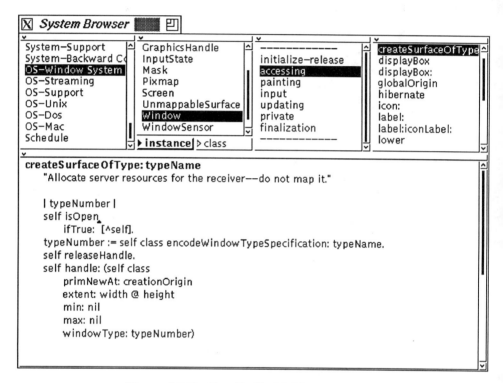

```
┌──────────────────────────────────────────────────────────────────┐
│ ⊠  System Browser  ▓▓▓▓  凹                                         │
├──────────────────┬───────────────────┬────────────────┬──────────┤
│ System−Support   │ GraphicsHandle    │ −−−−−−−−−−−−    │createSurfaceOfType│
│ System−Backward C│ InputState        │ initialize−release│ displayBox │
│ OS−Window System │ Mask              │ accessing        │ displayBox: │
│ OS−Streaming     │ Pixmap            │ painting         │ globalOrigin │
│ OS−Support       │ Screen            │ input            │ hibernate   │
│ OS−Unix          │ UnmappableSurface │ updating         │ icon:       │
│ OS−Dos           │ Window            │ private          │ label:      │
│ OS−Mac           │ WindowSensor      │ finalization     │ label:iconLabel: │
│ Schedule         │ ▶ instance ▷ class│ −−−−−−−−−−−−    │ lower       │
├──────────────────┴───────────────────┴────────────────┴──────────┤
│ createSurfaceOfType: typeName                                      │
│    "Allocate server resources for the receiver−−do not map it."    │
│                                                                    │
│    | typeNumber |                                                  │
│    self isOpen                                                     │
│        ifTrue: [^self].                                            │
│    typeNumber := self class encodeWindowTypeSpecification: typeName.│
│    self releaseHandle.                                             │
│    self handle: (self class                                        │
│        primNewAt: creationOrigin                                   │
│        extent: width @ height                                      │
│        min: nil                                                    │
│        max: nil                                                    │
│        windowType: typeNumber)                                     │
└──────────────────────────────────────────────────────────────────┘
```

Figure 10.5   Smalltalk-80 Class Browser

Complex interfaces consisting of major subcomponents also follow the MVC paradigm: overall the complete interface is structured as a triple; in addition, each subcomponent is a triple, too. For example, consider the Smalltalk-80 class browser (see Figure 10.5) [Gol84]. It consists of five panes, four in the top part and one in the lower part. Overall, this user interface is structured as a triple of (1) model: the Smalltalk class organization as the application; (2) view: an overall window pane containing five subwindows; and (3) controller: an object that processes user input and modifies Smalltalk classes and their organization.

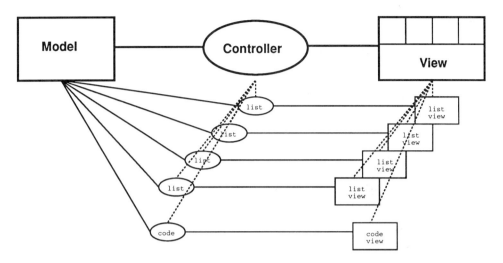

Figure 10.6   Hierarchy of Interface Components

Internally, this interface is built from five subtriples: one MVC triple is
responsible for the upper left-hand pane displaying the categories of Smalltalk
classes, and there is one for each of the pane's containing, respectively, the list
of classes in the selected category, the list of protocols in the selected class,
the list of methods in the selected protocol, and finally the body of the selected
method in the lower pane.

For example, consider the left topmost pane: the model for this user interface component is the list of all categories of classes; the view displays all
elements in a scrollable list, possibly highlighting a current selection; the controller accepts input from the user in the form of scrollbars and pull-down
menus from which the user can select commands. All user interface behavior
for this subpane is handled within this triple.

Each of the subtriples has a model, view, and controller that are part of
the overall model, view, and controller. The Smalltalk class organization —
maintained in a global object — serves as the common model for the triples in
the class browser interface. Figure 10.6 shows how the triples and subtriples
are connected. The solid lines show the connectivity within a triple and the
dashed lines show how the overall MVC triple is connected to its subtriples.
The overall view is composed of four list views and one code view. Smalltalk-
80 provides classes for these views: "SelectionInListView" and "CodeView,"
respectively. There are four list controllers and one code controller. The con-

trollers are specific to the views; i.e., they were created specifically to interact with their views.

The complete Smalltalk-80 class browser is made up of components that are reusable. These components can be used to quickly create new interfaces. Of course, Smalltalk-80 offers many classes for many styles of user interfaces.

10.5.2   The InterViews Toolkit for the X11 Window System

InterViews is a library of C++ classes that allow building user interfaces within the X11 window system. InterViews mandates a composition of user interfaces from four components [LCV88]:

1. Subject: a collection of objects representing the application domain of the user interface.

2. Interactor: a collection of interactive objects; they make up the view of the subject as presented to the user. An interactor has "sensor" and "painter" subcomponents to achieve its interactive behavior.

3. Sensor: a collection of input objects representing possible input media.

4. Painter: a collection of output objects representing possible output media.

Although it seems that this framework is different from Smalltalk's MVC paradigm, the logical composition is similar: the application is separated from the presentation, and a control component maintains the consistencies. Figure 10.7 illustrates the overall organization of any user interface built with InterViews and the flow of information. The interactor ("I") receives user input through a sensor ("S") and communicates with the subject ("S") and updates the presentation through a painter ("P"). Communication among the components is achieved via message sending. As with the MVC paradigm, established protocols of messages have to be followed.

For example, consider that a user issues a command to change data. The sensor receives and handles the input — the event — from the user. It then sends a message to the interactor to affect the user's request for a change. As a response, the interactor sends an appropriate message to the subject to affect the required change. Then the interactor inquires as to the new state of the subject and updates or redisplays the presentation on the screen by sending a message to the painter.

Composition of user interfaces is achieved with different classes of interactors. One class of interactors is a *scene*. It allows the interactor to have components that are interactors themselves. Scenes provide the functionality to add and remove interactors from the list of components; they also share and

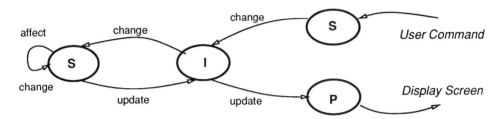

Figure 10.7   InterViews User Interface Framework

Figure 10.8   InterViews Example Interface

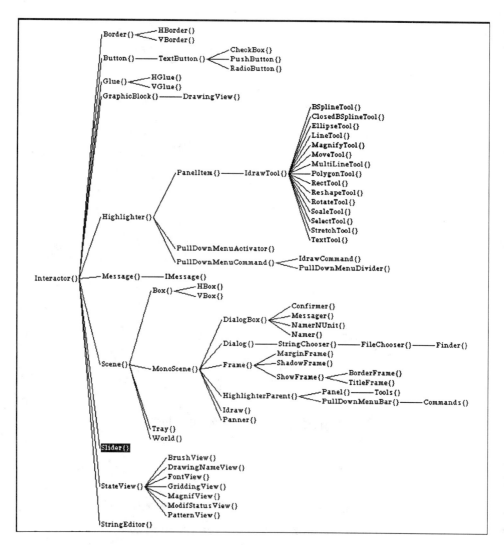

Figure 10.9   InterViews Class Hierarchy (partial)

Table 10.3   InterViews Code Example

```
int main () {
  World* world = new World();
  ButtonState* quit=new ButtonState(false);
  Dialog* browser = new Dialog(
    quit,
      new HBox( new VBox(
        new VGlue(0.3*inch,0.2*inch,1.0*inch),
        new Message("The quick brown fox..."),
        new VGlue(0.3*inch,0.2*inch,0),
        new HBox(
          new HGlue(0.3*inch,0.2*inch,hfil),
          new PushButton("Quit", quit, true)
        )
      )));
  world->InsertApplication(browser);
  browser->Accept();
  world->Remove(browser);
}
```

coordinate the sensor and painter objects of the subcomponents. How a scene organizes its components can vary. Subclasses of scenes allow for different composition strategies. Class *hbox* arranges its subcomponents horizontally; class *vbox* does it vertically.[1] A special class *viewport* allows the graphical depiction of the subject to be larger than its actual representation on the display screen and supports scrolling.

As an example of a small InterViews application, consider a simple interface that has the screen appearance as shown in Figure 10.8. A window contains a simple message and a button that a user can select. Again, the example follows the general organization of any InterViews interface. There is a subject, an interactor, painters, and sensors. Table 10.3 shows the C++ code that was used to create the sample user interface. The "World" is an overall interactor that encapsulates the structure and behavior of an X11 window, subject to a window managers operations. The "ButtonState" is a subject that will be used for a "PushButton" interactor; it has the appearance and behavior of a button that can be selected and pushed with the mouse input device. The "Dialog" object "browser" is also an interactor that allows active components. Its constructor is used to guide the layout of the screen appearance. Glue is used to center and arrange a "Message" and the "PushButton" interactor. Next,

---

[1]The horizontal and vertical arrangement of elements into boxes and the use of *glue* is similar to boxes and glue in TeX [Knu86].

the "browser" dialog interactor is inserted into the "world" interactor, and the application is started by sending an "Accept()" message to the browser. After its return, the "browser" is removed from the "world" interactor, and the example is done.

While space does not permit it here, it is also conceivable to model complex user interfaces with InterViews. A user interface similar to the Smalltalk-80 class browser (see Figure 10.5) could be structured as a tree of scenes in InterViews. The top scene would be a *vbox*, consisting of one subscene for the four top panes and one for the lower pane. The scene for the four top panes would be an *hbox*, consisting of four subscenes each of which holds a *viewport* scene to allow for scrolling within the lists. Each of all these scenes would share the same subject — the class organization — and participate in the input and output media through their sensors and painters.

Of course, InterViews offers many more classes for many styles of user interfaces. Figure 10.9 shows a multitude of InterViews classes.

10.6   User Interfaces: The Next Generation?

Object-oriented user interface technology has been touted as a major step in increasing the productivity in designing and programming modern direct-manipulation user interfaces, e.g. [FGKK88], because of the clear decomposition of structure and functionality. Several user interface programming environments (e.g., Smalltalk-80 and InterViews) that follow the "Seeheim User Interface Model" are in use and have demonstrated a gain in user interface quality, as well as in programmer's productivity.

Object-oriented modeling allows mapping user-interface elements like windows, icons, texts, etc., to objects and classes. Dynamic behavior is supported by message exchange between objects to activate methods, e.g., to open a window. The major advantage of an object-oriented approach to user interfaces is the clear decomposition of structure and functionality, which makes it easier for a developer to design, maintain, and reuse user-interface components. Since object-oriented systems support inheritance, new components can be specialized or extended from existing ones. Object-oriented user interfaces are therefore well suited for rapid prototyping.

Object-oriented user interface toolkits, in addition to providing a library of components that facilitate the construction of new interfaces, exhibit a similar framework that is imposed on any user interface built with them. Most toolkits follow the Seeheim model of user interface decomposition. However, there are problems when combining object-oriented modeling and the Seeheim model for user interfaces: As mentioned above, a user interface based on the Seeheim model is a triple consisting of presentation, dialog control, and application components.[2] To manage the complexity of large user interfaces, they are themselves constructed from smaller triples, each according to the model. Each of them has its own dialog control component that coordinates its presentation and application components. Any of these components of these triples may also be part of other triples.   For example, consider Figure 10.10; it shows

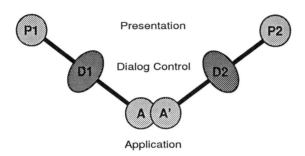

Figure 10.10   Connecting User Interface Subcomponents

triple ($P1$, $D1$, A) and triple ($P2$, $D2$, A'). Each of them implements a particular aspect of a larger interface, and they share their application component (A and A' are intended to denote the same set of application objects). Since the dialog component $D1$ controls A in the context of triple ($P1$, $D1$, A), any change that occurs within this triple is not reflected by the triple ($P2$, $D2$, A). In effect, $D2$ does not control A; instead it controls a different A, namely A'. To connect the two triples correctly, both dialog components need to communicate. This can only be done by passing messages (in effect, procedure calls) among them.

Although object-oriented user interfaces support message passing, a negative aspect remains: the components that are connected in such a way need to follow a precise protocol (sequence) of how the messages are sent and received, in order to maintain the appropriate context. The need for much detailed information depreciates the usability of components from a library, and has to be recognized as a hindrance to further improvement of productivity in creating user interfaces based on a purely object-oriented design.

10.6.1   Declarative User Interfaces

Other approaches to linking library components together (into triples, as mentioned previously) to form a user interface involve using declarative techniques.

---

[2]These components are called model, view, and controller in Smalltalk, and subject, interactor, and sensor/painter in InterViews.

The idea is to declare the connections between user interface components. The connections are formally declared or specified. With a formal specification it is possible to provide an automatic mechanism to maintain the connections. Examples of such systems are ThingLab [MBFB89], the FilterBrowser [EMB87], the RTL window manager for the X window system [CSI86], the Constraint Window System for Smalltalk-80 [EL88], and JADE [ZM90], which are all based on the use of constraints. A constraint — such as: $a = b + c$ — is distinguished from an imperative assignment statement in that it is a declarative specification of *what* is the case, without restricting *how* that state is reached. Whenever a, b, or c are changed the constraint is re-satisfied. There are several techniques for constraint satisfaction: local propagation (local information is used to maintain a constraint), transformations (constraint graphs are considered globally), and relaxation (iterative evaluation of sets of constraints).

Constraints are very useful in the context of user interfaces. They can be used to declaratively specify the relationships that exist within a triple: for the example in Figure 10.10, the triple $(P1, D1, A)$ can be phrased as $P1 == A$. The operation "$==$" denotes a constraint: it specifies that the presentation $P1$ reflects application A, and vice versa, in all cases. Now, if this triple is used in composition with $P2 == A$, it yields a combined user interface component $P1 == A == P2$ where the presentation $P1$ is constrained to reflect application A, which is constrained to reflect presentation $P2$, and vice versa. The composition yields a complete user interface component without a need for further communication. Any triples become connectable, without each knowing in advance in what context they are employed.

Constraints can be applied at all levels of user interface development. For example, consider two subwindows that are joined at one edge: if the user repositions one subwindow, we expect the adjacent subwindow to be repositioned, too (preserving the fact that they are joined). To achieve this behavior, the programmer explicitly has to consider the adjacent window when coding the "move" procedure. In contrast, if we state the fact that the two subwindows are joined as a constraint and provide a constraint-satisfaction mechanism, then the programmer does not have to consider the adjacent window, making the programming task much easier.

10.7   Summary of Chapter

This chapter explained how object-oriented concepts can be applied to user interface technology. Object-orientation improves user interfaces: (1) by allowing flexible construction and dynamic behavior in a uniform programming framework, (2) by producing reusable and extensible components, and (3) by achieving multiple levels of device and platform independence. The logical organization of the Smalltalk MVC paradigm and the C++ InterViews toolkit were described and illustrated with examples.

Chapter 11

Object-Oriented Databases

Object orientation can also be applied to database technology. An object-oriented database management system differs from an object-oriented programming language in that its focus is on efficient management of a large amount of data and on providing for data access and manipulation. The typical overall organization of an object-oriented database and its relationship to the application is explained in this chapter. The classes that are defined for such a database reflect the classes that exist in the application. Examples illustrate how to benefit from the persistent storage of objects offered by the database that also offers database-specific features such as handling of transactions, data access authorization, locking, and concurrency. The state of the art in commercially available object-oriented database systems is discussed.

11.1 Introduction

As we have discussed in the previous chapters of this book, object orientation views a system as a collection of objects, where each object models an entity or event in an application problem. Object-oriented programming environments allow the use of objects and classes of objects. Objects and classes allow the modeling of application concepts and their relationships in a natural way. They support not only structural definition, but also the modeling of natural behavior. Modern applications, such as office information systems, computer aided design and manufacturing systems, complex documentation systems, knowledge bases, and scientific applications, require an environment that supports the management of complex information.

As we have also pointed out repeatedly, the objects within such an environment, however, exist only for the duration of the program run. They must be created at the outset and saved (or destroyed) at the end. Conventional means of saving data are to write data onto files in a file system, or to store them in a database system. With conventional file and database systems, however, objects loose their nature as objects when being stored. They have to be recreated when loaded back into an object-oriented program. Recently, object-oriented methodology has been applied to database technology [CM84, BM91]. With the advent of object-oriented databases it is possible to extend the "life" of objects beyond the run-time of a program.

Conventional database systems are record based, where records are sequences of bytes. Over the years, the technology to logically organize and manipulate the records has changed from hierarchical and network type systems to the current era of relational database systems [Dat81]. In a relational database, data are organized into fields that together form records. Records are actually tuples containing fields. Similarly structured tuples (or records) are grouped into tables. Tables that contain records represent a "relation"; that is, the fashion in which the fields are arranged into tuples represents a certain relationship among them. For example, in a relational database, an employee may be represented as a tuple consisting of employee identifier, name, and address fields. All employees together are maintained in a table. The table represents the "Employee" relation. Access to data in a relational database is achieved through operations that build subtables, project columns, and merge and join different tables [Mai83].

Object-oriented database systems are based on the object-oriented model. The idea is to replace the concept of "relation" with the concept of "class." A class describes the structural properties of all records in a tuple. In addition, a class also describes the operations that specify its behavioral properties. In an object-oriented database an employee would be represented as an instance of an employee class. The employee class would define fields for name and address. There is no need to define an employee identifier, since an object always carries a unique object identifier. In the relational database the employee address would be represented by a string, since only simple types are allowed for attributes. In an object-oriented database there is no such limitation: fields in an object (member fields) can be instances of classes themselves. For example, the address field of an employee object could be an instance of the address class.

Applying object-oriented concepts to database technology has more advantages: On one hand, it promises an improvement in modeling capabilities since the modeling concepts of classes and class hierarchies bridge the semantic gap between problem domain and application; on the other hand, it also promises an improvement in processing speed since the application program model is much closer to the permanent storage model of data in the database, which requires much fewer conversions when objects are transferred to and from the application program and the database.

In the following sections, we will illustrate the overall capabilities, functionalities and organization of object-oriented databases. We will also show how they can be incorporated into object-oriented programs, either indirectly via an interface, or directly by making the database part of the programming environment. The chapter closes with a summary of the concepts and a discussion of the current state of the art in commercially available object-oriented database systems.

11.2 Organization

Not unexpectedly, an object-oriented database uses the object-oriented data model [Mai89, ABD+89] as its conceptual basis. Such a model provides support for complex objects, object identity, encapsulation of behavior, classes, and class hierarchies. In the following we will briefly reiterate the key aspects of the data model, and then discuss the various aspects of access and manipulation of objects in the database.

11.2.1 Data Model

The units or entities that are stored in the database are objects. In representing an entity with an object, its structure can be composed freely. An object can have fields that hold records, sets, arrays, or other objects. Every object has a unique identity. The identity of an object does not change. Two objects may contain the same data but are still distinct. The identity of an object is sufficient to identify an object within the database. The structure, or data content, of an object is only one aspect of its nature. An object also has operations, or behaviors. The code for operations, called methods, is packaged together with the data content of an object. The data content of an object is only accessible through the public features of an object.

Rather than describing each object, objects of similar data content and behavior are grouped together. This grouping is called a class. Objects are then instances of a class. The main advantage of the object-oriented data model is that it considers relationships among classes of objects: one class can be a special case of another class; one class can extend another class. Related classes form hierarchies of super- and subclasses. The subclasses inherit the data structure and behavior definitions from their superclasses. The class and class hierarchy doubles as the "schema" — the description of how the data is organized in the database. Moreover, encapsulation measures, i.e., the possibility to determine which features are public versus private for objects, give the database administrator the capability to regulate access to objects.

Another advantage of the object-oriented data model is that it allows multiple implementations of an operation (polymorphism). Each class of objects can implement its own idea of how to achieve an operation. The implementation of an operation is selected based on the class (type) of an object when the operation is invoked.

11.2.2 Access and Manipulation

Entities in a database are usually accessible in two ways: (1) the database provides a query language that allows the user to state query and manipulation requests; and (2) a call interface is usable from an application programming language.

Generally both types of access use the same underlying strategy in retrieving, traversing, and updating data from the database. The strategy depends on the specific database technology being used. For a relational database, the SQL query language [Dat81] allows the ad hoc formulation of retrieval and update requests. The call interface provided for traditional application programming languages usually follows the same idea, in that it allows the program to make selections and updates. An interesting aspect is that in order to traverse logically related data, for example to access the "teacher" data item for a "course" data item, it is necessary to employ the same retrieval mechanism through the query language or call interface of the database.

In contrast, in an object-oriented database there is no need for a complete and separate query and update language. The object-oriented programming language that serves to describe the behavioral aspects (the member functions) of database objects can double as query language.

Access

The first aspect of access and update of the database is access: to affect any change to any object, it needs to be retrieved first from the database into an application program. In an object-oriented database, access is achieved in two ways: (1) the database provides a set of global objects that are always accessible, and (2) the public features of these global objects provide access to objects that are referred to by the globals. Access is "navigational." The set of global objects, of course, is definable for application specific purposes.

For example, consider a potential database to store university scheduling information for the application discussed in Chapter 5. Figure 11.1 shows a snapshot of the database containing student, professor, schedule, course, and

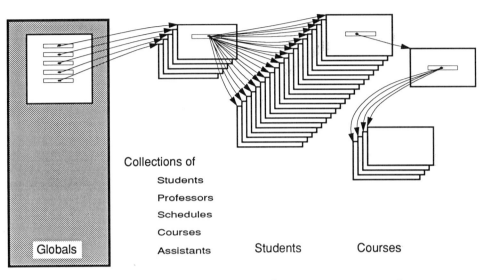

Figure 11.1   Database Objects for University Example

assistant objects. In addition, one of the global objects defined for this application might be a "university" object. Its class specifies public fields to hold and make accessible the collection objects that hold all professors, schedule, student, teaching assistant, and course objects in the university.   Table 11.1 shows the class interface for class "University." To reach an individual course that a specific student is taking, the following steps can be taken:

1. Access the public field "studentBody" of the university object to to reach the collection of all students.

Table 11.1   University Class Interface

```
class University {
 public:
   Collection *allProfessors;
   Collection *allCourses;
   Collection *allAssistants;
   Collection *allSchedules;
   Collection *studentBody;
};
```

2. Use the student identification to select the correct student from the collection.

3. Access the "taking" field of the student to reach the collection of courses the student takes.

4. Finally, select a course from that collection.

The result of this traversal is a specific course object. The logical relationships among objects is used to navigate the database. As member fields of objects are accessed it is the database's task to fetch the necessary objects from secondary storage. The physical access to the database is hidden. Traversal of logically connected objects is done as if all objects were within reach and scope of the application program and session that issued the access requests.

Update

Manipulation and update capabilities are also provided by the public functions available for objects as defined by their classes. To remove a student from a specific course in the above example, first access the correct collection, then send a "remove" message to the collection that contains the courses that a student is taking and indicate in the parameter which course to delete. The "taking" collection for the specific student is changed within the scope of the application program, but that change actually affects the persistent objects in the database. The database reflects the new state of the objects. The collection no longer contains the course object. The life of objects extends beyond the single run of the application.

11.2.3 Database Features

Object-oriented databases, like their conventional counterparts, also offer conventional database features. For example, we expect that they support the transaction concept, authorized multiple and simultaneous access to the stored data, and even the distribution of physical storage across multiple storage devices and media.

The transaction concept allows an application session to proceed with making data changes, i.e., altering objects that it had reached, but without immediately affecting the data stored in the database. A database transaction can be viewed as a sequence of alteration to objects. All changes to data base objects are made permanent; i.e., the changes are reflected by the new state of the database, or none of the changes are made. In the first case, a transaction completes successfully by "committing" all its changes done to objects to the database. In the second case, the transaction "aborts" and none of the changes take effect. The database is still in the same state as if the transaction was never started.

Multiple and shared access to database objects is also provided by object-oriented databases. Locking schemes are typically employed to resolve conflicts among application sessions that access common data. The protection mechanism is based on the object, which is the natural access unit. In addition, the physical database might be distributed among multiple devices, media, and locations. The database system presents a view to an application as if the database were a uniform collection of objects. The database system coordinates access and updates to the physical objects throughout the network of distributed storage media.

In the following sections, we will present two typical examples of how programs access an object-oriented database. In one example, the data base is loosely coupled with the application program. In the second example, the database is logically incorporated into the application program.

11.3 Accessing a Separate Database

Object-oriented database technology is still emerging. Early systems implement a model in which the database system incorporates the data storage and also all data access and manipulation aspects. An example of such an object-oriented database system is GemStone [MSOP86].[1] GemStone is a database system that implements an object-oriented data model similar to Smalltalk. Even the syntax used to describe classes, their instance, and class variables and methods resembles Smalltalk. The execution model also reflects the Smalltalk ideology; for example, messages are always dynamically bound to methods at run-time. Table 11.2 shows an example of a short GemStone class description.[2] It defines a simplified version of the student class, with one instance variable "taking." The variable is made public by providing an instance method with the same name that returns the variable.

While GemStone can be used as a complete programming environment, it is rarely used that way. Applications are typically written in an object-oriented programming language, and therefore it is necessary to access, retrieve, and manipulate objects in the GemStone database separately.

GemStone is available with an interface to Smalltalk.[3] The database pro-

---

[1]GemStone is a trademark of Servio Logic, Inc.

[2]Note that the variables are specified by their names only — their types are unspecified. GemStone does allow the use of constraints to place restrictions on what an instance variable can contain.

[3]The GemStone database system can be accessed in three different ways: (1) using a text-based interactive interface that allows the creation, retrieval, and update of objects and

---

Table 11.2   GemStone Class Description

```
Person subclass: 'Student'
  instVarNames: #('taking')
  classVars: #('')
  poolDictionaries: #[]
  inDictionary: UserGlobals
  constraints: #[]
  isInvariant: false

taking
  ^ taking
```

---

vides facilities to login and establish a session. A GemStone database session provides a global object "UserGlobals" that allows keyed access to session-specific objects. The "UserGlobals" object is an instance of class "Dictionary." A dictionary contains (key, value) pairs. It provides a keyed entry point to persistent objects in the database as described in the previous section.

11.3.1 Import and Export

In addition to all methods that are accessible for individual database objects, each object in a GemStone database understands the message "asSmalltalkObject," which imports the object from the database into the Smalltalk object space. The object that is an instance of a GemStone class is converted into an instance of a Smalltalk class. The Smalltalk class needs to be similar to the GemStone class. It is therefore necessary to duplicate the class description of those classes that can have instances which need to be imported into Smalltalk.

GemStone also allows objects that exist with the Smalltalk object space to be exported into the database. Smalltalk is extended to allow the message "asGemStoneObject" to be sent to any Smalltalk object: the receiver of the message is replicated as an instance of a corresponding GemStone class in the database. Of course, the conversion of objects to and from the database can be controlled. GemStone maintains tables to track how classes within Smalltalk and GemStone correspond to each other.

Table 11.3 contains a small fragment of Smalltalk code that illustrates access to the GemStone database. The code implements the simple query to

---

their classes; (2) using an extension to Smalltalk that incorporates the GemStone classes and objects into the normal Smalltalk run-time environment; and (3) using the C call interface, which allows access from the C programming language.

Table 11.3   Smalltalk – GemStone Query

```
| u s |

    GemStone login.
    u := GemStone execute: [
            (UserGlobals at: #university)
                asSmalltalkObject
        ].

    s := u students select: "John Doe".
    s taking remove: "COP 3223".
    u asGemStoneObject.

    GemStone commit.
    GemStone logout.
```

remove a student from a particular course in the university example. The GemStone session is started with a "login" message, which will prompt the user for his access privileges. After the login, the next statement instructs GemStone to execute a statement. The statement selects the university object from the global objects of the session. The university object is imported as "u" into the Smalltalk world. The object "u" now belongs to a Smalltalk class and responds to the message "students" with the collection of all students. The collection then receives the message "select," which returns the student object "s" with name "John Doe." In the following statement, object "s" receives a "taking" messages to gain access to the collection of all courses a student takes. The collection is then asked to remove the course with number "COP 3223". The "remove" message affects the receiving collection. The effect of the change is made permanent by exporting the objects back into the database and committing the transaction. Of course, for the example to work properly, corresponding classes (similar to the C++ class described in Chapter 5 for the university course scheduling application) need to exist in GemStone and Smalltalk.

11.4   Incorporating Database and Language

A newer generation of object-oriented database systems tightly incorporates the database into a programming language. The goal is to make the use of database objects transparent to the programmer. Instead of paying special attention to database objects, they are treated exactly the same way as "local" objects within the application program. The database objects just happen to persist beyond the termination of the specific application program where they were last used.

There are several commercial database products on the market that provide object-oriented functionality and facilities for the C++ programming language. Instead of using a specific product in an example, we keep the syntax general and concentrate on the concepts common to this new era of databases.

The first place to look for database objects is when instances of classes, i.e., objects, are created in a C++ program. In C++, objects are typically created with the "new" operator. For example,

```
Course *c = new Course;
```

creates a new instance "c" of class "Course." In the presence of a database, we want to be able to create database objects in a similar way. One way to achieve this is to use a special new keyword operator. For example,

```
Course *db_c = persistent Course;
```

uses the keyword "persistent" to denote the creation of a database object. The object "db_c" is created as an instance of class "Course"; any applicable constructor is invoked to initialize it. Moreover, the object "db_c" is accessible within the C++ program in the same fashion as object "c". Object "db_c" may receive any message that is defined by the "Course" class, and it may be changed. However, if it is changed, these changes are then reflected by the database.

The database also needs to allow access and retrieval of objects that already exist in the database and to assign them to local variables in a C++ program. A possible syntax allows the class constructor to be invoked with a selection criterion. For example,

```
Course *old_db_c = persistent Course("name == 'COP 3223'");
```

would retrieve a course object from the database. The database selects the course object that stores the value "COP 3223" in its name field. The course object is then accessible as "old_db_c", which can receive the public messages defined by the "Course" class.

Other database objects can be accessed from known objects. For example, since we already have an existing course object, it is also possible to retrieve objects that can be reached from the course object. In our university course scheduling example, a course has no public member fields. Its private member fields, however, can be reached via public member functions defined for the "Course" class. As an example of how to reach other objects through objects that are already imported into the world of the application, consider the "university" object (as discussed in the previous two sections): it can serve as an

---

Table 11.4 C++ Database Access

```
Database db("university");

db.login();

Student *s = persistent Student("name == 'John Doe'");
Course *c = s->taking->select("COP 3223");
s->taking->remove(c);

db.commit();
db.logout();
```

---

entry point into the database. It has fields that hold the collection of students: through the public features of a collection, "select" for example, it is possible to retrieve a single student object. The retrieval is hidden from the programmer, and if changes are made to the state of an object, the database system will ensure that the changes are automatically reflected in the database (of course, subject to a successful commit of the transaction).

Table 11.4 shows a small fragment of C++ code accessing an imaginary object-oriented database. In the code, after a successful login to the university database, a specific student is retrieved from the database. The student object is stored as object "s" and is used to retrieve the collection of courses the student is taking. The message "select" retrieves the course object "c", which is then removed from the student's "taking" collection. The "db.commit( )" call commits the changes made in this small transaction to the database, and the session is terminated with a "db.logout( )." As in the Smalltalk example, we also assume that the necessary classes are defined in C++ and in the object-oriented database.

11.5 Summary of Chapter

An object-oriented data base management system can be defined as a database system that directly supports a model based on the object-oriented paradigm. In this chapter we illustrated the concepts on which object-oriented databases rely. They extend the life of objects that occur in applications beyond a single run of a program. We discussed the general organization of such databases, and explained their functionalities to access, retrieve, and update objects. An example of a detached database and an example of a coupled database illustrated the use of an object-oriented database with an object-oriented program.

The field of object-oriented database systems is still subject to intense research [KL89, BM91]. Quite a few commercial systems are emerging [ABD+89]. Examples of commercial object-oriented database managenent systems are Avance [BH89], Encore [Zdo90], Gbase [LeN88], GemStone [BMO+89], Iris [WLH90], O2 [ea90a], Orion [ea90b], and Vbase [AH87] . Some of these systems have already shown that a significant gain in performance can be expected from applying object orientation to database technology. Applications that use the new database system have been shown to be at least one order of magnitude faster than a comparable relational database application.

Chapter 12

Object-Oriented Design

The application of object-oriented technology to programming calls for new techniques in software design. This chapter discusses object-oriented design. Object-oriented design techniques deal with how to best identify entities in the problem domain that can be mapped into objects and classes of objects. An important issue is how to identify objects and classes in an application problem, and how to make use of existing classes to gain the highest productivity.

12.1 Introduction

Object-oriented programming is the theme of this book. Throughout the book we concentrated on various aspects of the programming task in an object-oriented environment. Programming is, however, only one subtask within the overall task of producing software. The discipline of software engineering is dedicated to the process of producing software systems as a whole. These software systems can be simple, but most are complex. Most of the examples shown in this book are examples of simple software systems. For these simple systems, the programming task is the major portion of completing the software system.

Few applications, however, are simple and small. Software has the tendency to become very complex very rapidly. We argued throughout the book that object orientation is a tool to grasp and manage this complexity better. The obvious step after applying object orientation to programming is to seek out other tasks within the software engineering process as candidates for object orientation. Figure 12.1 shows the major phases of a traditional model of the software engineering life cycle. It shows the three major phases in software development: analysis, design, and implementation. We can view these three phases in light of our earlier argument that software uses computer concepts

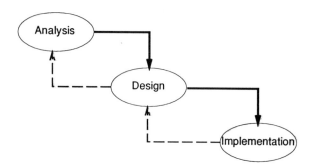

Figure 12.1   The Software Life Cycle

to model problem domain concepts: software engineering is the task of bridging the semantic gap between these concepts. Figure 12.2 shows the software life cycle and its relationship to the semantic gap between computer and application concepts. The "Analysis" phase of the life cycle analyzes the problem domain to yield an understanding of the problem that is to be modeled in software, and it lays the foundation for the software design phase. The design phase bridges the gap; it establishes a relationship between the problem and and the software solution.

In this chapter we will illustrate an object-oriented approach to software design. While object orientation will ease the task of software design, we should not forget that it — like any design activity — is an intellectual activity: it is more *art* than *science*. We will describe the underlying methodology and outline a method that can help the design task.

Object-oriented design differs from traditional design methods. Two categories of traditional design methods are "top-down structured design" and "data-driven design" [Som89]. Top-down structured design [YC79] looks at the problem as a single function that is decomposed into subfunctions successively in a structured manner to yield small enough function components that can be implemented as a module or software unit. Data-driven design [Jac83, Orr71] focuses on the input and output data of a problem, and derives the program design as a mapping from input to output data.

Both design methods are completely inadequate to yield a design that is to be implemented in an object-oriented programming language. Top-down structured design concentrates on the functionality of its units and neglects the data structure aspects. In effect, structured design tends to yield much data structure that is global [Mey87]. Data-driven design, on the other hand, focuses on data structure units and tends to globalize functions. Both ap-

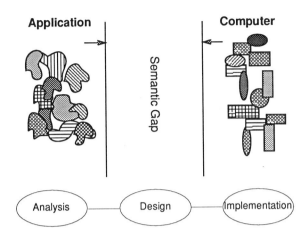

Figure 12.2   The Semantic Gap

proaches run counter to the object-oriented philosophy of associating data
and its functions into a single unit: the object.

Methods for object-oriented design are emerging [WPM90, Gro89, SS88].
These emerging methods have in common the basic assumption that a system
is a collection of objects that communicate with each other to achieve the overall goal of the system. The objects are instances of classes, and classes belong
to class hierarchies. This underlying basic assumption builds the foundation
of an object-oriented design methodology.

Object-oriented design is a method of decomposition. The design process
is a process of "divide and conquer." Where in traditional design methods
the overall problem is divided into functional subunits, or data subunits, in
object-oriented design the overall problem is decomposed into subunits that
have functional and data aspects. The subunits can be two things: primarily,
they are classes; secondarily, they are objects. The goal of object-oriented
design is to decompose a problem first into classes and then into objects.

As with any design technique, tools to support the method are very important. For object-oriented design these tools exist in the form of diagrams
for classes and objects, and a set of steps that guide a designer in the design
process.

In this chapter we will first discuss object and class diagrams that play an
important role in the conceptual realization of an application problem and that
help to translate it into a software solution. Then, we will discuss a sequence
of steps that form the heart of many object-oriented design techniques. The

chapter closes with a summary and remarks about the benefits that can be gained from using object-oriented design.

12.2 Design Tools

Diagrams are used in many design tasks. In object-oriented design, since it deals with objects and classes, we expect to find object and class diagrams. Throughout this book we accompanied most of our examples with diagrams to visualize the involved objects and classes for illustration purposes: diagrams (i.e., pictures) are able to convey more information quicker than many sentences.

The diagrams employed during the design task resemble the object and class diagrams from earlier chapters of this book. Due to the nature of the design process (i.e., information about the objects and classes is accumulated while designing), the diagrams tend to be less precise, i.e., show less information, at the beginning of the design phase and gradually become more and more detailed as the design progresses. Information about classes and objects

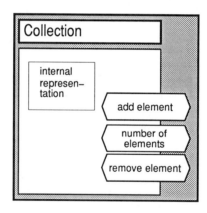

Figure 12.3   Collection Design Class Diagram

need not be depicted in much detail in the early stages of design. The diagrams reflect important properties of objects and classes. For example, there is no need in the early stage of design to determine whether the property "number of elements" for a "Collection" class is an attribute or a function. It is more important to convey the nature of the feature and the fact that it is publicly visible. Figure 12.3 shows a design class diagram for a "Collection" class. In addition, the diagrams have less focus on individual objects and classes, but show groups of objects and classes to visualize their relationships, interactions, and interdependencies.

12.2.1   Design Class Diagrams

Design class diagrams play an important role in identifying classes that are part of a software solution to an application problem. The class diagram shows the existence of a class, its major properties, and the relationship of the class to other classes. Figure 12.3 is an example of a design class diagram for class "Collection." During the design process it is important to consider classes in the context of other classes. Classes have relationships that can be depicted. Classes and their relationships form a semantic network that can also be depicted. The two relationships among classes in object-oriented

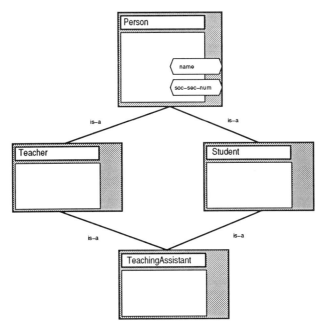

Figure 12.4   Design Class Hierarchy Diagram

design are "is-a" and "part-of." The "is-a" relationship models the subclass-to-superclass relationship: a subclass "is-a" superclass, or, instances of a subclass "are" also instances of the superclass. Figure 12.4 shows design class diagrams with "is-a" relationships. The classes shown are part of a design for the university course scheduling example (see Chapter 5). Class "Employee" "is-a" "Person," "Student" "is-a" "Person," etc. Instances of "Student" are also instances of "Person." The purpose of the diagram as a whole is to depict class relationships. These relationships are being developed during design and will yield class hierarchies in the object-oriented implementation.

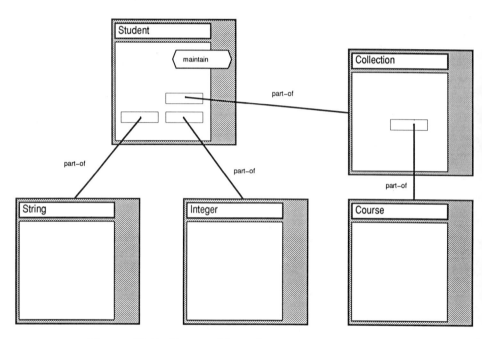

Figure 12.5   Design Class Components Diagram

The "part-of" relationship models part-whole or client-server relationships. Figure 12.5 shows design class diagrams with "part-of" relationships. The "Collection" class is a part of the "Student" class; it serves to capture the collection of courses that a student takes. Likewise, the "String" class captures a student's name, and the "Integer" class is used to represent a student's social security number. The "part-of" relationship yields attributes for classes that can refer to the component classes. Another way to phrase the relationship is as a "client-server" relationship. For example, the "Collection" class serves the "Student" class: the "Student" class is one of its clients.

12.2.2   Design Object Diagrams

Design object diagrams are also important to identify the existence of objects

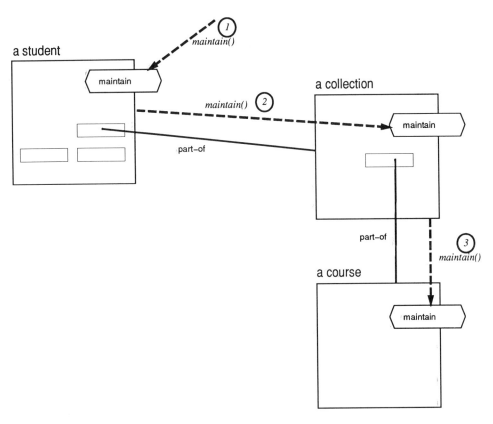

Figure 12.6   Design Object Diagrams

and their relationships. While the structure of objects is better depicted with class diagrams of their respective classes, object diagrams can show a snapshot of objects as they might occur in the problem domain. Design object diagrams can therefore depict behavioral relationships among objects. They can show the timing and sequence of messages that are sent between objects. For example, consider the student-to-course relationship in our sample application. Figure 12.6 shows a student object that receives a "maintain( )" message. The figure shows how the message results in further messages being sent to other objects. For practical purposes, it helps to number the messages to reflect the sequence in which the messages occur. The figure shows how a student is maintained:

1. A student object receives a "maintain( )" message. Maintaining a student is done by maintaining the collection of courses that the student is taking.

2. A collection receives a "maintain( )" message. The course object selects from among its elements which course is to be maintained.

3. A course object finally receives a "maintain( )" message.

Together, the three steps illustrate how a student-to-course relationship is achieved in our sample application. The information gathered with this design object diagram will be reflected in the respective methods that are to be defined for the student, collection, and course classes.

Object and class diagrams are at the heart of any object-oriented design method. One such method is discussed in the next section.

12.3   A Design Method

As we wrote earlier in this chapter, design is an intellectual activity: it is more an art than a science. Therefore, one cannot expect to look up a prescribed method to tackle any application problem to yield a satisfactory design for a software system. Instead, what can be done is to provide guidelines to help a designer through the process of design. In this section we will describe one such method, which was first presented by Grady Booch [Boo90], extended with the notion of responsibility-driven class design [WBWW90].

Before we describe the method, which consists of four steps, we need to realize that software design is an incremental and iterative process. Several passes through the steps might be necessary to arrive at a satisfactory design. Each pass through the steps will add new information and understanding of the problem. While the ultimate goal is to produce a system that consists of a collection of objects, the focal point of the design task is to determine and specify those classes that govern the structure and functionality of these objectives.

Step 1: Find Key Abstractions

The first step in object-oriented design is to identify the key abstractions that occur in the problem domain. An examination of the application problem yields the key concepts that need to be represented in the software solution.

In our course scheduling example, candidates for such key abstractions are the concepts of "Course," "Teacher," "Student," and "Schedule." These concepts represent the abstract components of the overall application. They are abstract since we consider only essential and high-level concepts, rather than petty details.

The result of the first design step is a list of class candidates. The class candidates may already be depicted as design class diagrams. At this point, the information about the class candidates consists of their names, perhaps some written comments or annotations on their class diagrams, and the problem understanding of the designer.

Step 2: Establish Class Responsibilities

The second step in object-oriented design is to establish the features and properties of the classes identified in the first step. The features and properties of a class are its responsibility. For example, consider a "Teacher" class. Its properties are which courses a teacher can teach and which courses a teacher teaches in a particular semester. A teacher also has a name, social security number, etc. The features that are identified for the teacher concept become the responsibilities of the "Teacher" class: the class has to define these features so that its instances exhibit the correct behavior and state when they collaborate with other objects. A good exercise in this context is to "walk" through the life of a specific instance of a class in question. For example, a teacher instance of the teacher class needs to be able to report its name and social security number, as well as add and remove courses from the list of course preferences and courses taught. The needed functionality is reflected by responsibilities defined for the class.

The product of the second design step is a more detailed list of class candidates. The class candidates evolve into classes that are annotated with their necessary properties. The classes can be depicted in the design class candidates. Specific objects may be depicted with the design object diagrams showing how their properties appear.

Step 3: Relate Classes

The third step in object-oriented design is to recognize relationships that exist between the concepts within the application problem. The goal is to recognize patterns that may give rise to generalization, specialization, or inheritance. These relationships exist at the class level and at the object level. At the class level, these relationships are the "is-a" and "part-of" relationships described earlier. It is most likely at this stage in the design that the first iterative cycle of these design steps occurs. In recognizing "is-a" relationships, one comes across the need to recognize new classes. For example, in one case we might have recognized a "Teacher" and a "Student" class in the first step and added their properties of having a name and social security number in the second step. Now in the third step, we recognize a commonality among the two classes. This gives rise to a new class "Person" with "is-a" relationships to "Teacher" and "Student." For class "Person" we repeat steps one and two of the design method.

The "part-of" relationship may also lead to more classes. The name of a person, for example, can be represented by a string. "String" is another candidate for a class for which steps one and two are repeated. It is also significant to recognize classes that have a "server" role within class relationships. These classes need special attention since they are prime candidates for reuse in different parts of an application. For example, consider the "Teacher" class: two of its parts are lists of courses. We can recognize a server class to model "lists of things" and name it "Collection." The "Collection" class is a server class that can be used and reused throughout the application at hand and many others. It deserves special care to make it as useful and general as possible.

Relationships among objects are also an important element of what is discovered or designed in this step. The pattern of messages that can be sent and received among objects plays a significant role in what responsibilities are assigned to the classes. Object relationships will have a definite impact on the features defined for the individual class. Therefore, it is most likely that more iterations to step two will occur. At this stage it is also helpful to consider groups of objects of different classes and to trace their collaboration. In our example, we can consider a student, a course, and a teacher object, and trace the behavior of each object as a student is added to a course. How a student is added will affect the properties needed for the "Student," "Course," and maybe even the "Teacher" class.

The product of the third design step is a description of class and object relationships. Very suitable tools for this description are the design class and object diagrams. The increase of problem understanding at this stage of the design will also change and amend the products of the previous two steps.

Step 4: Specify Classes

The fourth step in object-oriented design is to provide a detailed class specification that is the basis of an object-oriented implementation. The information gathered in the first three steps culminates in this last step. Do not expect to be done when this step is reached. Instead, as part of the class specification, expect to identify more classes that will yield yet more iterations of the four design steps. The classes recognized may be component classes, or they may represent lower-level details. The design is complete when all classes are completely specified down to components that are predefined or available from libraries.

The product of the fourth step is the class specification for all classes in the design. Of course, the products of the previous steps are also part of the complete design product. The design class and object diagrams are also an important component of the class documentation used in programming, testing, and maintenance.

Overall, the four steps of this object-oriented design method, while demonstrated here only for a small example, are useful and capable of addressing large problems. A large application problem is usually tackled by groups of software designers. The nature of the decomposition of the problem into classes and subclasses allows the identification of self-contained, i.e., encapsulated, subproblems. These individual subproblems can be assigned to smaller groups of designers. The interactions among the subgroups follow the needed interactions among the addressed subproblems. Object-oriented design is well suited to solve large and complex application problems.

12.4 Summary of Chapter

In this chapter we illustrated the application of object orientation to the process of designing software. It is recognized that object-oriented programming is an improvement over traditional programming techniques. This is even more true for the design task within the whole software engineering process. Object orientation bridges the semantic gap that exists between application and computer concepts: it is the design process that achieves the bridge. The design process is now part of an overall object-oriented view of the complete software life cycle: object-oriented analysis that examines and recognizes problem concepts, object-oriented programming that provides computer concepts, and object-oriented design that marries the concepts of both. The software solution will closely resemble the original problem, which eases not only the understanding of the system but also its testability, maintainability, and usability.

Conclusion

Programming languages have come a long way since their invention. A major breakthrough was achieved in the 1970s with the introduction of control and data structures as supported concepts in programming languages. In the same way, we feel that object-oriented programming was, is, or soon will become, the major innovation to programming languages in the 1980s and 1990s.

In this book we introduced the basic concepts of object-oriented programming. Everything centers around the "object," which combines data and control structure in one identifiable unit. An object hides its local state and methods, supporting the software design principle of information hiding. Similar objects are grouped into classes that are used to hold the description of its instances. Classes can be related through inheritance, which allows the definition of new classes, just by slight specialization of existing ones. Inheritance fosters a new philosophy for programming, in that new programs need not be defined from scratch, but instead can start at a "default beginning."

The first part of this book was dedicated to the foundation and basic concepts of object-oriented programming. The second part illustrated how this foundation is used to improve common abstractions and algorithms, and how to apply these concepts to a complete programming environment with object-oriented user interfaces and data bases. The last chapter of the second part was devoted to object-oriented design, which closes the semantic gap that forever is the target of all programming endeavors.

As with any innovation it takes some time for object orientation to be accepted by the large population of its users. The number of object-oriented programming languages and the large number of companies that produce commercial-grade compilers for them are a strong sign that slowly, industry is beginning to use the languages that support object-oriented programming. Soon, the industry will go through a revolution, as software managers will recognize the giant potential that object-oriented programming offers to all facets of software development.

Appendix A

Summary of Terms

The following alphabetical list is a glossary of object-oriented terms. It reiterates most of the terms that were defined throughout this book and may serve as a reference.

Abstract class:

A class that is not intended to have instances. It serves as a superclass to other classes.

Abstract data type:

An abstraction that provides data as well as functional aspects. A class is an implementation of an abstract data type.

Base class:

A class that serves as the basis for inheritance. A base class is the superclass for all its derived classes.

Binding:

The match between a message received by an object and one of its methods. Can be done static, that is, at compile-time, or dynamic, that is, at run-time.

Class:

A class describes a group of similar objects. Elements of such a group are called instances. The class describes variables / member fields and methods / member functions that are common to all instances of the class.

Class method:

A global method defined for a class. It may operate only on class variables of the class. Also known as static member function or factory method.

Class variable:

A class variable is a variable defined for a class whose value is shared by all instances of the class. Also known as static member field.

Constructor:

Special member function of a class. It is executed whenever an instance of the class is created. Used to initialize member fields.

Current:

Predefined member field that refers to the object itself. Also known as self or this.

Derived class:

A class that inherits features from a base class. It is a subclass of the base class.

Factory method:

A global method defined for a class. It may operate only on class variables of the class. Also known as static member function or class method.

Feature:

Collective term for variable / field or method / function of a class. A feature of a class can be an instance variable or a method.

Friend:

A class can have friends. Friends can be other classes or functions. Friend classes or functions have access to all fields and functions of a class regardless of the specified access rights.

Inheritance:

When a class is a subclass of another class, it inherits variables and methods from its superclasses.

Instance:

An object that belongs to a class is an instance of that class. All objects are instances of some classes. The structure and methods of an instance are described by its class.

Instance variable:

Instance variables are variables that can have a specific value for each object in a class. The values for instance variables are local to an object. Also known as member field.

Instance method:

The function that implements the response to a message that is received by an object. Also known as member function.

Instantiate:

To make an object that is an instance of a class.

Member:

A synonym for instance; there are also member variables and member methods. In C++ member methods are called member functions.

Member field:

Variable that can have a specific value for each object in a class. The values for member fields are local to an object. Also known as instance variable.

Member function:

The function that implements the response to a message that is received by an object. Also known as instance method.

Message:

A request to perform a method for an object. A message results in the invocation of the method. The message contains a selector that identifies the method and any parameters from the method.

Method:

The function that implements the response to a message that is received by an object.

Multiple inheritance:

The fact that a class inherits features from more than one superclass.

Object:

The main element of object-oriented programming. Objects combine data and control structure.

Polymorphism:

The capability of program entities to belong to more than one type.

Protocol:

A standardized set of messages. Two classes whose instances respond to the same set of messages are said to follow the same protocol.

Receiver:

The object that is sent a message is its receiver.

Self:

Predefined member field that refers to the object itself. Also known as this or current.

Static member:

Collective term to refer to static member field and static member function.

Static member field:

A field that is defined for a class whose value is shared by all instances of the class. Also known as class variable.

Static member function:

A global function defined for a class. It may operate only on static member fields of the class. Also known as class method or factory method.

Subclass:

A class that inherits variables and methods from a superclass.

Superclass:

A class that has subclasses, that is, it has subordinates in a class hierarchy.

This:

Predefined member field that refers to the object itself. Also known as self or current.

Virtual function:

A member function that is bound at run-time rather than at compile-time.

Virtual base class:

A superclass that is not replicated for its subclasses. Avoids repeated inheritance.

Appendix B

Listing: The Hello World Example

We started the first chapter of this book with the description of a hello world object. The following is an example of how the hello world example can be stored in a file and compiled with C++. Assume that we edited the following code and saved it in the file "`hello.cc`". Different C++ compilers use different naming conventions for the source filename extension. Most C++ compilers allow the extension "`.cc`". Other extensions being used by other compilers are "`.c`", "`.cpp`", "`.CC`" or "`.cxx`".

file: hello.cc

```
#include <stdio.h>
class HelloWorld{    // comments start like this
public:
                     // constructor
    HelloWorld(){
        message = "hello world";
    }
    char *message;    // member field

    announce(){       // member functions
        printf("%s \n", message);
    }
    change(char *newmessage){
        message = newmessage;
    }
};

main(){
    HelloWorld hw1, hw2;     // two variables: hw1 and hw2
                             // of class HelloWorld
    hw1.announce();
    hw2.announce();
    hw1.change("this is hw1");
    hw2.change("different object");
    hw1.announce();
    hw2.announce();
}
```

Most C++ compilers, like C compilers, are organized into several phases. The first phase is a preprocessor that handles and eliminates commands to include files, define constants and macros. The second phase, usually called "cfront," translates C++ into C. The following phases — compilation, assembly, and linkage — are usually handled by a C compiler.

The command to invoke the C++ compiler depends on which C++ compiler is available on a particular system. There are many versions available, the command to invoke it may be CC, g++, c++, ccxx, tcc or occ. Assuming the first version, the compilation command is

```
CC hello.cc -o hello
```

The C++ compiler allows that the executable be named with the -o option. The compilation will be successful. It is then possible to invoke the program as

```
hello
```

which will print:

```
hello world
hello world
this is hw1
different object
```

Appendix C

Listing: A String Class

Throughout the book we used a "String" class that captured variable length strings. In this appendix we list a complete implementation as far as necessary for the examples in the book. The class implements two constructors, one to initialize a string of fixed length, and one to initialize a string from a "char *" character string. The class also implements member functions for string equality ("=="), concatenation ("+"), and string containment. The code also shows how to overload the two friend operators << and >> to allow C++ stream input and output for instances of the "String" class. For other, and more complete, implementations of this class consult the "String" class from the GNU C++ library or the "String" class described in the "C++ Primer" by Stan Lippman [Lip89].

String.h

```
#ifndef _String_h
#define _String_h

#include <iostream.h>      // stream i/o package
#include <string.h>        // C string handling
#include <bool.h>          // true and false

class String {
    char *str ;
  public:                  // constructors
    String(int l = 0){
      str = new char[l];
    }
    String (const char *s){
      int len = strlen(s);
      str = new char[len + 1];
      strcpy(str,s);
    }
                        // member functions
    bool operator==(const String &s){
      return (bool) !(strcmp(str,s.str));
    }
    String operator+(String &s){
      char *tmp =
        new char [strlen(str) + strlen(s.str) + 1];
      strcpy(tmp,str);
      strcat(tmp,s.str);
      return *new String(tmp);
    }
    bool contains(const String &s){
      if (strstr(str,s.str))
        return TRUE;
      else
        return FALSE;
    }
                        // friends of the class
    friend istream& operator>>(istream&, String&);
    friend ostream& operator<<(ostream&, String&);
} ;
#endif
```

String.cc

```
#include "String.h"

             // overloading insertion
             //  and extraction operations

ostream& operator<<(ostream& o, String& s) {
  o << s.str;
  return o;
}

istream& operator>>(istream& i, String& s) {
  i >> s.str;
  return i;
}
```

Appendix D

Listing: The Course Scheduling Example

In this appendix we illustrate how an application can be modularized. As an example we use a subset of the course scheduling application presented in Chapter 5. The class is the main structuring criteria in an object-oriented program. Since C++ is text-based, its modules, i.e., the classes, are stored in separate files. Class declarations are usually split up into two files: a header file with extension ".h" that contains the class declaration with the member fields and the member function headers, and a body file with extension ".cc" that contains the bodies of the member functions.

The header files contain preprocessor directives to avoid duplicate declarations of classes. It is common programming practice to start a header file with

```
#ifndef somename
```

If the constant `somename` is already defined, then the preprocessor will skip the header file. If not, then the second line

```
#define somename
```

defines the constant `somename` to ensure that the header file will not be processed again. The header file has to close the "if"-block with the statement:

```
#endif
```

The following pages list the header and body files for the Person, Teacher, Student, Course, and Schedule classes. Also listed are two possible main programs that use these classes.

Person.h

```
#ifndef Person_h
#define Person_h

// Class definition for Person

class Person {
  char* name;
public:
  Person();
  Person(char *n);
  virtual print();
};

#endif
```

Person.cc

```
// Body for class Person

#include <iostream.h>
#include "Person.h"

// constructor functions

 Person::Person(){
   name = "";
 }

 Person::Person(char *n){
   name = n;
 };

// member functions

 Person::print(){
   cout << "I am: " <<  name << endl;
 };
```

Teacher.h

```
#ifndef Teacher_h
#define Teacher_h

// Class definition for Teacher

#include "Person.h"

class Teacher: public Person {
  int courses;
  static int MaxCourses;
public:
  Teacher():courses(0){}
  print();
  bool assign();
};

#endif
```

Teacher.cc

```
// Body for class Teacher

#include <iostream.h>
#include "Teacher.h"

// initializing static member field

 int Teacher::MaxCourses = 2;

 Teacher::print() {
   cout << "am i a teacher\n";
 }
 bool Teacher::assign(){
    if (courses < MaxCourses) {
      courses++;
      return TRUE;
    } else
      return FALSE;
  }
```

Student.h

```
#ifndef Student_h
#define Student_h

// Student class declaration

#include "Person.h"

class Student: public Person{
 public:
   print();
};

#endif
```

Student.cc

```
// Body for class Student

#include <iostream.h>
#include "Student.h"

// constructor functions

 Student::print() {
   cout << "Student: ";
   Person::print();
 }
```

Course.h

```
#ifndef Course_h
#define Course_h

// Class definition for course

#include "Teacher.h"
#include "Student.h"

class Course {
  char *number;
  char* time;
  Student students[25];
public:
  Course();
  Course(char* n, char* t);
  Teacher teacher;
  assignTeacher(Teacher& t);
};

#endif
```

Course.cc

```
// Body for class Course
#include "Course.h"

// constructor functions
 Course::Course(){
   number = "";
   time = "";
 };
 Course::Course(char* n, char* t){
   number = n;
   time = t;
 };

// member functions
 Course::assignTeacher(Teacher& t){
   teacher = t;
 };
```

Schedule.h

```
#ifndef Schedule_h
#define Schedule_h

// Class definition for Schedule

#include "Course.h"

class Schedule {
  Course offerings[10];
  int offered;
public:
  Schedule():offered(0){}
  assign(Course&,Teacher&);
};

#endif
```

Schedule.cc

```
// Body for class Schedule

#include <iostream.h>
#include "Schedule.h"

// member functions

Schedule::assign(Course& c, Teacher& t){
  if (offered < 10) {
    offerings[offered++] = c;
    c.assignTeacher(t);
  } else
    cout << "Schedule full ! \n";
};
```

main.cc

```cpp
#include <iostream.h>
#include "Schedule.h"

main()
{
  Schedule s;
  Teacher t1("John Prof"), t2("Jack Dennis");
  Course c1("COP 4225","MW 1030-1200");
  Course c2("COP 6611","TR 1030-1200");
  Student st("Hugo Meier");

  cout << "It may begin\n";
  s.assign(c1,t1);
  s.assign(c2,t2);

  cout << "Teacher of first course: "; c1.teacher.print();
  cout << "Teacher of second course: "; c2.teacher.print();
  cout << "A student: "; st.print();
}
```

another **main.cc**

```
#include <iostream.h>
#include "Person.h"
#include "Teacher.h"
#include "Student.h"

main()
{
  Teacher t1("John Prof"), t2("Jack Dennis");
  Student st("Hugo Meier");
  Person *array[3] = {&t1, &st, &t2};
  int i;

  cout << "It may begin\n";
  t1.print();
  st.print();
  t2.print();

  for (i=0; i < 3; i++)
    array[i]->print();
  for (i=0; i < 3; i++)
    if (t1.assign())
      cout << "Course assigned\n";
    else
      cout << "Course not assigned\n";
}
```

The complete program can be compiled in several ways:

1. With a single compilation command:

```
CC Person.cc Teacher.cc Student.cc Course.cc
   Schedule.cc main.cc -o test
```

which will produce the executable test.

2. With separate compilation commands:

```
CC -c Person.cc
CC -c Teacher.cc
CC -c Student.cc
CC -c Course.cc
CC -c Schedule.cc
CC -c main.cc
CC  Person.o Teacher.o Student.o Course.o
    Schedule.o main.o -o test
```

Each individual command only invokes the compilation phase of the compiler by using the -c option. The last command links all object files together.

3. With a library:

```
CC -c Person.cc
CC -c Teacher.cc
CC -c Student.cc
CC -c Course.cc
CC -c Schedule.cc
ar c libsched.a Person.o Teacher.o Student.o
                Course.o Schedule.o
ranlib libsched.a
CC main.c -o test -lsched
```

The individual object files are kept in a library archive file. The library file is mentioned when compiling the main program with the -lsched option.

Appendix E

Listing: A Generic Collection Class

The C++ programming language does not directly support generic classes. Part of the current draft proposal to the ANSI standards committee is a class template construct that will add generic classes to C++. Until then, programmers can use a workaround involving the compiler preprocessor to simulate generic classes. Most current C++ compilers allow this workaround and provide a header include file to simplify the definition.

Generic classes are defined in terms of C preprocessor macros. A generic class definition involves three parts:

1. A macro to construct a special class name from the generic class name plus a type parameter. For example,

   ```
   #define Collection(T) name2(Collection_,T)
   ```

   defines a macro that will replace all occurrences of

   ```
   Collection(Something)
   ```

   with the string

   ```
   Collection_Something
   ```

   The macro name2[1] allows the concatenation of two strings together and is defined in the genric.h header file.

2. A macro that expands into a concrete class declaration for a given type parameter. For example:

---

[1]C++ compilers that are based on the AT&T release use name2 for this macro. We have seen other compilers that use different macros. Some compilers also allow the definition of more than one parameter.

281

```
#define Collectiondeclare(T) \
class Collection(T) { \
...
```

defines the preprocessor macro for the class declaration. Note that the lines of the class declaration all end with a backslash("\") in order to prevent the interpretation of the end-of-line character following it.

3. A macro that expands into a concrete class body for a given type parameter. For example,

```
#define Collectionimplement(T) \
int Collection(T)::GrowIncrement = 5; \
...
```

defines the preprocessor macro for the class body.

A generic class can be used, i.e., instantiated, with an actual type parameter. The generic.h include file defines two macros to produce a complete class from the class templates. For example,

```
declare(Collection,Person)
implement(Collection,Person)
```

is expanded into complete class description for the class Collection_Person. The class can be used in programs as class Collection(Person) according to the first step above.

In the following we will list the complete Collection class as a generic class template. The class is identical in functionality to the Collection class described in Chapter 5.

Collection.h

```
#include <generic.h>

#define Collection(T) name2(Collection_,T)

#define Collectiondeclare(T) \
class Collection(T) { \
   T **list; \
   int size; \
   int filled; \
   void add_alike(String &); \
   static int GrowIncrement; \
public: \
   Collection(T)() { \
     list = new (T *[GrowIncrement]); \
     size = GrowIncrement; \
     filled = 0; \
   }; \
   int get_size() {return filled;}; \
   void add(T *); \
   T* search(String &); \
   T* search(T *); \
   void remove(T *); \
   void print(); \
   void maintain(); \
   T* select(); \
};
```

Collection.cc

```
#define Collectionimplement(T) \
\
int Collection(T)::GrowIncrement = 5; \
\
void Collection(T)::add(T *element) { \
  if (filled >= size) { \
    T **oldlist = list; \
    list = new (T *[size + GrowIncrement]); \
    for (int i = 0; i < size; i++) \
      list[i] = oldlist[i]; \
    size += GrowIncrement; \
  }; \
  list[filled++] = element; \
}; \
\
T* Collection(T)::search(String &key) { \
  for (int i = 0; i < filled; i++) \
    if (list[i]->identify(key)) \
      return list[i]; \
  return (T*) NULL; \
}; \
\
T* Collection(T)::search(T *key) { \
  for (int i = 0; i < filled; i++) \
    if (list[i] == key) \
      return list[i]; \
  return (T*) NULL; \
}; \
\
void Collection(T)::remove(T *element) { \
  int j = 0; \
  T **oldlist = list; \
  for (int i = 0; i < filled; i++) \
    if (oldlist[i] != element) \
      list[j++] = oldlist[i]; \
  filled = j; \
}; \
\
void Collection(T)::print() { \
  if (filled == 0) \
```

```
      cout << "collection is empty\n"; \
    else \
      for (int i = 0; i < filled; i++) \
        list[i]->print(); \
}; \
\
void Collection(T)::maintain(){ \
  String selection, answer; \
  T *sel_element; \
\
  while (TRUE) { \
    print(); \
    cout << "Select an entry or enter 0 to exit: "; \
    cin >> selection; \
    if (selection == "0") break; \
    if ((sel_element = search(selection)) != NULL) { \
      sel_element->print(); \
      cout << "maintain (m) or delete (d) ? "; \
      cin >> selection; \
      if (selection.contains("d")) \
        remove(sel_element); \
      else \
        sel_element->maintain(); \
    } else { \
      cout << "not found,"; \
      cout << " do you want to create it (y/n) ? "; \
      cin >> answer; \
      if (answer.contains("y")) \
        add_alike(selection); \
    }; \
  }; \
}; \
\
T* Collection(T)::select() { \
  String selection; \
  print(); \
  cout << "enter name: "; \
  cin >> selection; \
  return(search(selection)); \
}; \
\
void Collection(T)::add_alike(String &name) { \
```

```
    if (filled == 0) \
      cout << "sorry, list is empty, cannot add\n"; \
    else { \
      T *element = list[0]->alike(name); \
      add(element); \
    }; \
  };
```

main.cc

```
#include "String.h"
#include "Collection.h"
#include "Collection.cc"
#include "Person.h"
#include "Course.h"

declare(Collection,Person);
implement(Collection,Person);

declare(Collection,Course);
implement(Collection,Course);

int main(){
        Collection(Person) p_col;
        Person *p1 = new Person("John");
        Person *p2 = new Person("Sue");
        p_col.add(p1);
        p_col.add(p2);
        p_col.add(p1);
        p_col.print();

        Collection(Course) c_col;
        Course *c1 = new Course("COP3223","good stuff");
        Course *c2 = new Course("COP4994","bad stuff");
        c_col.add(c1);
        c_col.add(c2);
        c_col.add(c1);
        c_col.print();
}
```

This main program produces the following output:

```
Person: John
Person: Sue
Person: John
Course: COP3223 - good stuff
Course: COP4994 - bad stuff
Course: COP3223 - good stuff
```

Bibliography

[ABD+89]   M. Atkinson, F. Bancilhon, D. DeWitt, K. Dittrich, D. Maier, and S. Zdonik. The object-oriented database system manifesto. In *Proceedings of the First Conference on Deductive and Object-Oriented Databases*, Kyoto, Japan, December 1989.

[AH87]   T. Andrews and C. Harris. Combining language and database advances in an object-oriented development environment. In *Proceedings of the ACM Conference on Object-Oriented Programming Systems, Languages and Applications*, Orlando, Florida, October 1987.

[BBB+88]   F. Bancilhon, G. Barbedette, V. Benzaken, C. Delobel, S. Gamerman, C. Lécluse, P. Pfeffer, P. Richard, and F. Vélez. The design and implementation of O_2, an object-oriented database system. In K. Dittrich, editor, *Proceedings of the Second International Workshop on Object-Oriented Database Systems*, Bad Münster, FRG, September 1988.

[BH89]   A. Björnerstedt and C. Hulten. Version control in an object-oriented architecture. In Won Kim and Frederick H. Lochovsky, editors, *Object-Oriented Concepts, Databases and Applications*, pages 451–485. Addison-Wesley, Reading, Mass., 1989.

[BI82]   Alan Borning and Daniel Ingalls. Multiple inheritance in smalltalk-80. In *AAAI-82, The National Conference on Artificial Intelligence*, pages 234–237. American Association for Artificial Intelligence, 1982.

[BM91]   Elisa Bertino and Lorenzo Martino. Object-oriented database management systems: Concepts and issues. *IEEE Computer*, 24(4):33–47, April 1991.

[BMO+89]   Robert Bretl, David Maier, Allen Otis, Jason Penney, Bruce Schuchardt, Jacob Stein, E. Harold Williams, and Monty Williams.

The gemstone data management system. In Won Kim and Frederick H. Lochovsky, editors, *Object-Oriented Concepts, Databases and Applications*, pages 283–308. Addison-Wesley, Reading, Mass., 1989.

[Boo90]   Grady Booch. *Object-Oriented Design with Applications*. Benjamin / Cummings Publishing Co., Redwood City, CA, 1990.

[Bro87]   F.P. Brooks. No silver bullet: Essence and accidents of software engineering. *IEEE Computer*, 20(4):10–19, April 1987.

[Bud85]   Timothy A. Budd. *A Little Smalltalk*. Addison Wesley, Reading, MA, 1985.

[CM84]   G. Copeland and David Maier. Making smalltalk a database system. In *Proceedings of the 1984 SIGMOD Conference*, Boston, Mass., May 1984.

[Cox86]   B.J. Cox. *Object Oriented Programming: An Evolutionary Approach*. Addison-Wesley, Reading, MA, 1986.

[CSI86]   Ellis S. Cohen, Edward T. Smith, and Lee A. Iverson. Constraint-based tiled windows. *IEEE Computer Graphics and Applications*, May 1986.

[Dat81]   C. J. Date. *An Introduction to Database Systems*. Addison Wesley Programming Series. Addison Wesley Publishing Company, Reading, Mass., third edition, 1981.

[DMN68]   O.J. Dahl, B. Myhrhaug, and K. Nygaard. SIMULA 67 common base language. Technical report, Norwegian Computing Center, 1968.

[DN66]   O.-J. Dahl and K. Nygaard. Simula - an algol-based simulation language. *Communications of the ACM*, 9(9):671–678, September 1966.

[DS84]   P.L. Deutsch and A.M. Schiffman. Efficient implementation of the smalltalk-80 system. In *Proc. 11th POPL*, pages 297–302, Salt Lake City, Utah, 1984.

[ea90a]   O. Deux et al. The story of o2. *IEEE Transactions on Knowledge and Data Engineering*, 2(1):91–108, 1990.

[ea90b]   Won Kim et al. Architecture of the ORION next-generation database system. *IEEE Transactions on Knowledge and Data Engineering*, 2(1):109–124, 1990.

[EL88]   Danny Epstein and Wilf R. LaLonde. A Smalltalk window system based on constraints. In *Proceedings of ACM OOPSLA'88 Conference*, San Diego, September 1988.

[EMB87]   Raimund K. Ege, David Maier, and Alan Borning. The Filter Browser: Defining interfaces graphically. In J. Bézivin et al., editor, *Proceedings of European Conference on Object Oriented Programming (Springer Verlag: Lecture Notes in Computer Science No. 276)*, pages 155–165, Paris, France, June 1987.

[ES90]   Mary A. Ellis and Bjarne Stroustrup. *The Annotated C++ Reference Manual*. Addison Wesley, Reading, MA, 1990.

[FGKK88]   J. Foley, Ch. Gibbs, W.Ch. Kim, and S. Kovacevic. A knowledge based user interface management system. In *CHI'88 Proceedings*, pages 67–72. ACM/SIGCHI, 1988.

[Gol84]   A. Goldberg. *Smalltalk-80: The Interactive Programming Environment*. Addison Wesley, Reading, MA, 1984.

[GOP90]   Keith E. Gorlen, Sanford M. Orlow, and Perry S. Plexico. *Data Abstraction and Object-Oriented Programming in C++*. John Wiley and Sons Ltd, New York, NY, 1990.

[GR83]   Adele Goldberg and D. Robson. *Smalltalk-80: The Language and its Implementation*. Addison Wesley, Reading, Mass., 1983.

[Gre85]   Mark Green. Report on dialog specification tools. In Guenther E. Pfaff, editor, *Workshop on User Interface Management Systems (1983: Seeheim-Jugenheim, Germany)*, pages 9–20. Springer Verlag, 1985.

[Gro89]   HOOD Working Group. Hierarchical object-oriented design (HOOD) reference manual. Noordwijk, The Netherlands, September 1989.

[Ing86]   Danial H. Ingalls. A simple technique for handling mulitple polymorphism. In *Proceedings of ACM OOPSLA'86 Conference*, Portland, OR, September 1986.

[Jac83]   Michael Jackson. *System Development*. Prentice-Hall, Englewood Cliffs, NJ, 1983.

[Kir89]   Bjørn Kirkerud. *Object-Oriented Programming with SIMULA*. Addison-Wesley, Reading, Massachusetts, 1989.

[KL89]   Won Kim and Frederick H. Lochovsky, editors. *Object-Oriented Concepts, Databases and Applications.* ACM Press, Reading, Mass., 1989.

[Knu86]   Donald E. Knuth. *The TeXbook.* Addison-Wesley, Reading, Massachusetts, 1986.

[KR88]   Brian W. Kernighan and Dennis M. Ritchie. *The C Programming Language, 2nd edition.* Prentice Hall, Englewood Cliffs, New Jersey, 1988.

[LCV88]   Mark A. Linton, Paul R. Calder, and John M. Vlissides. Interviews: A C++ graphical interface toolkit. Technical Report CSL-TR-88-358, Stanford University, July 1988.

[LeN88]   Yannick LeNoan. Object-oriented programming exploits AI. *Computer Technology Review,* April 1988.

[Lip89]   Stanley B. Lippman. *C++ Primer.* Addison Wesley Publishing Company, Reading, Mass., 1989.

[LVC89]   Mark A. Linton, John M. Vlissides, and Paul R. Calder. Composing user interfaces with InterViews. *IEEE Computer,* 22(2), February 1989.

[Mai83]   David Maier. *The Theory of Relational Databases.* Computer Science Press, Rockville, MD, 1983.

[Mai89]   David Maier. Why isn't there an object-oriented data model? Technical report no. cs/e-89-002, Oregon Graduate Center, Beaverton, OR, May 1989.

[MBFB89]   John Maloney, Alan Borning, and Bjorn Freeman-Benson. Constraint technology for user-interface construction in ThingLab II. In *ACM OOPSLA'89 Conference Proceedings,* pages 381–388, New Orleans, LA, October 1989.

[Mey86]   Bertrand Meyer. Genericity versus inheritance. In *ACM OOPSLA'89 Conference Proceedings,* Portland, OR, September 1986.

[Mey87]   Bertrand Meyer. Reusability: The case for object-oriented design. *IEEE Software,* 4(2):50–64, March 1987.

[Mey88]   Bertrand Meyer. *Object-Oriented Software Construction.* Prentice Hall, 1988.

[MSOP86]   David Maier, Jacob Stein, Alan Otis, and Alan Purdy. Development
           of an object-oriented dbms. In *Proceedings of the ACM Conference
           on Object-Oriented Programming Systems, Languages and Applica-
           tions*, Portland, Oregon, September 1986.

[Orr71]   K. Orr. *Structured Systems Development*. Yourdon Press, New
           York, NY, 1971.

[SB86]   Mark Stefik and Daniel G. Bobrow. Object-oriented programming:
           Themes and variations. *The AI Magazine*, pages 40–62, 1986.

[Som89]   Ian Sommerville. *Software Engineering*. Addison Wesley, Working-
           ham, England, 3rd edition, 1989.

[SS88]   E. Seidewitz and M. Stark. *An Introduction to General Object-
           Oriented Software Development*. Millenium Systems, Rockville,
           MD, 1988.

[Ste87]   Lynn Andrea Stein. Delegation is inheritance. In *Proceedings of
           ACM OOPSLA'87 Conference*, Orlando, FL, October 1987.

[Str86]   Bjarne Stroustrup. *The C++ Programming Language*. Addison Wes-
           ley, Reading, MA, 1986.

[WBWW90]   Rebecca Wirfs-Brock, Brian Wilkerson, and Lauren Wiener. *De-
           signing Object-Oriented Software*. Prentice Hall, Englewood Cliffs,
           NJ, 1990.

[WLH90]   K. Wilkinson, P. Lyngbaek, and W. Hasan. The iris architecture
           and implementation. *IEEE Transactions on Knowledge and Data
           Engineering*, 2(1):63–75, 1990.

[WPM90]   A.I. Wasserman, P. Pircher, and R.J. Muller. An object-oriented de-
           sign notation for software design representation. *IEEE Computer*,
           23(3):50–63, March 1990.

[YC79]   E. Yourdon and L. Constantine. *Structured Design*. Prentice-Hall,
           Englewood Cliffs, NJ, 1979.

[Zdo90]   S. Zdonik. Object-oriented type evolution. In F. Bancilhon and
           P. Buneman, editors, *Advances in Database Programming Lan-
           guages*, pages 277–288. Addison-Wesley, Reading, Mass., 1990.

[ZM90]   Brad Vander Zanden and Brad A. Myers. Automatic, Look-and-
           Feel independent dialog creation for user interfaces. In *CHI'90
           Proceedings*, pages 27–34. ACM/SIGCHI, 1990.

Index